The Fasnion of Football

Paolo Hewitt is the author of 12 books, including *The Sharper Word: A Mod Anthology*, *The Soul Stylists: Six Decades of Modernism — from Mods to Casuals*, *Alan McGee and the Story of Creation Records: This Ecstasy Romance Cannot Last*, *The Greatest Footballer You Never Saw: The Robin Friday Story* and *The Looked After Kid: Memoirs From A Children's Home*. He now wants to go on holiday.

Mark Baxter is a former shop and club owner with a passion for '60s clothing, Tubby Hayes and Millwall Football Club. This is his first book.

THE FASHION OF FOOTBALL

FROM BEST TO BECKHAM, FROM MOD TO LABEL SLAVE

Paolo Hewitt
and Mark Baxter

MAINSTREAM
PUBLISHING
EDINBURGH AND LONDON

This edition, 2006

First published in Great Britain in 2004 by
MAINSTREAM PUBLISHING COMPANY
(EDINBURGH) LTD
7 Albany Street
Edinburgh EH1 3UG

ISBN 1 84596 050 5

A catalogue record for this book is available from
the British Library

Typeset in Apollo and Frutiger
Printed and bound in Great Britain by
Cox & Wyman Ltd

■ ■ ■
Dedications and Acknowledgements

This book is for my Dad, John 'Sid Boy' Baxter. He passed on his love of football and clothes to me, for which I will always be truly thankful. 'To live on in the hearts of those you leave behind is never to die.' Love ya, Pop.

Many thanks go to the following: Brother Will, for his friends in high places; O'SH, my getaway driver; Dean P and his amazing mobile; Paul H and Noj; Bomber Wild, Gavin A, Danny Walters; Nick for stalking Ian Wright; Mum and Dad Nic, and Jan; Ginger Dave, Mr Gumby, Keith P; my NB lovelies, Betty, Doris and Keely; Rhys, Kate, Vicki, Dave O, Sam, Tracy and Matt, and Sir Brian of Harlow; the Freemans crew of Lisa Baby, Noella, Darryl, Bugsy and Mark E; Will at Whitehall; Georgie the Tailor, Freddie the Shoe, Uncle Gudge, Audie, Jess and Terry O; Stuart at Duffer; Wardy, Wisey, Chris and Deano at the 'Wall; Jen and Sam at Empics; Kathryn at Berg; Wendy, Dons, and Gillian at Man Utd Museum; Tony Mottram for his photo of The Accent; Martin Ellison; Iain Munn; all the interviewees and all at Mainstream.

Love to the following: my mum, for her unconditional love, Tracey, Toots and Clods.

Finally, the two people without whom this would never had happened: PH, I can only say thank you, Mon Brave. One for the road, son? And last but certainly not least, my wife, Lou, who has supported me in every way with this and so much more. As Brian Wilson once sang, 'God only knows where I'd be without you.'

Mark Baxter

I second those emotions and send out big thanks for their support and kindness to the following: George 'Smiler' Georgiou, for being so upbeat; the estimable Simon Wells for the annuals and indefatigable support; Nipper Harris, David Rosen, Mark Powell, Dean Powell, Andy Rigg, that Feeney gal, William Hunt, Gary Kingham, Audie and Jack the dog, Doug Hayward, the Owen brothers and their fellow Welsh Boys; Irvine Welsh, Sir Chalfont of NW3, and Sir Peter Blake of the Royal Academy of Arts; the Guigs and his famiglia — wife, Ruth, and son, Patrick; Greg and Helen Gordon; all at John Simon; Frank McLintock and his sons, Neil and Ian; Tommy Sheehan; Bill Nicholson just for being Bill Nicholson; and my man, Stevie Perryman. A big *salut* to Deborah Hicks for her sterling work with a mountain of tapes, to another Debs, Deborah Warner, for her meticulous editing work, and another one to Kevin Francis Rowland for his time and memories.

I wish to thank big-time my superb midfield holding player, the Millwall maestro, Signor Mark Baxter, his family and, of course, his wife Lou — may love follow you both, for ever and a day.

This one is for the silent S — another work you've helped send out into a world made so much better by your presence.

Both authors wish to publicly acknowledge the kindness of that great Mayfair Orphan, Mr Terry O'Neill.

Paolo Hewitt

■ ■ ■

Contents

PART THREE Second Half: Terrace Ghosts – The Fashion Fans

INTRODUCTION

A Minute Before Kick-off . . .

He calls it his 'office', the rest of the city knows it as Bar Italia, on Frith Street in the heart of Soho. Whenever we had to meet, my co-author and I, this was the spot we settled on, without fail. It was, after all, his office.

Bar Italia is opposite Ronnie Scott's famous club, which was apposite. Mark was, as I would soon discover, a big jazz nut. The British musician Tubby Hayes was his hero and soon after we began work on this project, he began badgering me to write a biog on the man.

'You should do it, son,' he'd say. 'Tubby was the man. Fifteen years old and he blows Ronnie Scott off stage, goes to America, becomes the toast of New York, then bang, gone! Went on the needle. Tremendous story.'

It probably is, I'd reply, but writing books is a soul-sapping experience and the sales of a Tubby Hayes biog were hardly going to compensate for the effort.

'So why you doing a book about football and fashion?' he'd jokingly ask.

'Because a Millwall season-ticket holder asked me to and I thought he might beat me up if I said no,' I joked.

'Careful on the Millwall references, son,' he replied. 'Your team, Spurs, ain't exactly the dons these days. Fact is, the only table they top these days is the hooligan one.'

Mark always arrived at his office before me. Didn't matter if I was super-early or just early, every time I walked into the joint, he'd be there, sitting on his usual stool at the back by the fruit machine and the video screen.

Spotting me, Mark would always smile, stand and walk towards me. 'Want a drink, son?' he'd say. 'My shout. Cappuccino? Mocha? What do you fancy? Not on the piss again last night, were you? You look a bit weak, son.' (Mark started off calling me son. Later, London street slang changed and I became 'bruv'.)

Mark's a big man, a man of presence, clean-shaven, and always neat and tidy in his appearance. His accent is deep South London, his vocabulary peppered with slang from both London's past and present. He smokes, but not ciggies or doobie-doos, his were dark, thin cigars which in a pub or bar he would dip into his vodka and Diet Coke.

Like me, he was a football man, a music man, a clothes man. His taste was '60s and Modernist in flavour. He was from Camberwell, South London, and proud of the fact as well. Michael Caine grew up near him and one of his dreams was to escort the man round his old stomping ground, see what treasured memories he could elicit from the veteran actor.

I had previously met Mark on about four or five different occasions but couldn't say I knew him well. It was always business stuff, like photos for book covers he might be able to access. That's why, when he called in early September 2002 and said he had an idea I might be interested in, and could we meet, I was intrigued enough to say we could.

At that first meeting in Bar Italia, Mark handed me the proposal he had written. 'Might be something in there, might not,' he said in an offhand manner. His easygoing tone masked the work he had already put into the project. For the previous year, Mark had been sending the proposal here, there and everywhere, and got the same reply every time – nice but no cigar and certainly not a book you can wet your beak with.

It was frustrating. He knew he was on to something but the publishing world disagreed. It normally does.

'Have a look, tell me what you reckon. Can't hurt, can it?'

I read it on the Tube home. Mark didn't have one idea for a book. He had three.

I emailed him the next day:

> Mark, seems to me that there are three different ideas going on here:
> a) A 'where are the famous footballers of yesteryear now'-type affair
> b) Football kits and their development
> c) (which I think is the strongest) A look at footballers' fashions over the years – start with the '50s and demob suits, into the '60s with Bobby Moore, the '70s with Charlie George, Alan Hudson etc., Hoddle and Waddle in the '80s, Ian Wright, John Barnes and the '90s, and so on.
> Those are my first thoughts. Call me to discuss further.

Which he did.

In that conversation was born the idea of writing a history of the links between fashion and football, detailing the clothes worn by the players and fans, starting in 1962 and ending in the present day.

'You know what else we could do?' I added.

'What's that, son?'

'We could provide a parallel history of British menswear at the same time,' I said.

'Oh, yes. I like that, like that a lot.'

'Means a lot of research.'

'Don't worry me. I love all that. You watch, once I get hold of an idea, that's it. Bosh. I'm off on it.'

He was good on his word. Soon as we had secured a deal, Mark started bombarding me with large brown envelopes packed with information. Even though he held down a day job, working for a man from the property trade, his energy was impressive. He sent me fanzines, pictures, newspaper articles, magazine articles. He set up interviews, conducted interviews, phoned a million people, sorted out the photographs. He also began putting together a website for the book.

'Once this is finished, the whole world is going to know about it,' he told me.

A Minute Before Kick-off . . .   11

As the book took shape, I began to think of its subject matter as a large pool of spilt coffee, our work as the tissue which absorbs it all.

Unlike standard works, this is quite a loose book. Although there is a structure, we have not presented the research in a linear or obvious manner. For example, we begin with a history of football, before we go on to a major Scottish writer, two great Scottish players, the maximum-wage affair, Jimmy Hill's revolution, the inside of a '60s wardrobe, the history of Modernism, the importance of the button-down shirt, then travel into a punk musician's memory, all before we really get going. This book brings together fashion history and football culture and all points in between. We have expanded the story itself to take on many other aspects connected to both football and fashion: fandom, loyalty, belief, one-upmanship, the wonder of the loafer, the despair of defeat.

In many ways, this book is a diary of two guys going off to meet a wide variety of people with a common interest — football and fashion — and then reporting back to the world as to how they got on. Like the Spurs team under Ossie Ardiles, its loose formation is such that you can dip in, dip out at will. Mark thinks of this work as a free-form jazz book; I think of it more like a classic Blue Note record — one that starts with a solid riff and then sees what develops from there.

Either way, hope the book sends you. It did us.

PART ONE
■■■■■■■■■■■■

FIRST HALF

The Lion, the Genius
and the Wardrobes

■■■

The Whistle-blower

I thought: annuals, football annuals, a good place to start. Friends went into attics and brown boxes and sent me their precious, slightly tattered football picture books, their pages soaked with their teenage memories.

I received *Charles Buchan's Soccer Gift Book* (apparently the world's greatest annual), the *Topical Times Football Book* from the 1971 season and two copies of the *Tiger Book of Soccer Stars*, one from 1971, the other 1972. All of them contained the names that defined their era – Best, Law, Charlton, Chivers, Peters, Osgood, Shankly, etc. – but I noted others, such as Gerry Queen from Crystal Palace, Willie Anderson from Aston Villa and George Ley of Portsmouth; saw them as names now only remembered by the faithful few and wondered where they were now.

Unfortunately, not many of these annuals featured players in off-duty clothing. All the pictures were on-field action shots. So, one welcome and rare summer-in-winter afternoon in February, with the sky blue and the air warm, I took a stroll to my favourite second-hand bookshop to see if they had anything of value. They did.

Norman Barrett's *Purnell's Encyclopedia of Association Football* was not filled with great pics of well-dressed players but it did contain a history of football that I found highly enlightening. It certainly changed my view on matters and, as we have enough time, all the time in the world, in fact, it's worth repeating here. The first statement to catch my eye was this:

> The Chinese and the Japanese can claim some of the earliest
> references to football. In the history of the Han Dynasty,

which covers the period in Chinese history from 206 BC to AD 25, mention is made of 'tsu chu': 'tsu' meaning to kick with the foot, 'chu' meaning 'the ball made of leather and stuffed'.

I was shocked. All my life, I'd been taught that England invented the game. Never thought to question it. In fact, I'd read a reference to it just the other day. Now I was being told that if football ever went home, then it would be on a slow boat to China. Amazing.

From China, *Purnell's* went on to say, variations of the game travelled to Ancient Greece then on to Italy. The Romans called the game *harpastum* and according to our man Barrett:

> . . . this game may well be the ancestor of modern soccer, for it is almost certain that the Roman legions would have taken the game with them when they conquered Britain. Centuries later men were still chasing a ball, using either hands or feet.

Maron! Heating systems, bathing, straight roads, orgies, wine – not only did the Italians single-handedly civilise England but most importantly of all they gave them their national sport. This was not a fact that I had heard before. All my life I'd heard from sour English commentators that the Italians were cynical, defensive cheats but never that they had brought the game here and popularised it.

The English people certainly loved the game the Roman Empire bestowed upon them but those who ruled them thought differently. They hated football. On 13 April 1314, King Edward II banned the game after being deluged with complaints from rich, influential merchants unable to carry out their business successfully.

'For as much as there is a great noise in the city,' read his decree, 'caused by hustling over large balls . . . we command and forbid on behalf of the King, on pain of imprisonment, such game to be used in the city in the future.'

Edward's successor, Edward III, also hated the game, as did Richard II and Henry IV. These kings shared one compelling reason for their stance – soccer took the men away from archery practice. You can see their point of view: an Army of men kicking leather balls into the faces of the viciously armed oncoming enemy wasn't

　　　　　　　　　The Fashion of Football

really going to cut it in battle. A ball, a ball! My kingdom for a ball! I think not.

Ironically enough, it was only in the nineteenth century that the public-school system popularised the sport most associated with the working class. Barrett reports:

> Eton, Harrow, Winchester and Rugby did much to organise football. Each school had its own variations. Some permitted holding and running with the ball, bodily tackling and hacking (the unpleasant practice of kicking an opponent's shins). Others, because they played on courtyards and in cloisters, preferred a dribbling game with little bodily contact.

In October 1863, the Football Association (FA) was formed. Their first job was to establish a set of rules, one of which made handling the ball an offence. When they presented these rules to the clubs, a schism immediately opened up. Quite a few clubs preferred the handling game, so broke away from the Association and, in doing so, formed the game of rugby. Undeterred, the FA grew in power. In 1871, they launched the Challenge Cup, which would later be named the FA Cup, and in 1872, they organised the first official international between England and Scotland.

'The Scots had a profound influence on soccer in two respects,' Barrett states. 'They initiated the passing game and they gave football its first professionals.' Again, the myth of England as the fount of all football shattered. It was the Scots who taught them how to pass.

The mention of professionals by Purnell intrigued me. Our book was to begin with the abolition of the maximum wage in 1962 and the subsequent change in players' contracts. Those developments in soccer also paralleled the boom in British menswear which began in the late '50s.

We get ahead of ourselves.

Back in the 1880s, football was still an amateur sport and professionalism of any kind was severely frowned upon. Yet *Purnell's* states that it was not uncommon for Northern clubs to regularly use financial incentives to entice talented Scottish footballers to play for them. In such a manner, Blackburn and Preston became as powerful as Man United and Arsenal are today.

In 1885, unable to control the clubs' unlawful financial practices, the FA legalised professionalism. They had to. They had no choice. 'Three years later, the Football League was founded,' Barrett concludes, 'and the modern game was well on its way.' The modern footballer wasn't. He would have to wait until 1962, and the efforts of two players – George Eastham and Jimmy Hill – before he could take centre stage.

* * *

He was an unlikely revolutionary, George Eastham. Reports from his time as a player in the mid-'50s refer to him as 'soberly dressed' and state that 'he would not have been out of place behind the counter of a bank'. Born in Blackpool in 1936, Eastham started his career in Northern Ireland, playing alongside his father, George, at club level for a season. In 1956, he went to Newcastle. They paid £8,000 for him. It's where the story begins.

At the time, all clubs operated a retain-and-transfer system, the method by which they exerted total control over their employees. Players were signed for life and only let go if the club so desired, or by mutual consent. A player could not leave a club by his own volition. To do so meant that he was instantly banned from playing for anyone else. Effectively, his career was over.

The clubs not only controlled their players, they made a mint out of them. Football was immensely popular. Since the setting up of the Football League, clubs had seen their terraces invaded by crowds numbering 80,000 or more. Week in, week out, they poured through the turnstiles, paying money which rarely reached the very people they had come to watch, to admire. The professional footballer was paid a pittance for his endeavours. Furthermore, he operated under a maximum wage limit that all clubs imposed. At the time of the limit's abolition in 1962, that wage was £20 a week. If the players complained about their low wages, clubs delighted in reminding their workforce how lucky they were that the club even gave them a living. After all, they would point out, look at the alternative. You could always go back to the factory, the Army, the mines or, worst

The Fashion of Football

of all, the dole queues that stretched for miles.

On that point, they could not argue. These were working-class men who, through their playing skills, had evaded a life of back-breaking work, of tough living. Playing football gave them a life that the majority of their friends and families could only envy. To be robbed of this privilege was a risk no one was prepared to take. In this manner, English football clubs made millions of pounds for many, many years. Then came George.

After four years with Newcastle, George Eastham was unhappy. He didn't like his club or his employers. He put in a transfer request. Newcastle refused him. He put in a second time. Again, no. On his third refusal, Eastham decided enough was enough. He told his employers, tough luck, I'm going.

Charlie Mitten, the Newcastle manager, responded with an unequivocal, you're going nowhere, son.

Want a bet? Eastham replied, and walked out. Newcastle immediately banned him from playing and George went to work for a firm importing cork for refrigeration plants. Neither club nor player would talk to the other.

It was a stand-off that would have huge repercussions for the game. One organisation that was delighted by this turn of events was the Players' Union, latterly the Professional Football Association (PFA), formed in 1907. Weak and ineffectual in the face of the clubs' overall grip on their players, the PFA was smart enough to realise that, finally, they had a man they could use to spearhead long-overdue change. They put their full support behind Eastham.

After six months of silence, Newcastle broke the ice and made Eastham an offer. He could stay in London and work for his cork plant but at weekends he would be obliged to travel up to Newcastle and play. Eastham refused the offer. Then he turned the tables on his former employers. He instructed his lawyers to serve papers on Newcastle Football Club for unreasonable restraint of trade.

Newcastle terminated his contract and Eastham was able to sign to Arsenal for £47,500. He received a hefty £20 signing-on fee and waited for the court hearing that would decide not only his future but that of the game itself.

These things come in pairs. As Eastham fought with Newcastle, a young man by the name of Jimmy Hill was launching his bid to have the maximum wage abolished. Hill was a South London boy, born in 1928. He had left school and worked in finance as an insurance agent and a stockbroker. He joined the Army and was spotted playing football at the Blackdown Garrison in Hampshire by the former Arsenal legend Ted Drake. Drake persuaded Hill to play amateur football for Reading.

Six months later, Hill moved to Brentford. Three years at Brentford and then on to Fulham, where he played centre-forward and was good enough to make over 300 appearances, playing alongside highly skilled Fulham legends such as Johnny Haynes.

Hill was a man of the future, a model pro, an enthusiastic man who would have trained all day and all night if he could have done. He possessed a vociferous character, had huge self-belief and was driven by an Englishman's sense of fair play. These traits naturally drew Hill into the PFA. In 1956, he was appointed chairman of the union and within two months he had instigated his first battle with the FA.

At the time, most players were involved in the illegal practice of taking 'under the table' payments. These were cash treats from various sources to supplement wages, to help make ends meet, and it was a widespread practice. When the FA swooped on several Sunderland players and charged them with illegal behaviour, the growing sense of militancy against the FA rose to the surface. The Sunderland players refused to answer or acknowledge the charges set against them. The FA suspended them from playing football. Hill immediately stepped in and asked all his members to publicly declare their financial dealings. He was banking on so many players owning up to these payments that it would render the FA powerless to continue their action against the Sunderland gang.

He was right. The FA was so overwhelmed by footballers 'fessing up to taking small cash gifts that they backed down. If they had charged everyone, the game would have vanished within a day. The ban was lifted and the FA fined the Sunderland players instead. Even that stricture proved useless. Hill had the fines overturned six months later.

Emboldened by his success, Hill turned his attention to the maximum wage limit. His resulting plan was both simple and direct. In 1961, Hill held a strike ballot amongst his members. Again, every one of his members supported him. Hill then went to the FA and informed them that unless they abolished the maximum wage, there would be a national strike. 'You can no longer expect a footballer to be a serf six days a week and an executive on the seventh,' he was quoted as saying.

Once more, the FA had been totally outmanoeuvred. In the face of such opposition, they capitulated, although some officials remained outraged and publicly contemptuous of such developments for the rest of their lives.

Tough luck. Hill had won. Players could now negotiate their own wage packets. Within months of this historic breakthrough, the wages of Hill's teammate Johnny Haynes shot up to £100 a week.

'When I got my money,' Haynes said recently, 'there was outrage in some quarters. There were a lot of people in the Football League who were absolutely mortified that the maximum wage was finished. They fought tooth and nail not to let it go, but Jimmy Hill simply wouldn't take no for an answer and, in the end, we won quite comfortably. The Football League secretary, Alan Hardaker, was very bitter.'

Fulham responded by giving Hill a free transfer, a bitter thank you for having so successfully unlocked the club's vaults.

A year after helping to abolish the maximum wage, Hill, PFA secretary Cliff Lloyd and George Eastham had their day in court. On Thursday, 4 July 1963, Mr Justice Wilberforce delivered his 16,000-word judgment pertaining to the case of *Eastham* v. *Newcastle FC*. Contained within was the one sentence that mattered: 'The rules of the Football Association and the regulations of the Football League . . . are an unreasonable restraint of trade.' Eastham had won.

The professional footballer now had freedom of work, plus a potential to earn beyond anything his predecessors had ever imagined. They could now start to compete financially with their contemporaries in the entertainment world. They could also start to dress like them . . .

■ ■ ■
The First Metrosexual

One of the first interviews conducted for this book was with Frank McLintock, the former Arsenal captain and Millwall assistant manager. At the end of our chat, the Glaswegian suddenly exclaimed, 'Gordon Smith! That's your man. You should find out about Gordon Smith. Played for Hibernian. He was an absolute legend. He was really talented, but he was also one of the best-dressed footballers of his era; looked great every time you saw him. Fantastic style about the man.'

Hibernian. There was only one man I knew who I could contact for information about Hibernian: the writer Irvine Welsh. I had first met Irvine back in the '90s at a place called The Social, a ground-breaking club whose original venue was The Albany pub by Great Portland Street station. After a year of inactivity in bookshops, his first novel, *Trainspotting*, had just taken off and he was about to become the poet laureate of the E generation.

After the club, we went back to Jeff Barrett's house (Barrett ran The Social) and chewed each other's ears until dawn. I saw a lot of Irvine in those early days, liked him a hell of a lot. I thought it great that not only had he brought the waifs and strays of council-estate living firmly into the spotlight, but that he had been so successful with his effortless style, his challenging approach to language and his brilliant humour. Irvine was both artistic and commercially successful and it remains a source of great pride to me that my only novel, *Heaven's Promise*, would influence his finest book, *Marabou Stork Nightmares*. I decided that one day I would write the definitive biography of the man. Of course, when I approached him about this idea, he ran a mile. Irvine has the writer's temperament, secretive as hell.

In the mid- to late '90s, we didn't see as much of each other as we should, went off on different journeys, our paths occasionally crossing. I bought his every book, really liked some – *Glue*, *Porno*; didn't like others – *Ecstasy*. But through them, one thing became very apparent indeed: Hibernian Football Club meant the world to him.

A week after meeting McLintock, I emailed Welsh:

```
Irvine
Hope you're well. Started football and
fashion book now. Spoke to Frank McLintock
last week. He raved on about a Hibernian
player from the '50s, a Gordon Smith. We've
checked into it but nothing coming up at
present. Do you know of this man? Do you
know where we can get info?
    OK, mio amico, look forward to hearing from
you.
    Paolo
```

This reply from Irvine arrived the next day.

```
    The Famous Five forward line played for the
first British club to play in the European
Cup, losing to Rheims of France in the semi,
who went on to get beaten by Real Madrid in
the inaugural final.
    More importantly, they played an exhibition
match in the 1950s in Brazil (first UK side to
play there) and the game against Vasco da Gama
in particular was a showpiece for Brazilian
coaches and journalists. The Hibs team's
interchanging style was reckoned by one
influential Brazilian football journalist to
be the inspiration behind the great Brazil
team of 1970. [I have to interject and say I
love that line. No Hibs, No Pele. Proper.
P.H.]
    Smith fucked his leg up and was released by
```

Hibs after winning three League flags with them. Bad mistake. He signed to Hearts and promptly won another League title with them. He was ancient when they released him but then he signed for Dundee. Although he scarcely could run by then, he provided the pinpoint crosses for young soon-to-be-Tottenham-legend Alan Gilzean's then-still-hairy dome and Dundee won the League that year! So that's five Championship medals over three clubs, not one of which was Rangers or Celtic, an incredible record for Scottish football.

Also, Hibs' Famous Five took on Man United's 'Busby Babes' in 1952 when both clubs were respective champions of their leagues. The game was played at Easter Road and doubled as Smith's testimonial match. He scored a hat-trick as Hibs fucked Man U 7-3. They wanted a replay at Old Trafford and Hibs obliged, winning 4-0 down there with a depleted side which didn't include the injured Smith.

The other members of the Five were Bobby Johnstone, who won an FA Cup medal for Man City against Newcastle; Laurie Reilly, Scotland's highest international goalscorer until Law equalled and Dalglish surpassed his total; Eddie Turnbull, manager of the good Hibs and Aberdeen sides of the '70s, who were obscured a bit by Stein's great success at Celtic; and Willie Ormond, who recovered from three leg breaks in his playing career and went on to manage Scotland in the 1974 World Cup in Germany.

I once planned to write a book on the Five, I've loads more information on Smith. Old boys go starry-eyed in pubs in Edinburgh when you mention his name. Those that saw him reckon that he really was one of the greatest players of all time.

    Sorry for the rant,

    See you soon,

    Irvine

This was my reply:

Rant? A wealth of information, my man, and many thanks for it. But was Mr Smith a good dresser or not? Was he as sharp as his crosses or as scruffy as Ralph Coates's barnet? His story sounds fascinating. Was he the guy you told me about, the Hibs answer to Robin Friday? And where can we get pics do you think?

    PH

And his response to that was as follows:

Paolo

The answer is an emphatic yes. He was the first metrosexual, always well turned out with a dandy-like elegance evident in both his play and his dress and grooming. This wasn't the Hibs' Robin Friday. Smith was a massive talent but disciplined (never booked in his career), a kind of old-school Corinthian who fulfilled all his potential. The lack of TV media and that he chose to stay in the relative backwater of Scottish football (although Hibs crowds under the Five were around 50,000 regular) means that he's not so known as Matthews and Finney in England. Had Hibs accepted the blank cheques both Newcastle and Man U offered, then it would have been a different story.

    Hibs' Robin Friday was a guy called Willie Hamilton who played for them in the '60s. Jock Stein, who managed him at Easter Road, described him as the best player he'd worked with, some accolade when you consider Stein had Johnstone

etc. from Celtic's 'Lisbon Lions' in his charge.
He took the piss out of Jim Baxter (4-2 v.
Rangers) and Frederick Puskas (2-0 v. Real Madrid
– the first time Real had lost to a British side
when a young Peter Cormack hit Hibs' opener) in
one week. He died in Canada.

I've got loads of Smith pics. Obviously, my
stuff is boxed up but I'll dig something out for
you when I get back. I'd like to talk to you about
Smith 'cause I have my own left-field theories
about him.

All the best
Irvine

Then I made my mistake. I emailed Irvine saying we should meet soon. I had things to talk to him about, one of which was my proposed biog on him. Like I said, mistake. He never got back to me, retreated into his shell. A biog obviously didn't sit well with him.

Soon after, I saw a picture of another Scottish player in the same mould as the Hibs boys Irvine delighted so much in exposing to the world. His name was Jim Baxter, a man who also dressed as he played, with élan, style and cheek. In the pic, Jim wears a leather trilby with a leather coat, three buttoned. He looks tremendous, smiling just as he must have smiled that famous day in 1967 when Scotland beat England, the world champions, 2–3 at Wembley and the fans poured onto the pitch to dig up mementoes that are still looked upon with immense pride by their owners.

In that game, Jim Baxter took on the English with vengeance in his heart. About 20 minutes into the match, the ball came to Baxter in the English half. He controlled it, looked around with disdain and then walked away from the ball, knowing full well that his teammate Denis Law was nearby and would reach it before any Englishman. Not long after, Baxter again took the ball and to everyone's astonishment juggled it with both feet for several seconds. 'The proud England players,' a report said, 'were reduced to the level of a clumsy bull before a matador.'

There were recriminations, not least from Scottish managers. Bill Shankly opined that the team would have done better to score more

The Fashion of Football

goals that day than spend their time extracting the urine. Jim Baxter ('Slim Jim' as he was known then, before alcohol swelled his stomach to an unmanageable size) disagreed.

Baxter once related the story of his first cap for the Scottish Under-23s. He had been selected to play against Wales. 'A big day for me,' he said. 'I was with Raith then. I go over to Edinburgh, full of myself, all dressed up in my best gear. Really sharp. And I see these players from Glasgow and Edinburgh, now they really look something, and suddenly I'm a country yokel. I'm a nobody. All the kids are queuing for their autographs. Me, I'm asked a couple of times, and they look at my signature to see who I am. Well, that was the day I made up my mind – I was going to be noticed.'

Interesting how Baxter straight away understood the impact of his teammates' clothes, how their look immediately singled them out from the crowd. Baxter, a miner's son, who played with grace for Raith, Rangers, Sunderland and Nottingham Forest, learnt his lesson that day, and learnt it well. During his years on the pitch, he dressed as he played: to be noticed, to be admired. Then he stopped playing, hit the bottle and the wardrobe lost its significance.

Just seven months after humiliating the *Inglese* at Wembley, Baxter played his final game for Scotland, a 3–2 victory against Wales. In 1970, he retired from playing and managed a pub, as a lot of footballers were wont to do in those days. In 1994, this Scottish legend underwent two liver transplants and, in 2001, at the age of 61, he passed away. Cancer had claimed him.

Today, we are still writing about him. Tomorrow, we will as well.

* * *

Not long after my correspondence with Irvine, I had to go to Croydon to pick up some photographs from Tom Sheehan, a photographer I had spent many pleasurable times with during my time at *Melody Maker*. I went to his home and, whilst I was there, told him about this book. Immediately, he said, 'Bobby Keetch, you've got to get Bobby Keetch in, he was the man. I used to watch him at Fulham. He was a great dresser, a real Mod footballer.'

On my return home, I phoned Mark, put him on the case. He soon put facts at my fingertips. Although his was not a long playing career, for those who followed Fulham in the early '60s, the late Bobby Keetch inspires nothing but admiration. He played 127 times for Fulham, moved to QPR, then quit the game aged 27. Yet such bland facts obscure a bigger truth – off the pitch, Bobby Keetch was in no way a typical footballer. At the time, players tended to be men of simple tastes, who were paid for doing something they loved and were happy to return to their families or the local pub at night. Bobby Keetch was different. He was a man fascinated by art, by culture, a man who would think nothing of rushing off to Paris after a game to spend time in that fine city's many museums.

On the pitch, however, it was a different story. In his biography, *Bring Back The Birch* (top contender for 'worst title for a biography'), Alan Birchenall, the ex-Chelsea winger, described Keetch shouting to him during a game, 'If you do anything, I'm going to break your effing legs.' Yet he also adds that the Fulham man:

> . . . smelt as if he had emptied the entire contents of a crate of aftershave over his body. You didn't need to see him coming, you could smell him a mile off. His hair was big and bouffant and he wore more jewellery than Mr T. He sported a big, gold necklace and matching rings on his fingers . . . he clanked while jogging up to take a corner.

One Fulham supporter who regularly saw Keetch play was the great artist Sir Peter Blake. 'Bobby Keetch was a very good looking man, with a fighter's face and very blond hair, which he may have dyed,' he told me. 'The art gallery owner Robert Fraser liked him a lot. He used to come with me to Fulham just to watch Keetch. Later on, Keetch hung out with Fraser and his arty crowd, which was a very strange thing for a footballer to do.'

Not many pics of Keetch off-duty seem to exist, although we did access one shot of the man, resplendent in a three-piece suit, shirt and tie. Things were warming up for us.

After football, Keetch went into several business ventures, not least the sports bar he helped launch on the Haymarket in London in 1996. Keetch's status as a Fulham hero and a fascinating character brought to mind two other footballers who have both worn Fulham shirts and stamped their own unique clothing style on the public consciousness: Bobby Moore and George Best.

■■■

The Mod Formal's
Dressing-room, 1963

His hair is college-boy cut, parting high on the left, hair sweeping across the scalp, but with a little bouffant visible at the back, thus bringing together America and France.

His suit is tailor-made. Could be from Bilgorri in Bishopsgate or Mr Eddie on Berwick Street. Either way, the Mod Formal will have obsessed about this number from the minute he chose its material. The jacket will have three buttons at the front, a vent at the back. Italian tailors Brioni, who have introduced a box jacket that is tighter and shorter than the usual cut, have inspired its overall design. Brioni are world famous. Every male American film star who visits Rome visits Brioni, then styles it to the rest of the world.

His shirt is a button-down, made by the American firm Brooks Brothers. This company, formed in 1818, sold its first suit in 1845, made a coat for Abraham Lincoln in 1865 and mass-marketed the button-down shirt in 1896. They are the main purveyors of the ever-influential Ivy League look, worn by both British working-class kids and American businessmen.

His shoes are Bass Weejun loafers. Bass, the company, was formed in 1876 and brought this shoe onto the market in 1936. The design had been inspired by a Norwegian moccasin (thus the name weejun *which echoes the word Norwegian). In 1960, a newspaper produced by the University of North Carolina stated that Weejuns were the hippest shoe on the campus. Within months, every college-boy student for miles around was wearing them. By 1966, the demand for the shoe is so high that company employees can't even score a pair. One of the shoe's most distinguishing features is the semi-pocket featured on the vamp (known as a saddle in the trade). Students started putting a penny coin into the vamp. Some believed it was good luck, others used the device as a travelling wallet for spare change. Either way, the Weejun got the nickname 'the penny loafer'.*

■ ■ ■

The Target Man

Two greats, two very differing looks. The '60s styles of Bobby
Moore and George Best remain one of the most authentic reflections
of British working-class fashion from the time, styles that reside
under the umbrella term 'Mod'.

The British youth cult known as Modernism began at an English
polo match attended by John Brooks. History argues with itself over
the date of this particular game – it is either just before the turn of
the twentieth century or ten years into it – but, either way, Brooks,
the president of the prestigious American clothing firm Brooks
Brothers, is about to make history. He has observed how the collars
on the players' shirts are held down by buttons to prevent them
flapping up in their faces. This neat stylistic invention plants itself
firmly in his mind, stays there until he can get back to New York and
start making shirts with a similar collar.

The shirts are an immediate success. By the mid-'40s, early '50s,
the button-down shirt (with a tab on the back pleat to hang it with
and a placket front to strengthen the buttons) will form the basis of
a look that will be known as the 'Ivy League' style. Its first
proponents are students attending universities in and around New
York, a collective known as the Ivy League, hence the title.

Head to toe, this look begins with the hair, which is college-boy
style. A button-down shirt, a tie, a suit made from mohair-type
material and penny loafer shoes finish off the ensemble beautifully.

Ivy League style is soon noted and then brilliantly appropriated
by jazz men such as Miles Davis. His use of this look remains one of
the great fashion statements of all time. By dressing in the clothing
of those who fiercely resent their culture, their music, the colour of
their skin, Miles and his peers are playing the enemy beautifully,
walking amongst them whilst changing the landscape forever. You

think he's a bank manager, in fact Miles is a revolutionary in silk and mohair.

In 1947, in London, a gang of jazz players – Ronnie Scott, Pete King, Tony Crombie and Eddie Harvey – start emulating this style, flashing their suits and sunglasses at all-night Soho clubs, most of which they opened themselves. It was the birth of Mod. Soon, the children of London would adopt this look and customise it. 'We were the initiators of Mod culture,' the stylist John Simon once wrote. He was right. Simon's own immersion into the world of Ivy League began in the East End when he came face to face with an American soldier dressed in a smart uniform jacket, gabardine trousers and brogues so shiny that when you looked into them your reflection seemed to go right to the centre of the world. Simon was mesmerised by the vision. It would burn itself onto his consciousness and never leave him.

Simon was lucky as well. He had uncles who had just returned from America and they too had been taken by the Ivy League look. They took their nephew to shops such as David's on the Charing Cross Road or Austin's on Shaftesbury Avenue, bought him button-downs and chino trousers.

'It's not surprising that in this atmosphere I became hooked on fashion,' he wrote. One day, he would open up the Ivy Shop in Richmond and footballers, such as Alan Hudson, would travel there to buy brogues and Harrington jackets, Sta-Prest trousers and button-downs.

The stage is set, the time right. In the late '50s, a small group of London teenagers took their cue from their jazz elders and began calling themselves Modernists. They were into jazz and cool attitude, later on RnB and cool attitude. They spent hours discussing clothes, the detail always the most important aspect of their outlook. Detail, detail, detail, detail – for the Mods, details are where the truth is hidden. Other influences are European cinema (especially the clothes worn by Italian actor Marcello Mastroianni), French hairstyles (Jean-Paul Belmondo in *À Bout de Souffle*), Italian scooters and the culture of the cool Continent.

From these influences, the art of customising developed: telling your tailor you want the jacket this way, not that way; the buttons here, not there; the vent at the back this long. Mods changed

London. Clubs that once ran jazz turned into RnB hotspots to accommodate their passion for the music. Georgie Fame moved into The Flamingo on Wardour Street and spent four years there. The Scene club, with Guy Stevens DJing the best in soul, opens up close to Ham Yard. Near Carnaby Street, Count Suckle hosts the Roaring Twenties, where a young Pete Townshend hears ska and an early form of scratching. John Stephen, a young Glaswegian Mod and pioneer, opens up a clothes shop on Beak Street.

In the richer areas of London, other vibrations. Vidal Sassoon cuts hair by day and studies architecture by night. Soon, he combines the two and the first geometric cut is born. Mary Quant designs girl clothes and sells them at her Bazaar shop on the Kings Road in heavy numbers. The miniskirt takes to the streets of London, the papers start calling the world of the young 'the permissive society'. As Aretha Franklin might have sung, 'Change, change, change – change of rules'.

Mods are everywhere and the two footballers who will dominate the '60s, Bobby Moore and George Best, will come to represent both sides of Modernism's nature.

* * *

In all of the reports Mark gave me on Bobby Moore, one facet of his character kept repeating itself – his fastidious style. Time and time again, he is described as 'immaculate' and 'clean', obsessed with appearance. 'His training gear was always spotless, even when he was young,' states Ted Fenton, the West Ham manager who signed Moore. In 2004, Mike Summerbee said, 'Someone once said to me, how do you epitomise Bobby Moore as a person? I said, he is the only person I know who gets out of the bath dry.'

Moore, the England and West Ham stalwart, is Mod Formal – always in charge of himself, never out of control. From an early age, he is meticulous about his appearance. He rarely dresses casual, preferring a smart look. Handmade suits by Dougie Hayward, shirt and tie, smart trousers with a cashmere polo neck, jacket, formal trousers, never jeans.

You could not imagine Moore at a rock gig (too unruly), nor can you picture him pouring champagne into a mountain of glasses. Yet

Moore drank, and drank well. According to close companion Terry Venables, it was Moore's innate shyness that led him to the glass. 'He was such a lovely man,' Venables said, 'but sometimes, if you introduced someone new to his company, he would be stiff and edgy. Then he would have one lager, maybe two, his face would relax and his eyes would start to shine. He needed that lubrication. He never had a problem with drink, but maybe he could have done if he hadn't been so strong, if he hadn't had a sure knowledge of who he was and what he always wanted to be.'

A sure knowledge of who he was — whether he knew it or not, Venables had just expressed the essence of great dressing and of life itself, no less. In all philosophy down the ages, the same order repeated again and again — know thyself. From that point onwards, all wisdom flows.

Moore had a 'sure knowledge of who he was' and that brought him success, which in turn gave him an unassailable confidence. He expressed his belief through his clothes. His wardrobe was his soul and his style located itself at the very heart of Englishness. Moore had a reserve about him, a distrust of emotion that was typical of his countrymen. His cool manner brilliantly symbolised his people. It made him the perfect English captain, the master of control, the one to follow Kipling and keep his head when all about him were losing theirs. It was why he was so revered, so well thought of.

Typically for a clothes stylist of the '60s, he was born in the East End, in 1941.

'He really was the boy next door,' a neighbour said. 'If he saw me he'd say, hello, how are you? Polite, you see. I remember, too, how he never hurried when he walked down the street but seemed to glide. I suppose naturally athletic people do that.'

He was sports mad (could have been a pro cricketer, they say) and joined West Ham in 1956, aged 16. A year later, he made his debut for the England youth team and won a further 17 caps at that level. Ron Greenwood came to manage West Ham, told Moore he was going to build his team around him. Some viewed this notion with real distrust. Moore, they pointed out, did not have any pace, and speedy strikers would make mincemeat of him.

Moore was astute, though. Why? Because he knew himself. Very early on in his career, Moore sought out his mentor, Noel Cantwell,

The Fashion of Football

and asked him directly if lack of speed spelled lack of greatness. Cantwell's response was to tell Moore to study the Fulham player Johnny Haynes. Haynes lacked pace as well but he was clever. He visualised what he was going to do with the ball *before* it arrived. That covered his tracks. Moore began practising this technique and, in this manner, developed a peerless game that would take him to the pinnacle of world football.

In May 1963, he was made the youngest-ever England captain in a game against Czechoslovakia. Three years later, the England team, under his captaincy, famously beat West Germany at Wembley to win the World Cup. As he walked to the stairs to meet the Queen and the Jules Rimet trophy, typically, Moore was not consumed by excitement or wild pride. Instead, he was worried. Would his slightly soiled hands dirty the Queen's immaculate (that word again) white gloves?

I can think of no other player who would think this way having just won the biggest prize in football. It suggests a magnificent obsession. When you look at pictures of Moore celebrating, held aloft by his teammates as he clutches the Cup, his face is not suffused with ecstasy or joy but with quiet, controlled happiness. The smile is wide but held back. It's as if he is thinking, OK chaps, we've won, but life goes on. Now on to the next game.

It was apposite that England should win the Cup in the mid-'60s. This was their decade, the decade that changed the country forever, brought it teenagers, fashion, drugs, pop music, new attitudes, new visionaries.

Football was no exception. Thirty million people watched the World Cup − a figure that equalled viewing figures for Royal occasions. It was a fact that could not go unnoticed. The first man to work Moore's commercial potential was the agent Bagenal Harvey. He netted Moore a Brylcreem poster for which the footballer earned £450. Bagenal also landed Moore and his teammate Martin Peters a commercial advertising pubs, suitably enough. A TV ad for Bisto gravy was then followed by an ad for Vitasil hair tonic. Moore then moved on to clothes.

He was photographed modelling suits for the royal tailor, Hardy Amies, in 1966 but it was a David Walker who took matters further. He approached Moore and, in 1968, the Bobby Moore Shirts and

Ties operation was launched with Walker at the helm. There was also a tie-up (sorry) with Mike Summerbee's shirt-making operation in Manchester. 'Moore and Walker opened a shop up,' the Manchester City legend recalled. 'There was a laundry business there and a bespoke shirt-making business. They used to measure the people up and we made the shirts but we didn't have enough machinists.'

The business soon fizzled out. It was said the only profit Moore made from the venture was a dozen monogrammed silk shirts and ties. The failure of the business set the tone for Moore's future investments. He was a man touched by the hand of unluckiness.

A Hatton Garden jeweller launched the Bobby Moore jewellery line. Outcome? No income. Meanwhile, Moore went into business with Freddie Harrison and Morris Keston. The trade was men's leatherwear. Moore put five grand into the operation – never saw it again. The product they manufactured was high quality and was sold through big-name retailers such as Harrods and Liberty's, and their customers tended to be footballers that Moore tapped up at matches, or film stars, pop people, those irresistibly drawn towards Moore's fame. For his part, Moore designed some of the items, keeping a pad and pencil at hand when he went on his travels in case he spotted a garment he liked.

Business was good, so good that Moore was persuaded to keep putting his profits back into the operation. The business bought a factory in Cyprus and then the curse struck. The introduction of the three-day week in Britain and the invasion of Cyprus by Turkey dealt such crushing blows to the operation that it never recovered. The firm went bankrupt, debts of £373,697 to its name.

Moore waved his five grand goodbye and moved on. The press were overjoyed. They often filled their newspapers with cruel jibes at Moore's lifestyle: the French maid and gardener at his home in Chigwell, his two dozen Savile Row handmade shirts and suits, the manicures he took on trips to the West End. In that sense, the press were as English as Moore.

A Bobby Moore sports shop opened up on Percy Road, opposite West Ham's Upton Park. It did quite well but came nowhere near yielding the anticipated profits. This failure was nothing compared to what came next. At the 1970 World Cup, Bobby Moore was arrested in Bogota, accused of stealing a gold bracelet. He was locked up in a South American jail for days.

Yet, if there was one man to keep his cool in such nerve-racking circumstances, it was Moore. When he came home, his image as the quintessential Englishman was immeasurably strengthened. Johnny Foreigner could never ruffle our boy.

After the World Cup, Moore holidayed in America and was exposed to the huge chains of restaurants and clothing lines from which American baseball legend Mickey Mantle was reaping millions. It was suggested that Moore could start similar enterprises in England. A meeting was arranged between the two stars but nothing came of the venture. Worse, none of Mantle's success as a businessman would rub off on Moore.

Age began to take its slow, inevitable toll. In a 1973 World Cup game against Poland, Moore made a mistake on the pitch that was so out of character the whole nation knew in a second that the end was approaching. He was caught in possession just inside his own half by a Polish forward, who then drilled the ball into the England goal. A year later, Moore's England days were finished, his collection of 108 caps a record number for the time. Only goalkeeper Peter Shilton would better him.

Not long after, Moore was transferred to Fulham, took them to an FA Cup final against West Ham (naturally) and lost 2–0. Moore refused to stick around after the game, went home engulfed in black. Regular defeat on the football field was a taste he was yet to get used to.

He finished his playing days in America, then moved into management. He worked at Southend, Oxford and Swindon. Moore wasn't a managerial success, never got the hang of it. My bet is he was too cool for the players' likings. His bad luck in business continued, never abated. He invested in sports clubs, restaurants, country clubs – and they all went belly up. But, like his clothes, he never lost his style or dignity. Great Britain never woke up to find Bobby Moore splashed all over the morning papers, lamenting his run of misfortune.

Finally, he moved into media and commentating but just as he was finding himself, cancer struck. He died a national hero in 1993, his lifelong love of clothes reflecting not only the dignity that informed his whole career but also the dignity of the class he sprang from. Many now believe that the inability of the football world to help Moore after his playing days was a national scandal. It is a notion that was given much credence when, in 2001, a cap he had earned playing for England against a FIFA team in 1963 was rescinded. Even in death, the national hero was not safe.

* * *

A friend George is a West Ham man, a consistent advocate of the club's academy system which, over the years, has produced the likes of Moore, Hurst and Peters, later on Joe Cole, Rio Ferdinand, Frank Lampard, Glen Johnson and Jermaine Defoe, all of whom have now left the club. As Oscar himself might have noted, to lose one of these players might look like misfortune; to lose the whole bunch . . .

As part of my research, George lent me a Bobby Moore picture book, edited by one David Emery. I decided to show it to the tailor Mark Powell. Powell is one of Soho's colourful characters and a fervent supporter of West Ham. He had attended many games and knew the club's history well. In business, Powell had opted to set himself up as the gangster's tailor. Now he was starting to rue his decision. Such an image is great when it's trendy, not so good when it is out of favour.

'The big stores, they won't even look at me because of my rep,' he complained. Powell's office was on Brewer Street, surrounded by Italian delis, porn shops and markets. Every time I saw him, Al Capone came to mind. It wasn't the physical likeness, I think it was the various chains strung across the waistcoat of his pinstripe suits that clinched it for me.

I met Mark at his office, strolled round to Bar Italia with him. Along the way, a succession of people hailed him. 'What is this? You the king of Soho?' I asked. 'Something like that,' he said, with a gentle, proud smile.

Paolo Hewitt: When did you first see Bobby Moore play?
Mark Powell: I started going to West Ham around 1967. I went to the game West Ham beat Sunderland 8–0. Hurst scored six that day, Moore scored one and Brooking scored one.

The Fashion of Football

PH: I wanted you to look at some of the pics of Bobby Moore in this book and just tell me what comes to mind.

MP: [Turns pages, sees pic of Moore casually dressed in a flowery shirt and trousers] This is an interesting period, the early '70s, because he never really went with it totally, he went with it a little bit, as everyone had to, but you could see in his heart he was a lot more conservative then.

PH: You think he's uncomfortable with the shirt, the open neck and no tie?

MP: He went for it like everybody else but for me the look that exemplifies Bobby Moore more than anything is that mid-'60s period when he used to wear a classic three-button suit or a nice three-button blazer with a pair of casual trousers, and a shirt and a tie. Even his hair at this point is a Perry Como cut grown out a bit.

PH: My theory is that all footballers play how they dress. It's their character that determines their style of play.

MP: I agree. I think one of the classic things about Moore is that when he met the Queen he wiped his hands. He was a very sharp, articulate man. I mean his mum ironed his laces. [Laughs] That says it all really. In the '50s, they used to wear white or yellow laces and she would iron them for him. So, in many ways, he really exemplified the whole mentality and philosophy of what a Mod was.

PH: I think he represents the formal side of Mod.

MP: You spoke earlier about that formal side, which was very much the early modernist look. Modernist rather than Mod. Jazz rather than RnB. Ronnie Scott, Brooks Brothers. He wouldn't have been part of it, as he would have just been growing up, but if you had to define his look, it is that look. His image comes across in that way.

PH: His tailor was Dougie Hayward.

MP: Yeah, I remember. I would have thought that earlier on he would have used a good East End tailor. Some of the tailors round the East End were very good. He probably would have gone round East Ham, Barking, for a tailor in the '50s and the Dougie Hayward thing would have happened probably round the '66 World Cup when he became an established player, because

Dougie Hayward was a celebrity tailor, he did Tarbuck, Dave Allen, Michael Caine . . .

PH: Terence Stamp.

MP: That's right. So it made sense that someone like Bobby Moore would go to him. I wouldn't be surprised if Dougie Hayward had approached him.

PH: There wasn't really anyone to compare with Bobby Moore's style at the time, was there?

MP: Not in the '60s, there wasn't. Alan Hudson was very stylish in the '70s with Chelsea. He was the first footballer to have the shorter Vidal Sassoon haircut.

PH: Mike Summerbee described West Ham to me as 'the Mod team of the '60s'. Why was that?

MP: West Ham as a supporters' club was a Skinhead club, plus the club recruited players from the East End, so there was always a strong street fashion within the club. I can remember people like Johnny Ayris, who used to play on the wing, he was a Skinhead.

PH: As a player, how did you see Moore? A lot of people speak about his lack of pace . . .

MP: It was only in 1973, '74, like the game against Poland, that he showed his lack of pace. Before that, it was never an issue because he was always thinking one step ahead of everyone. That's why his vision was amazing, although sometimes it would work against him because he could actually think too much about what to do and make a silly mistake. He rarely did, which is why it was really noticeable when he did. [Looks at a pic of Moore in 1966 at the hotel prior to the World Cup final.] Even when you see him casual, like this pic, and he's got a Slazenger jumper on, he still looks smart.

■ ■ ■

The Mod Casual's
Dressing-room, 1965

He has on the classic white Fred Perry top, the one Fred Perry launched in 1952. Fred Perry, born in 1909, was a working-class boy from Stockport whose dad was a prominent left-winger. The Perry family came to London in the early 1920s. Fred fell in love with table tennis as a boy and turned professional as a tennis player in 1929. He was great. He won the Wimbledon men's singles title in 1934, 1935 and 1936, the first British tennis player to win three titles on the trot. He was a national hero and the Wimbledon authorities hated him. 'Not one of us,' was their considered opinion of this national hero. (Example: on the occasion of his first victory, a Wimbledon official entered his dressing-room, handed Fred's American opponent a bottle of champagne and said, 'Congratulations, this was one day when the best man certainly didn't win.' Fred was sitting in the bath next door listening.)

He travelled to America, won tournaments there and taught the game to Hollywood stars such as Chaplin and Errol Flynn. In 1950, he was approached by Tibby Wegner, an Austrian businessman. The following year, Fred Perry Sportswear launched the first-ever sweatband. Their next move was to produce a sports shirt, one made from white, knitted cotton-pique material with short sleeves and three buttons. The shirt was launched in 1952 and immediately took off. In the early '60s, due to demand from clothes-shop owners, the company started producing the shirt in different colours. These shirts had coloured piping around the sleeves and collar. It was said that the colours deliberately corresponded with the major football teams of the day.

His jeans are Levi 501s. Their history snakes right back to America and the Californian gold rush in the early 1850s. Loeb Strauss was born in Bavaria in 1829. He emigrated to America as a young man and did the wise thing – changed his name to Levi. In 1853, Levi arrives in San

Francisco. He has brought with him tons and tons of rough tent material which he intends to sell to the gold diggers. They sneer at his opportunism – tents ain't the problem here, they tell Levi, our fragile and ripped working clothes are. Levi goes home and gets thinking, and comes up with a multimillion-dollar idea. Levi takes his canvas and turns it into working trousers, not tents. The workmen buy them in their droves; Levi Strauss and Co. is born.

Around this time, a local tailor called Jacob Davis discovers a way to stop the pockets of his clients' trousers ripping. His solution is to place metal rivets on the stress points. It's a great invention but to patent the idea costs $68, a lot of moolah-doolah.

Davis approaches Levi in 1873 and suggests a partnership. Soon, Levi trousers are causing a sensation with this simple design. In 1890, using serge de Nîmes (a fabric from Nîmes in France; many believe this is the root of the word denim), the Levi 501 jean is launched. At this point, the market for Levi's is the thousands of workmen building America. Everyone else wears formal trousers.

In 1929, that all changes. The stock market crashes, millions of families are forced onto the breadline. In every aspect of their lives, they have to choose the cheaper option and that's how Levi jeans were picked up on and turned into an American symbol of working-class culture.

His shoes are Clarks desert boots. Shoemaker and Englishman Nathan Clark designed the original desert boot during the Second World War. He nicked the idea when he saw fellow soldiers in Burma wearing a similar shoe made in the bazaars of Cairo.

Clark came home and tried to put the shoe into manufacture but encountered a lot of resistance, eventually having to design the pattern himself. In 1950, he introduced them into America, where they had a much better reception. From there, the shoe spring-boarded into Europe ten years later.

The desert boot cut right across classes. You could ride your scooter wearing them because they didn't scratch the running board, you could wear your duffel coat with them and then walk for miles in aid of CND.

The Killing of Georgie

If Bobby Moore was a man in full control, George Best's impulsive nature, his wild-hearted temperament, led him to places Moore would never have visited, such as turning up drunk on national TV or finding himself senseless on early-morning pavements.

Best was both totally open and totally closed, a man of mystery and soul. He once chased a girl for months and months, and when she finally relented and appeared at his house to disrobe and entangle herself with him, she was a greeted by an empty flat and a note on the door from George that read, 'Nobody knows me.'

When Best arrived in this country, the son of a shipyard worker and an alcoholic mother, he was a callow 16 year old who dressed in black and white, very staid, very understated. Within a day, he was back in Belfast, convinced that not even his God-given talent could deliver that which was expected of him by manager Matt Busby. He was wrong. Within a year, Best had transformed himself into one of the most stylish footballers of his time, both on and off the pitch.

At first, Best adored his stardom, for it made his life a dream. Money, champagne, girls, applause, the whole country enraptured by your unique skills — was there ever a better buzz, or curse, for a working-class boy from Belfast? Best played football with extraordinary flair and colour. His ability to create a wondrous magic on the field, to leave defenders in his wake and the crowd gasping at his ability to score goals of supreme imagination, gave British football a completely new dimension. Best brought something totally new to the game and in doing so achieved greatness.

Best was the supreme individualist, a man not given to a belief in tactics, only to faith in his lavish skills. His magic was instinctive, totally unexplainable. His national manager at the time, Billy

Bingham, once said of him, 'He contributes nothing [to team talks] . . . nothing at all. He sits and never utters a word . . . most players want to get involved but when I bring George into the discussion, he'll only say yes or no . . . I don't know why because he's an intelligent boy.'

Best's ascent to the highest levels of fame began in 1963, the year he made his debut for United. He learnt fast. By 1965, he had played fifty-eight League games for United, scored nine goals and made as many appearances for his country. He was not yet twenty. In 1966, United played Benfica away in the quarter-final of the European Cup. Busby ordered his players to contain them for the first twenty minutes at least. Defend, don't let them score. Defend, defend. Those were the strict orders drummed into the players' heads.

'George must have had cotton wool in his ears,' Busby later stated. 'Within the first quarter of an hour, he destroyed them on his own with two goals and made another for Connelly.'

Tactics, schmactics.

Best came home to find his face on the front and back pages of the *Daily Mirror*. He wore a sombrero. El Beatle, they called him. It was a smart move to link him with the Fab Four, for what The Beatles were to pop music, George was to football – an absolute phenomenon, a man of magic, a man who would change the way things were done forever. Just like John, Paul, George and Ringo.

Six days after the Benfica game, Best and close Manchester City friend Mike Summerbee (Best was best man at Mike's wedding) opened up a male boutique called Edwardia in Sale, Manchester. The 400 fans, mainly schoolgirls, who came to the opening nearly brought down the shop window under their collective pressure. For Best, the shop was a diversion whose main rewards were not financial, but those of the flesh.

'I ended up having a stake in three shops,' Best told writer Joe Lovejoy. 'Another one just off Deansgate and the third in the Arndale shopping precinct in Manchester. Summerbee and I were partners but it was Malcolm Mooney who ran the set-up. Mike and I didn't really have much to do with them; we used our names to promote them and popped in once in a while. Just another way of pulling birds I suppose.'

Clothes for the young were the obvious tool in the selling of

Georgie. He was soon being photographed carrying boxes of what he termed 'our new "Mod" stock' into the shop. He was also photographed posing in a white button-down shirt, Prince of Wales checked trousers and waistcoat, looking very Modish. 'I enjoy it and it's good for business,' he stated.

Best often posed with his partner, Mike, and that was good for business as well – United and City for once joined at the hip. Everyone welcome. In one memorable press shot, they wore suits made from 'kid mohair, with satin-faced lapel and cuffs. The trousers are slightly flared with satin-bound side seams. The price, about £42'.

The copy line also says that this is George's one and only suit. 'He always teams jackets with trousers but won't buy a suit.' George's attitude to suits is instructive. At that point in his life, suits to the young symbolised authority, were worn only by the staid, those who would keep talent such as his at bay. Suits were for squares and Best wanted nothing to do with the creaking world the suit represented at that particular point in Britain.

With the shop came further photographic demands. Here's a pic of Mike, modelling a checked umbrella for men, 'one of the first to break away from the traditional black umbrella image', and George sporting a double-peaked rainhat made by Edward Mann and costing 35s 11d. 'Thank heavens for a bit of imagination,' George's quote runs. 'Men tend to be so dull about accessories. They wear floral ties and things, why not stripes and zigzags on umbrellas or caps like this, instead of outdated trilbies?'

As on the pitch, so in the wardrobe. Best yearned for the new. The new coloured up the world, created a brave new future. It was the decade's strongest belief, designed to instigate the complete breaking away from the stiffness of the 1950s, the years of austerity, the years of kowtowing to the upper classes.

George Best, through his style and image, was as intrinsic a part of this shift in attitude as anyone else. Only one suit to his name but there were hundreds of colourful tops and shirts and trousers and shoes and jackets and coats that were issued under his name, the famous George Best clothing range. A man I recently spoke to in Sheffield remembered one George Best shirt – a purple number with red patches on the elbow.

The shops fizzled out in the '70s. They sold men's clothes but females visited the premises far more than males, and most of them were not shopping for their boyfriends. When George and Mike remember this time, their memories have nothing to do with the selling of men's clobber, rather they concern the removing of girls' clothes. As the man said, just another way of pulling birds.

By now, Best was a national phenomenon and knee deep in advertising work. Along with Moore, he was one of the first footballers to be sold by the pound. Amongst the items issued bearing George's name were a range of kids' shoes with an imprint of a footballer on the sole, and then the famous George Best football boot, manufactured by a company called Stylo.

Stylo gave George a good deal. He got £20,000 on signing and 5 per cent from every pair sold. For the first year, the company budgeted on selling 2,000 to 3,000 boots. They ended up selling nearly 30,000. The boots sold well for years.

Best kept going. He promoted a chewing gum called Match. Then he made TV adverts for an aftershave called Fore, in which he walked through a park catching an apple. Pretty girls from miles around suddenly smell his Fore scent and race to embrace him, chasing George down the road. One wonders if a comedian by the name of Benny Hill was watching at the time.

It couldn't last, never does. First, Best's relationship with United started to unravel. In 1971, he disappeared before a game against Chelsea. At the time, United were on a heavy losing streak. No one gave them a chance against the Blues *sans* Best – yet they scored a surprise victory.

'The reason we went so well today,' said an unnamed United player, 'was that George wasn't there hogging the ball. We all got a chance to play with it.'

Dissent in the ranks. Not good. It was known that Bobby Charlton disapproved of Best's lifestyle, the life of short-skirted girls and fast cars and noisy nightclubs. Charlton was old school, British in much the way Moore was. Best annoyed him, exasperated him. Others felt that way as well. 'He's one of the finest footballers I've ever seen,' said teammate Denis Law, 'but he would be twice as good and would score twice as many goals if he got it into his head that there are other players to pass to and he'll get the ball back.'

Best's relationship with his manager, father-figure Matt Busby, began to dip. From an early age, Best understood that his magic protected him, that no one would dare rid United of this turbulent man − just as long as he was unlocking defences, scoring goals, creating victory. When he stopped doing that . . .

After he walked out of the team in 1971, a national media hunt tracked him to actress Sinead Cusack's London flat. A live broadcast was set up outside as the world waited for George to appear. This was fame gone crazy and George knew it. He apologised to his employers, got back in the team, but the tone of his life was now set. Best and United were slowly separating from each other. In the end, Best did the job himself and instigated the final separation. In May 1974, he left United; left behind the dreams he had made so real for so many people and began his travels. And what travels they were . . .

For eight weeks and eleven grand, he plays for a South African team called the Jewish Guild. He returns home and George Best, the man of the '60s, the athlete who, with Muhammad Ali, caught the times, turns up to play at Dunstable, then Stockport, then over to Ireland to play for Cork Celtic. The man obviously doesn't give a fuck. He is destroying his image, killing the smiling man with the girls and the cash and the carefree life, telling the world it is all bullshit. Soon, he starts on himself, dowsing himself in a sea of alcohol to forgive and forget. In an interview, he once joked, 'I saw an advert for Canada Dry tonic water which said, Drink Canada Dry. So I thought, why not?'

Just like Beau Brummell, as he gives his life over to his demons, his fashion sense is cast aside. When he wakes up in the morning, he cares not what he pulls on. He goes to the States, plays for the Los Angeles Aztecs. His drinking gets wilder. One day, driving down the freeway, his wife, Angie, spots a tramp in the pouring rain, trying to get home. Then she recognises him − her husband. She leaves soon after.

Best returns to London, joins Fulham, and sparks of skill and magic fly between him and Rodney Marsh. So good is Best at this point that Billy Bingham takes a chance, puts him in the Northern Ireland team to play Holland. Cruyff versus Best. George versus Johan. The game finishes two all. A fair result.

Best hops on a plane to America, signs for Fort Lauderdale, leaves, then joins Detroit Express. Fulham are enraged. George is still their man, still on their books. They complain to FIFA and Best is given a worldwide ban for signing to different clubs. In March 1978, the ban is lifted and George goes back to Fort Lauderdale. Put simply, he needs the money because he needs to keep drinking. He rows with the coach, then flies to Scotland, joins Hibernian. His play now exists at a low level but the Hibs people are happy. He's putting thousands on the gate every week. Soon after, Best leaves again, travels back to the States and joins the San Jose Earthquakes.

He gets a phone call – Middlesbrough are interested and there's a chance that Bingham might take him to the 1982 World Cup in Spain. He has to get fit, though, has to leave off the booze for six weeks. No way, the very thought causes his body to go into uncontrollable trembles. But Best is clever. Instead, he goes to the World Cup as a commentator, watches Italy take their third World Cup trophy.

At 30 even years of age, he joins Bournemouth, plays a little and then flies to Australia. His final game is with the Brisbane Lions, the latter part of his career as wayward as his drinking.

Alcohol has not let him settle in any part of the world. It brings him into arguments, makes him restless. He comes home and, in 1984, Christmas-time no less, is arrested for drink-driving. He claims the policeman called him an 'Irish wanker' and that's why he head-butted him. The judge couldn't care less. Best is given a three-month sentence and spends the festive period behind bars. It is safe to assume he is not wearing cords, a flowery shirt and a nice jacket as he completes his sentence.

After his release, the pub beckoned. One night in 1990, so did chat-show host Terry Wogan. Best came on wearing a horrible green suit, a beard and a cruel smirk. He was off his trolley.

'What do you like to do?' the genial Irish host asked the drunken Irishman.

'Shagging, Terry, I like shagging,' was Best's reply. The interview was quickly terminated but still broadcast.

No longer was Best a symbol of the times but a man bloated by alcohol, a far cry from El Beatle, the slim Mod of the '60s. He spent his days in pubs, earning the odd coin here and there through after-dinner speaking. There was little else for him to do. Then, symbolically, the game he had helped create came to rescue him.

The formation of the Premiership in 1992 not only brought incredible amounts of money into the game but also fuelled an interest which burns as bright today as it ever did. The past, the present, the future of football — all of it endlessly debated and written about, day in, day out. Luckily for George, this development took place. Suddenly, he was in demand — after-dinner speaker, talker and raconteur, just show up and be George Best and we will give you money. Lots of it.

A whole Sunday night on BBC2 was given over to Best, with screenings of film after film of his amazing on- and off-field exploits. Offers from abroad came to him and so did a young 23-year-old stunna, Alex. He married her in 1995 but the drink still haunted him. He went with her to detox clinics and recovery houses but, in 2002, the inevitable. Best was rushed into hospital, given a liver transplant.

I'll never drink again, he swore. In public. Again. And, for a while, he was good for his word. Pictures of him, slim and trim, were released to the press. Alex, triumphant, by his side. But it wasn't the fairy tale we all wished for. It rarely is when the bottle is at the centre of the story.

Then came some news about George that made Mark and I look at each other and reach for that phone.

* * *

In 1968, George Best and Danny Bursk, George's agent at the time, itemised for a teen magazine the clothes they were taking on holiday to Spain that summer. George's list included half a dozen soft roll-collar American shirts, a white wide-zip-front cardigan by Jaeger, lightweight jackets, trousers and sweaters for the evening, denim shorts in orange and red stripes, and matching shirts by Ben Sherman. Next to this list was a pic of George supping on a bottle of coke and wearing brown towelling striped shorts, again by Ben Sherman.

Over 30 years later, George would resume his relationship with

Ben Sherman by agreeing to the company launching an exclusive George Best range of clothes. Since its inception in 1962, the famous shirt company had flourished thanks to its button-down shirts. Of late, though, there had been a growing realisation that to survive in today's label-led market would mean expanding their clothing range. The shirts became part of an extensive Ben Sherman wardrobe that included items such as hooded tops, T-shirts, trainers and desert boots. The George Best range included similar items but with George's autograph strategically placed on the cloth.

Mark rang the company, grabbed some time with their PR girl, Sarah Feeney, and marketing director, Andy Rigg. Feeney was bright, bubbly, anxious to help. She promised us a Best interview, and Mark and I went away happy.

It wasn't to be. Two weeks after our meeting, Best attacked a photographer in a Surrey pub he was boozing in. From here, his life unravelled. His wife, Alex, threatened to leave, then came back. Then another girl appeared on the cover of a tabloid claiming that she and George had been more than just good friends. The following week, that was amended – she was carrying his baby.

Alex threw a complete fit and left for Australia to appear on the TV show *I'm a Celebrity Get Me Out of Here*. That was the last straw for Best. A week later, another young blonde girl appeared in a tabloid and told of her sexual liaisons with George. Alex filed for divorce and then, to really piss him off, posed for *Loaded* magazine in a skimpy bikini. Best went out on the town, brought two hookers back to his hotel room, then in the morning discovered they had disappeared with two grand of his money.

Most men would have kept their mouths shut, covered up the crime with a blanket of guilt. George? He marches into the nearest police station and reports the theft. The following day, Best is on the front page again, relentlessly smearing the '60s sunshine image that he once epitomised.

'Don't reckon he'll be much in the mood for talking about clobber now,' Mark said drily to me over the phone.

'Shame we're not the coppers who interviewed him,' I replied. 'Could have killed two birds with one stone.'

'I think he did that last night,' Mark shot back.

'Could have said to him, Mr Best, when you awoke, how long

The Fashion of Football

before you discovered your money was missing? Really? And when you ran the Edwardia shop in 1966, what kind of clothes did you have on sale?'

'He probably just wants to sink a few sherbets and be left alone,' Mark pointed out.

'True. What we need is someone who went to his shop.'

And a month later we found him. His name is Steve Diggle; he is the guitarist with a group called The Buzzcocks. The band formed in the mid-'70s, released some striking songs, some big, some small. Nearly 25 years later, they are still a concern.

Diggle had just released a biography called *Harmony In My Head*. I had skimmed through the book on the way to meet him. Given the stories of excess contained within, I was not surprised by most people's amazement that the man is still functioning in such a lively manner.

As a kid, Diggle visited George Best's Edwardia shop and was a big United fan. We met him in The Spice of Life pub in Soho, Diggle with his mate Welsh Pete. Even though I was meant to be off the cigs, I brought a pack of ten along. I know what I'm like. One drink, got to light up. I smoked three in the interview, Diggle had a couple as well. When we left, I nodded to the half-empty pack on the table. 'You can have those, mate,' I said. 'I don't want them any more.'

'Don't give them to him,' cried Welsh Pete suddenly.

'Why not?' I asked.

''Cos he's got bloody emphysema.'

Diggle sat there with a cheeky grin on his face, the little boy caught red-handed. The man obviously needed to take it really easy, relax, detox a bit.

On the Tube home, I remembered where he was going the next day – to America for a 20-date tour.

* * *

Mark Baxter: How long have you been a United man?

Steve Diggle: By rights, I should have been a City fan. In 1962, my dad took me and me brother to Manchester City. They lost to Preston North End. Then we moved to Bradford. Also, in that street, I first came across The Beatles. The girl across the road had long, blonde hair and a hairdryer, which I'd never seen in my life – it was like a Russian Sputnik – and she's listening to the first Beatles album and I'm there with my mate watching her dry her long, blonde hair in a mirror listening to 'Please, Please Me'. I got a guitar when I was about seven and looking at the girl with the long, blonde hair in the mirror and this Russian Sputnik hairdryer drove my first sexual experience, and all that soaked in with playing football in the street. So, certainly George Best to me was the fifth Beatle, like he was to many people. That was my background to it.

Paolo Hewitt: How old were you in '62?

SD: I'd be seven. We used to play football in the street and hit people's windows. Somebody would come out and go, 'Fucking ball. Now look what you've done. You'll get a good hiding off your folks.' Or you'd get a clout off the bloke if he caught you. Then, suddenly, it was like, let's go to United. You could take your banners, the rattles, the scarves. I remember buying a rattle off a kid and it was a work of art, you know.

MB: Haven't still got it, have you?

SD: No. I wish I did. I left it in a fucking house in a box with a lot of stuff, you know.

PH: Can you remember what the United fans were wearing at the time, '61, '62?

SD: Real early days? It was the scarves, the rattles, the plastic United badges. Always a scarf and a bobble hat. There were plastic star badges, with like a plastic sheriff's star with the individual members on them, like Denis Law. I'm just trying to remember the clothes. I remember having a suede, what do you call them, windjammer jacket, you know, and my cousin being a rock 'n' roll geezer with pointed shoes and a white plastic jacket.

Getting on towards '64, '65, it was like Levi's with the darkest blue we'd ever seen and the little turn-up. We used to buy brown Oxford shoes which not many people had, and what they called a surfer jacket. I guess because of The Beach Boys and that. I know they sell them now with the elastic in them. They used to be called surfer jackets. And so you'd have something like that with the badges, these plastic badges. But when you were walking down to Old Trafford, kids would run by and pull the fucking scarf or your hat. Particularly the hats, so you had to hold onto them.

PH: Did you travel away with United?

SD: Not really because I was really young. [Pauses] We had the banners in those days, you know. You used to paint the banners with either the Union Jack on the white bedsheet or whatever. And, of course, when you were in the ground it was always in the wet. And it was the same about the rattles. I mean 60,000 rattles going – it was phenomenal really. Even if you did it in a terraced street, it was enough to make a deafening sound, you know. So, that was the kind of scene. [Pauses] But I think probably '62 it would have been those jeans which you'd either get off the market or the shops. They were either ice blue or dark blue, with an axe on the back. We'd get 'em for 10 shillings, you know. And that was your standard, like rock 'n' roll Elvis-type jeans.

MB: Tesco, Tesco bombers.

SD: Tesco specials. Actually, ice blue were cool looking back then. As a kid, you normally wore the denim ones because they were ice blue.

PH: And was Best your man?

SD: Oh, yeah, because like I was telling you about The Beatle thing, it went hand in hand with music. And I was only seven, and I heard The Beatles and that was it for me. The English teacher couldn't give you the insight that The Beatles were giving you. Then I'm going to Old Trafford. I'm watching Bobby Charlton, you know. Respected footballer but he's bald-headed, you know what I mean. And, in rock 'n' roll, if you haven't got hair, it's unforgivable.

MB: Big trouble, ain't it?

PH: Unless you're Isaac Hayes.

SD: Unless you're Isaac Hayes. But if you're white, it's pretty tricky. Maybe fucking Coldplay can get away with it but you've got to have hair. At United, Denis Law was the industrious Scotsman, he was kind of stylish in a man's man way but Best was slightly effeminate. I remember on the terraces, if he lost the ball when he was running down the wing, they'd go, 'Where's your handbag, Georgie?' This is from United fans and I couldn't understand it. I suppose they were the older ones, in their 50s. To them, he was a little bit effeminate. He had the long hair.

Charlton had no hair. Denis Law had a regular, sensible kind of cut but Best was glamorous. He had a suntanned thing. He was obviously going to Majorca when it was new. And there was sex. It was like, I'm looking at a team of just regular footballers who kind of look all right and there's this guy who was like sex, like The Beatles.

Then you realised you could actually get the autographs. You could queue up for Bobby Charlton, same with Denis Law but it was like, where's George Best? We want him, really. He's the glamour one. Forget Charlton, we're after George Best. So, it was like running after a Beatle. And you'd see his car. In '65, he had a blue Sunbeam Alpine soft-top car. And it was always dirty. It was a work of art really because it had 'I love you, Georgie' and all this stuff all over the car. The other players probably cleaned their cars or had a cleaner or something but his was fucking dirty. And it looked fantastic. It was like John Lennon's Rolls-Royce, the psychedelic one. It was like that, covered everywhere in kisses, 'I love you, Georgie' or 'George you're best', all that stuff. There would be loads of girls going, 'George, George,' and he would say, 'No, I ain't got the time,' and they loved him even more because they thought, 'Fucking hell, he won't even give you an autograph.' Whereas Bobby Charlton is plodding away going, 'Next one, please.'

As much as I love Bobby, it was like George was untouchable. And, in a way, you almost didn't want to meet him because you knew he'd either tell you to fuck off or he'd say, 'Get away from the car' or something, so you didn't want to meet him in a sense. And when you realised that George Best had a Sunbeam Alpine, then moved on to Jaguars and Lotus Elans but still went back to his landlady, Mrs Fullaway in Chorlton, I always loved that as well. Then I discovered he had a shop, you know.

PH: What year was this?

SD: It was Who time and Modtastic time. I remember seeing collarless shirts in the window, those Dave Clark Five ones, although even as a kid I realised Dave Clark wasn't cool. When you watched *Ready Steady Go!* in black and white, you knew

Mick Jagger was cool and The Beatles were cool but Dave Clark . . . So I remember seeing those shirts in the window and being really disappointed, thinking, 'Is that the George Best collection, or is it a bit too much Dave Clark Five, because I ain't seen The Beatles wearing them,' you know.

PH: Did you go into the shop?

SD: Yeah, but I was only a kid and you didn't have the money to buy stuff in those days.

MB: Did you ever see Best in there?

SD: You always went in the shop in the hope. You always wanted to say, 'Is George in?' but you couldn't say it because you knew they'd just laugh at you. But there'd be some cool dudes there with their arms folded in really cool gear, you know.

MB: Whereabouts was the shop?

SD: I think it was Brown Street, just off Market Street.

MB: Is that in central Manchester?

SD: Yeah, very central. There was another one. Gets a bit hazy. By the Village Barber in, fucking hell, just off Deansgate somewhere. I'm just trying to think where. It used to be a little bit more upmarket there. I think the initial one . . . I'm trying to, you know, the drugs and the years . . .

PH: I find that funny, having a shop with Mike Summerbee of Man City. I mean, it's a bit like Tony Adams and Steve Perryman opening up a shop.

MB: But he was best man at his wedding, so they were obviously . . .

SD: It was a weird thing. It was like when you saw him on the news and he didn't turn up for training and on *Granada Reports* you had Bob Greaves going, 'They're looking for George Best. They don't know where he is.' Then they would find him and it would always be, 'I've had a word with the boss and I'll be back tomorrow.' And then some days, he didn't go back the next day. You think, 'That's even fucking better.' You know there's pictures of him like the Small Faces, in a magazine trying on shoes. You think, 'Wow, this is amazing.' That made him a lot more fucking interesting than Sir Bobby Charlton.

PH: Would George's shop have been comparable to what John Stephen was doing in Carnaby Street, where you could go and get all these up-to-date clothes?

SD: Yeah, it was Carnaby Street definitely. You had high-vented coats, button-down shirts and the long-sleeved button-down ones, those Dave Clark Five shirts I mentioned earlier. All the tasty stuff, yeah.

PH: Were there other shops in Manchester doing the same thing?

SD: Well, we had the Brown Street shop and I think there was this shop called Stolen From Ivor. That was the joke, a marketing thing. They sold bright-green bags with Stolen From Ivor written on them. That was a prophecy because, later on, by the time you get to the Happy Mondays, it was all fucking stolen.

Welsh Pete: Do you remember the sheepskin coat, the George Best sheepskin? It had a label inside with a picture of George Best's face. George Best – his label, his coat.

SD: That's right because the logo, wasn't it like half a globe or something? A round circle cut in half in the centre and one half was like a grid. And that was the whole George Best Collection. And so everything you bought from there had that label. And also I remember getting a card as well and it had a shot of him with a black double-breasted coat on, black trousers, it was all dark against a white background with a cup of tea, 'Join the Tea Set'. Might even have got that card from the shop. You walk in, 'Have one of these.' He'd obviously done a deal with fucking Typhoo Tea or British Tea, British India Tea Company or whatever it was at the time.

PH: He was doing deals with everyone at the time, wasn't he?

SD: That's right. That advert in Hyde Park, what was that for?

MB: That was his aftershave, a men's range called Fore, like in golf. And then there were the George Best football boots, the Stylo boots.

SD: Oh, yeah. I had some of them at school as well, actually. White soles, yeah?

WP: A mate of mine had some pairs of them. He got seven hundred quid on eBay. They had George Best written on them in gold writing. Boxed. Unworn. They're beautiful.

SD: He was such a rebel. He was a Sex Pistol before the Sex Pistols, do you know what I mean? He didn't turn up to the rehearsals, the training. He was with glamorous birds, he could drink, it was like, what more do you want from a footballer? And he had that dark intriguing bit. 'Oh, I'll sleep on the railway tonight.' It was like, 'You got a big match tomorrow.' He wasn't going home to a wife and family and all that kind of stuff.

PH: Did you go to the house he had built?

SD: I didn't actually go there. I sort of passed it in me dad's car and they'd go, 'There's George Best's house,' and you're, 'Wait a minute,' but you'd be on your way to Chelmsford because we used to have some relations there. That's where I watched the World Cup final in '66.

PH: How did you feel when George left United?

SD: That's when I kind of left football as well because they won the Double really. It was '68, wasn't it, I think.

PH: You won the European Cup.

SD: European Cup and the League. I was in the Stretford End and I thought, 'They've done it all and Best is leaving,' and that for me was like a departure. It was like I was tired of queuing, especially for the United against City matches. You'd queue all fucking day round the ground. As soon as you got near the box office, there'd be fights breaking out. You'd get a police horse in your face. It would be raining. And you'd be at the back of the queue again, and you don't want to be there, so I rekindled my interest in music.

MB: Should have stayed really, shouldn't he?

WP: He was only 27, weren't he?

PH: And, after him, you get all these lookalike players. Remember Peter Marinello?

SD: Yeah, and Willie Morgan. They were the Inspiral Carpets to the Happy Mondays.

PH: It's like in music now, somebody does something and they all repeat it.

SD: Do you remember when he ran off with Miss World, Marjorie Wallace? Well, a mate of mine was in the fire brigade and he took me in this fire brigade van. I'm sat in the back and I looked out the window and saw a white Jaguar behind. And it was George Best with Marjorie Wallace. He looked so glamorous. He was driving a white Mark II Jag. I thought, 'I'm touched by the hand of God or the fucking toe of a genius.' [Laughs]

But that was telling me something. I followed a white-line highway to a rock 'n' roll band and I always thought at the end of the white line would be the white Jag with Marjorie Wallace and George Best going, 'Come on in. You can't go wrong here. There's champagne.' I can't think of a footballer before George Best that really was doing anything. There weren't any. They had sensible haircuts. They went home to their wives, you know. They got married when they was bloody 18. They didn't go to clubs and they always turned up on time, and played the game. It was that old-fashioned school, you know. Whereas Best broke the mould of everything really, and a lot more than he's credited for.

■ ■ ■

A Vodka and Cranberry Is Good for the Joints

I hated getting older, hated the way my energy levels started dropping. I didn't care much either for hangovers that now lasted half a week, not half a day, or that my stomach was starting to fight with my shirts. There was only one option open to me: I joined the local gym. Started New Year's Day and within a week I was buzzing. It was like shaking off tired dust that had been clinging to my bones for years.

And then after an hour-long morning session, my back went. I thought it might. To cut a long story short, ever since a famous New Romantic vocalist put his knee into the base of my spine in a football match (and after all those wonderful things I used to say about his band in the *NME*), it had never been 100 per cent. What's more, it was a bad time to get hurt. That day, Mark and I were due to talk to the Chelsea icon Alan Hudson. I spent the morning resting, willing my back to heal, but come two o'clock I was still stationary. I slid off the sofa, crawled to the phone. 'It's me. I'm sorry, mate, you're going to have to interview him alone. My back's gone.'

'What? You're winding me up, aren't you?'

'Went to the gym, done my back. I can't move.'

'You are joking, aren't you?'

He knew I wasn't, knew it wasn't a wind-up. I could already hear the worry in his voice. 'Look, it'll be fine. Get a tape recorder and just be natural with him.'

'Be natural? Be natural? I've never done this before. How about telling me what to ask?'

Do anything long enough, it becomes second nature. I had spent 25 years interviewing people. Unless I was going head to head with a Mike Tyson or Nelson Mandela, nerves were no longer part of the equation. That obviously wasn't the case with Mark. He had been a printer for 14 years, lived the good life. Then Fleet Street changed, so did Britain. Murdoch and Thatcher had his meal ticket confiscated. Now he worked for a property developer in posh Piccadilly. He was not used to sitting down with celebrities and interrogating them. He was used to working with clients and deals. I could hear his mind screaming down the phone: What if I fuck it up? What if I make a prick of myself? Nightmare.

'OK,' I said softly. 'First off, ask him where he and Osgood and the rest of the Chelsea team got their clothes from. Ask him why they were the most fashionable team of their time. One thing I'm interested in is whether they used clothes as a kind of psychological bait.'

'As a what?'

'As a wind-up, to annoy the other teams, especially Leeds. What did Leeds wear? Straight stuff. And there was Chelsea with the cravats and the flares and the loud jackets and the Rod haircuts. It had to be a wind-up on their behalf.'

'Gotcha.'

'Don't worry about the biographical stuff, we can get that elsewhere.'

'You mean *I* can get that elsewhere.'

'*Scusa mio. You* can get that elsewhere.'

'You sure you can't make it?' he suddenly asked.

'Mark, mate, I can't move.'

'Getting old, son, ain'tcha? You won't be any good down White Hart Lane soon.'

'Thanks for the reminder. Honestly, you'll be fine. Look, any problems, just call. I'll be here, won't be going anywhere in this state.'

'OK, I'll do my best. But when we do the Tubby Hayes book, you better not do this to me again.'

I put the phone down and thought to myself, imagine if you had to do Mark's work for a day and everything depended on it. How would you feel? Like he did round about right now.

Alan Hudson was due to attend a boxing press event, we were scheduled to talk to him afterwards. And it was important that we did. If any player symbolised the Chelsea team of the '70s, it was Hudson. With his grown-out Mod haircut, his Squire suits, his Ivy

Shop brogues, his face that spoke of debauchery, of naughtiness, Hudson was the player to whom the fans gravitated. He was Chelsea through and through. He was born near the ground and stood on the terraces as he grew up. He knew the crowd and they knew him, for he was they as they were he, and they were all together.

Naturally, it helped that Hudson was such a gifted player, a man who could drift past opponents with ease, score goals with style and create countless opportunities for his teammates. Like his clothes, Hudson's skills were based on panache and style. This fact did not go unnoticed. In March 1972, under Terry O'Neill's lens, Hudson posed for the best football and fashion photo ever – a shot of Hudson with Dave Webb, Geoff Hurst, Terry Venables, Terry Mancini, Alan Ball and Rodney Marsh taken in a London restaurant. 'Look at Hudson in that photo,' David Rosen had instructed me. Rosen is a man immersed in fashion history and football – you will meet him later. 'Out of all the players, how smart is he? He's the smartest by a mile.'

In the photo, the players are gathered around a restaurant table. There are glasses of brandy in front of them and Hudson is wearing a two-button, checked suit from Squire with a dark polo-neck jumper, clutching a cigar. Happy days.

In 1974, Hudson was sold to Stoke and the Chelsea era came to a close. He caused ripples there and then moved to Arsenal in 1976. He briefly returned to Chelsea and again to Stoke in the early '80s before age, the footballer's curse, rendered his body unworthy of the battle. Later on, he wrote his autobiography, and gave it one of the best titles ever: *The Working Man's Ballet*.

In 1997, he was involved in a crash which nearly took his life, and came close to having both legs amputated. He swears he would have finished his life then and there if that operation had taken place.

He appeared in London's *Evening Standard* recently, in an excellent piece by Emine Saner, complaining that the council were going to move him from his flat and that he was finding it hard to make ends meet. He would never go cap in hand to Chelsea for financial help, though. Some things never change.

Mark met him in his local social club in Chelsea. Hudson wore a camel-coloured coat, dark-blue strides and a pair of brogues. Mark also wore brogues. The two had something else in common –

Hudson calls the club his 'office'. Mark offered him a drink, Hudson took a vodka and cranberry, then took many more. 'Good for the joints,' he explained.

Mark Baxter: Alan, can you give us a bit of background as to how you got involved with Chelsea Football Club?

Alan Hudson: Well, all through school I was in the school football team, and when I reached 13, my dad took me to Fulham to have a trial. They told him I was too small for them. Of course I was too small! I was only 13. Anyway, from there I ended up playing for a team called the Chelsea Boys' Club, aged 14, which was a very high standard of schoolboy football. I had a trial for London, but didn't get selected, and then I had a go at Chelsea, and they took me on aged 15. I signed schoolboy forms for them and then I became an apprentice shortly after in 1966.

MB: Around then, what clothes were you wearing?

AH: I was part of the Mod scene, really, and bought most of my clothes from Just Men. Harrods had an in-store boutique called Way In where the styles were straight out of Carnaby Street, but affordable to me. I particularly remember the matching shirt and tie being a big style around then. I once wore a matching shirt and tie with my club suit, and got slaughtered by the rest of the team for doing so.

MB: When did you break through to the first team?

AH: That was aged 17, and it wasn't anything to do with me playing well at the time. It was more a result of a few of the first-team squad having had a 'heavy lunch' in Barbarella's restaurant and being incapable of turning out for the club.

MB: Who among the first team were well dressed around that time?

AH: Well, Birchenall fancied himself and tried a few haircuts; Eddie McCreadie was into his clothes and was known to turn up at training in a three-piece suit on more than one occasion; Osgood was basically an old Windsor farmer and really didn't have a lot of idea on what to wear. He got me to take him down the Kings Road and show him where to get some gear.

I took him to I Was Lord Kitchener's Valet and also to Just Men, where I was well known to the staff. I left him in there whilst I went for a drink in Alexander's across the road. He finally came back to me with loads of suits and shirts, etc. A couple of days later, he's going around the changing-room telling everybody that if they needed any gear, to see him, as he knew all the places to go. He knew nothing, just a big old farmer, cheeky c*nt!

MB: Who else around those times was well turned out from other teams?

AH: Well, obviously Terry Venables, George Graham and Mooro, Bobby Moore, who was immaculate . . . immaculate.

MB: I found out he was getting his suits made down in Savile Row at one point.

AH: Yeah, looked like it. Mind you, you have to wonder where he got the dough, 'cos he wasn't getting that great money. Maybe he did a couple of deals, helped people out with tickets and got a good price down there. I used a tailor called Major in Dawes Road, between Fulham and Hammersmith.

MB: Why there?

AH: Oh, everybody who was anybody went there. Anyone you noticed who was well dressed in a pub, say, nine times out of ten, had a Major suit on. Expensive in there. I had a jacket which I wore to the 1970 Cup final, a blue and black check from there that cost me £200, which was a hell of a lot of money back then. Word had it that Dougie Hayward [celebrity tailor to Michael Caine, Sean Connery . . .] did a lot of work for them.

MB: Did any other players use them?

AH: When I went to Stoke, I introduced Geoff Hurst and Peter Shilton to them.

MB: There's that classic photo of 'The Clan' around the early '70s, taken by Terry O'Neill. Tell me about that.

AH: Great photo, that. I got a call to shoot down to this restaurant, down by the Ritz, which I would never find again, and the guys were already in there – Bally, Marsh, Hurst, Mancini, Venables – all with the cigars on the go and a brandy in hand. Wouldn't go down too well with today's managers, would it?!

MB: What about George Best?

AH: Had everything, the only player who had it all. Even his name was perfect. Best. Hollywood stars would pay a fortune to have a name like that. If he played today, and kept his nut down for a couple of years, he'd be a multi-multimillionaire. He told me a story once, where he was getting a bollocking from Matt Busby over something he had done. After 45 minutes of being ranted at, he had counted every flower on the wallpaper, hadn't taken a blind bit of notice. Basically, Busby couldn't control him any more, a bit like Beckham and Ferguson. Beckham had outgrown all of that.

MB: Talking of which, what do you think of Beckham?

AH: Fucking fantastic. Handles it all very well. Good player, a bundle of energy and has become an icon. He's quite effeminate in a way. Him and Best are totally different, ain't they? George – dark, birding it up – and Beckham – blond, married young, two kids – different people really.

MB: I'm interested in the rivalry with Leeds back in the early '70s. Tell me about that. Did you dress up a bit to wind them up when you all went up there for a game?

AH: Not sure about that. There was definitely a rivalry with them, but that had been there for years. I went to watch us play them once and I stood on The Shed and got pelted with coins by some of their mob, so there was always something there. We really used to dress up for the games in Manchester to be honest, 'cos we always used to end up at George's club Bestie's after the game, and wanted to be well turned out for that.

MB: How about later in your career, did you always keep up with the fashions?

AH: [Smiles] No, no, not really . . .

MB: Thanks, Alan, it's been a pleasure.

■ ■ ■

The Chuckle Brother

Question: How did the 18-year-old Alan
Birchenall celebrate signing his first
contract as a professional footballer with
Sheffield United? Did he (a) go to the nearest
bar and drink himself to oblivion, or (b) go
home and celebrate with a cup of tea and an
early night?

Answer: Neither. This is what he did . . .

'I decided the best way to celebrate my new-found wealth was to invest in a made-to-measure suit. In those days, only pop stars and film stars had special suits and, of course, impressionable young footballers. Although the money might not sound tremendous, the average wage was only £10 a week. Bear in mind that at that age – 18 – I was now earning more money than my dad at Bartons Transport. Off I went to the tailor's in The Moor, the main shopping area of Sheffield. I felt like a million dollars as I picked out the roll of grey mohair cloth from which my suit would be made.'

This revealing quote is taken from *Bring Back The Birch* (still hanging on as the worst ever title for a biography . . .). Mark showed it to me on the train to Leicester City, the football club Birchenall has supported all his life and the place where he now works as a kind of talisman, showing people around, arranging various matters, generally livening up the place with his sunny optimism.

'He's another from that culture,' I pointed out to Mark. 'Working class, always look smart, suit when you're 16. So many of these '70s players have gone through the same thing.'

I didn't really have to tell Mark this. He was from exactly the same background. The codes and rituals handed down to Birchenall and his generation were exactly the same as those Mark received growing up in South London.

'I hope that Muzzy Izzett is around when we get there,' I said. 'I want to have a word with him.'

The week before, Izzett had scythed down our in-form striker, Freddie Kanouté. The latest report suggested that the Tottenham striker would be out for a month. With Robbie Keane's form drying up and Hoddle's last two signings – Bobby Zamora and Helder Postiga – out of their depth, the month ahead did not look good for Spurs, especially with the Cup games due to start.

'Did you see that foul? Last minute of the game, harmless ball, and bang, Izzett's put our best striker out for a month.'

'Gonna struggle now, son. He's been playing well, that Kanouté. But you know what you need, don'tcha? New manager, son, new manager.'

'I know. Pleat's better than Hoddle but that ain't saying a lot. Be honest with you, a lot of games, like that Leicester one, we've blagged it. Played crap for 80 minutes and then, bang, two goals from nowhere. We did it against Villa, and the only way we got a 0–0 up at Man City was because their best chances fell to Wanchope and not Anelka.'

I looked out of the window at the flashing green. 'It can't carry on like this,' I said.

At Leicester train station, we caught a cab to Filbert Street. We shouldn't have. The interview had been arranged to take place at the training ground, three miles away. It was another one of my mistakes. I had been told this in an email but had completely forgotten.

Mark had adapted to my forgetful nature quite easily. I knew that my haphazard organisational skills went directly against his grain. Mark was meticulous, organised. Everything he said he would do, he did, on the button, on time, without fail. Me? Half the time my head is in a book and my feet are in the penalty area.

We caught a cab. 'You can pay for this one, son,' Mark said. 'Teach you to remember little things like where to go when you arrange to interview someone.'

I couldn't argue back against that point.

At the ground, we asked at reception for Emma, who had arranged the meet with Alan Birchenall. The guy behind the desk made a call. As he did so, Mark nudged me. I looked to my right and there, plainly visible through two doors, sitting at a table with five other Leicester players, was Muzzy Izzett.

'Now's your chance, son,' Mark said.

'Damn right,' I replied and, before the receptionist could move, I went straight to the doors, barged through them and marched up to Izzett, who was picking at a half-empty dinner plate.

'What the fuck was that tackle on Kanouté all about?' I demanded. 'He's out for a month because of you.'

Everyone except Izzett stood up. He just looked at me, blankly.

'Oi, mate, what do you think you're doing?' one of the players shouted.

I took no notice. 'Come on, why did you fucking do it?'

All five Leicester players – I think Matt Elliot was one of them, Paul Dickov another – flung their arms out and grabbed me. 'Get him out of here,' they shouted, pushing me towards the doors.

'Where the fuck is security?'

'You bastard,' I shouted back at Izzett, struggling to get to him as the players hauled me away. 'You'll pay for that tackle. You wait and see. You'll pay.'

Mark nudged me. I awoke from my daydream.

Alan Birchenall's office was in the reception area. On the door, he had placed a sign which read 'The Honourable Alan Birchenall MBE', a reward he had been given in the New Year's honours list, 2002. As we waited for him, Micky Adams, Leicester manager at the time, walked through, nodded at us, complete strangers, and said, 'How you doing, boys?'

'Fine,' we both replied.

'Good,' he said, pleasantly. 'Good.'

A minute later, Alan Birchenall shuffled into view. He was wearing a dark-blue T-shirt, grey tracksuit bottoms and the inevitable trainers. His hair was still blond under an Admiral's cap with 'The Birch MBE' written on it, his face a happy-natured one.

'You the lads from London?' he asked, as we rose to greet him.

'Come to see The Birch, have you?' he chuckled. 'Come in here, then. Come into The Birch's office.'

We soon discovered that 'The Birch', as he kept referring to himself, tended to end most of his sentences with a laugh. It was an endearing trait, made you warm to him.

We walked in, settled down, Birchenall behind his desk, us in front of him. He had a slight tan, not much weight on him. He looked good for his age, although he walked at a meandering pace.

'What's this all about then?' he asked us.

'We're doing a book.'

'A book? Have you seen mine? It's called *Bring Back The Birch*. Great title, eh?' Another chuckle. I kept my counsel.

'The book is about football and fashion,' I explained, 'and obviously the Chelsea team you played for in the '70s is going to feature quite heavily.'

'We loved that quote of yours, about having a suit made the day you signed for Sheffield United,' Mark added.

'It took about bloody six weeks to make, you know,' he said, chuckle. 'And when you went to the Far East, you could have it made in 24 hours. Here, you went back for about five fittings, you know, and it were about a month to five, six weeks before your bleeding suit was finished, and that's when you could afford to do it. As a young kid, I was an engine fitter coming out with a fiver a week, £6, £7. All of a sudden, I'm bumped up to £40 a week or, if we had two games, I was coming out with £60. Fucking couldn't believe it. So, you could buy a roll of cloth. You bought the roll and then had the suit made.

'Mohair was a big fashion statement in the mid-'60s and then, of course, when I got down to Chelsea and Eddie McCreadie took me up. I always remember it was Eddie McCreadie, Chopper Harris [Ron Harris, club captain], Ossie [Peter Osgood] and I think it was "Sponge" Tommy Baldwin, I think, 'cos Cookie [Charlie Cooke] was a bit of a loner. He used to go off on his own and do his fashion statement. We used to go off mob-handed.'

'Where did you go? Which tailor did you use?' I enquired.

'It was in Soho. It was . . .'

'Mr Eddie?'

'Ah, that rings a bell. Think it was. I can call someone, I'll call

Chopper Harris for you in a minute. The thing was, when I signed for Chelsea I acquired one of the first agents and he completely stitched me up. I was doing things like modelling for Aquascutum, doing the macs and stuff like that. I didn't get paid because he fucked off with it all. Aquascutum was a good brand in them days. I was getting some free stuff, you know, from Aquascutum, and with the odd suits and that, of course. You know.'

Mark pulls out Birch's book, shows him a great photo of Birchenall, Osgood and John Boyle standing on the empty terraces in the Chelsea ground. Birchenall is wearing a beautiful grey suit adorned with a matching silk tie and handkerchief. His hair is cut in the Suedehead style that is a bouffant cut but grown out somewhat, and his shoes are buckled with sharp toes. Next to him, Boyle and Osgood look like drab accountants. Birchenall reaches for his glasses and studies the picture. As he does, memories start to hit him.

'That was a modelling job,' he says. 'It was a one of these teenie new books. You know, these girlie books or something. Football was just starting to become showbiz, like pop. I mean, they say now that footballers are overtaking pop but back then it was coming on. And if you were playing with Chelsea . . . Chelsea was, as you know, the showbiz side. So they always used to focus on Chelsea for anything like that, basically. I mean, that's a joke because we had to come into the training ground at Mitcham done up like that. The lads took the piss because that was done just after lunch down at Stamford Bridge. Normally, if you come in at Mitcham, you come in like this [points to his sporty clothes]. Although Eddie McCreadie used to turn up wearing three-piece suits. Come to training in a three-piece, eh! So me, Boilers [Boyle] and Ossie, who had been on the piss the night before, were hammered. We came in looking like this and Dave Sexton [the Chelsea manager at the time] thought we were going out again because we'd got the old whistles on.'

'What about Alan Hudson,' I ask, 'because Hudson was a big . . .'

'Huddy?' interrupts Birchenall. 'Yeah, Huddy was a dandy. And David Webb. He would always make me laugh. He was a cross between an East End gangster and a mafia spiv with a footballer rolled into it, you know. Dave Sexton introduced him. He walked into the dressing-room at Stamford Bridge and said, I've just signed this gentleman, David Webb. And I thought, fuck me, it's Al Capone. He had a long black Crombie on with a white silk scarf hanging down like this. I thought, he's got a fucking sawn-off shotgun under that.'

No chuckle this time but a roaring laugh. From all of us.

'Why did Chelsea look this way and not the other teams?' I wondered, out loud.

'What, how did we manage to get all the spivs?' Birchenall shot back, chuckling. Again.

Mark came in. 'Was this something to do with being near the Kings Road, do you think?'

Birchenall readily agreed. 'Well, yeah. I think the influence . . . I would say without a doubt that we worked as a team. If you wore the Chelsea kit that I wore in 1967–71, that kit would not look out of place today. That's how modern it was. If you look, it was the blue lightweight top, blue shorts, white socks. But it was so modern. I'd come from Sheffield United where the fucking shirts were this thick. Great big fucking things. Horrible nylon shorts and nylon socks. I get to Chelsea, funnily enough, and the first thing I thought when I put the kit on, fucking hell, I felt like an Italian, and that is going back to the '70s. So, I think it just transpired that you looked the bollocks on the pitch, which Chelsea always did. And the players liked to look the bollocks off the pitch.'

'Did that ensure you were hated everywhere you went?' I asked.

'Well, this was it,' Birchenall said readily and conspiratorially. 'That's why there was this warfare any time we went north of Watford because we were the Chelsea, the Kings Road boys, with a showbiz team. I mean, we had Dickie Attenborough bringing in all the actors and actresses. Steve McQueen, Raquel Welch, bloody Charlton Heston, Dustin Hoffman – he used to bring them all in. And we were in awe of them. I mean, after a game you would meet up in the Players' Bar upstairs and you would be rubbing shoulders with these people like The Stones, The Beatles.

'The Animals, they'd come in. Joanna Lumley would be over there and there'd be fucking Sue George there, there'd be a Beatle there, a fucking Stone there and that's what it was. It just carried over into your lifestyle. I mean, I always said I had three great years at Chelsea but it put thirty years on me fucking life. Do you know what I mean?'

Chuckle, chuckle. We get the picture.

'You'd finish training, straight up the Kings Road, in the Markham Arms, cottage pie and beans, sit by the window, seven Chelsea players and all the girls in the miniskirts walking by. It was fucking heaven. They didn't stay open all day in them days but they fucking did for us. They'd shut the door, lads, and we'd hammer on the window, do you two birds want to come in for a party? I mean, that was the old culture then. This lot here think they invented having a good time. No.' (Ironically, Birchenall was speaking just a few months before three Leicester players would be embroiled in a sex scandal at the La Manga resort and placed in a Spanish jail for a week.) 'You see, with all due respect,' Birchenall continued, 'Arsenal had a good side, Tottenham did in them days, West Ham did – but there was something about Chelsea that used to get up people's noses. They thought it was arrogance. Well, there was a bit because, players like Ossie, he extolled his own virtues, but that was through his ability. And Cookie, you know, taking the piss, doing drag-backs about 15 times and then just running round somebody. We'd play the football the way Dave Sexton wanted to play it. Flamboyant, you know. But we played like that on the pitch. I think, if you're playing like that on the pitch, you have to look like it off it. If you see a dull team, I bet there are some dull fucking dressers in that. If you see a side that plays great, then they often look like the bollocks.'

At the time of Birchenall's stay at Chelsea, their greatest rivals were Leeds United. The two teams were the yin and yang of early '70s football. Leeds, dour but tough, skilled and disciplined, grinding out results week in, week out, managed by Don Revie, a man who many disliked throughout the game. (When Sunderland beat Leeds against all the odds in the 1973 Cup final, the manager, Bob Stokoe, celebrated more than just a win. Stokoe maintained that Revie had once tried to bribe him and had never forgiven the man's underhand attempt to dirty the game he so adored.) Chelsea, on the other hand, were the wayward team, the Southerners, the preening peacocks, a team viewed in the same manner that English commentators see foreign players today – talented maybe, but totally lacking in temperament or good British grit. Don Revie's Leeds could win all the leagues they liked but Chelsea never seemed that bothered. Instead, they won cups with a balanced team containing flair and toughness. Players such as Hudson or Cooke, whose flashes of genius brought gasps from the crowd, applause from the gods, were backed up by the likes of Ron 'Chopper' Harris or David Webb.

'Say you were playing Leeds, would you actually go a bit more over the top dresswise just to wind them up?' I asked Birchenall.

'Yep,' he replied. 'I can't remember having orders to travel in the club suit but you had to have collar and tie for travelling, like, you know, unless it was tracksuits. But that was more or less the theme in them days, it was more that you travelled smart, you know. And, of course, the lads took, you know, full advantage.' Then he thought of something. 'I know, let's give Ossie a bell.' He reached for his mobile, hit some numbers, then placed the phone to his ear.

'Hello,' he said cheerily. 'The Birchenall here. MBE, HRH, MFI, speaking from Buck House. [Chuckle] Hello, darling. Yeah, listen mate, I've got a couple of guys who are up from London. They're doing a fashion book for the '60s, like, '70s, that Chelsea era. I couldn't remember, you know when we went up into Soho, Berwick Street, and got measured up for the gear and . . . yeah, I know, we weren't in Soho for suits. [Chuckle] Can you remember the tailor? No? I wanted to check with you, pal.

'So, are you all right anyway? Oh, well, I won't disturb you, pal. Ah, brilliant, mate. I'll speak to you soon, mate. See ya, Os.'

We had one last question on the agenda for the man – where did he get his haircut?

'Fucking hell,' he replied, 'I'll have to think about that.'

Mark pointed out a photo of Birchenall and a barber in the book. The Birch peered at the pic. 'You know who that was?' he said. 'That was one of the top Sheffield Wednesday players of all time cutting my hair, Johnny Fantham. He used to play for Sheffield Wednesday.'

'What about at Chelsea, who cut your hair there?' I asked.

'A guy called Franco Pizzolon,' Birchenall stated. At which point the door swung open and the Leicester defender, Matt Elliott, walked in clutching a smallish Louis Vuitton bag.

'Sorry,' Birchenall cried in a mocking voice, 'I forgot, this is Matty Elliot's office.'

'Sorry, Birch,' Elliot said, 'I just wanted to make a quick phone call.'

The Fashion of Football

Birchenall waved at him genially, told him to continue his mission. Matt settled down, picked up the phone. Birchenall turned to us. 'Lads,' he said, motioning to Elliott, 'just tell him. He's had a pop at me down there for massaging my own ego. He's been a lovely lad for years now but he's started having a pop. And you know why? Because his fucking career's coming to its end, to say the least. And you know what the difference is? I never got bitter. No. I never got bitter. The only difference is I was fucking skint and he can turn around and say, I'm a fucking millionaire. But can he talk to me about fashion, lads?'

'If he could,' I replied, 'he'd have a top day.'

'Hear that, Matty,' Birchenall shouted, and that was that. We shook hands and off The Birch went, chuckling to himself all the way down the corridor.

Fuck 4–4–2 – Collar and Tie! Collar and Tie!

The name of the last team I played football with before age started to seriously wither my blistering pace and talent was called Kosmos. It was easily the maddest team I ever played for, made up of deranged individuals for whom the words 'team unity' might as well have been spoken in an obscure Chinese dialect. Kosmos began life in the late '80s as a kickabout amongst friends on a Thursday night in Hyde Park. (To my delight, I later discovered that the tailor Dougie Hayward's team, the Mount Street Marchers, started in exactly the same place.)

They were great games of football, played in cool, summer air and fading sunlight until gathering darkness blew the final whistle. Most of us who played knew each other but there were other characters involved, like the one-legged defender who insisted on calling me Pedro all the time. It drove me mad but I kept my counsel until one game when, as I ran past him, he sent me sprawling to the ground. 'Sorry, Pedro,' he said, nonchalantly.

I exploded. 'It may begin with P and end with O,' I screamed, 'but it's Paolo, not fucking Pedro!' Happy days.

So enjoyable were these nights that an extra game was added on Sunday afternoons at Regent's Park. It was there that the notion of forming a club and entering a league became a reality. From the outset, it was obvious that Kosmos was packed with talented footballers. In our first season, we won the league and reached the cup final. But I'll be truthful – I have never played with a bigger bunch of moaning bastards in all my life. It was as though every player on the pitch, whatever his profession, was determined to demonstrate that he could have played professionally.

From kick-off to final whistle, they screamed at each other. Pass it here. Go there. Get stuck in. Tackle. Don't do that. What the fuck do you think you're doing? In one game, I received the ball, skipped past two defenders and whipped in a top cross. As our centre-forward headed the ball just wide, I heard one of my team shout my name in an angry manner. I turned round in a rage. 'What did you fucking say?' I shouted to him.

'I said, well fucking played,' he screamed back.

'Well, that's all right then, isn't it?' I replied at the top of my voice. Happy days.

Towards the end of my time with Kosmos, a player called Steven Harris joined. Everyone called him Nipper. I think I must have played one game with him, if that, before I quit the team. About six months later, I was in a bar when I felt a tap on my shoulder. It was Nipper. 'Just wanted to say that we were watching some old Kosmos videos the other day and that you were a bloody good player. You should think about coming back.'

It was a lovely gesture but I had no interest in rejoining that team, my ears were still stinging from my time there. However, two months later, I was more than happy to help Nipper out with his book, *Dear Alan, Dear Harry*, which remains one of the great undiscovered football books of our time.

Dear Alan charts Nipper's lengthy correspondence with the club he has supported all his life − Spurs. It contains letters from the Spurs chairman at the time, Alan Sugar, and his right-hand man, Claude Littner. It is a frank and witty exposé of the arrogance that permeated the upper echelon of Spurs at the time and demonstrates the lengths true fans are driven to when their beloved club is invaded by non-football people.

Working on Nipper's book solidified our relationship. We were both into the holy trinity of music, football and clothes (although in a different order), and we were both of the same mind. Nipper lived up the road from me but in 2003 he bought a new drum. Whilst his new flat was made ready, Nipper moved in with a close friend of his called Neil. He too supported Spurs, except that Neil's father was none other than Frank McLintock, the captain of the Arsenal team that came to White Hart Lane in 1971 and won the League with a 1−0 victory. A month later, they won the FA Cup to become the second team ever to win the Double. Of course, we had done it ten years before, just as we did everything ten years before them, such as buying foreign players, but still it was kind of strange that Neil supported his father's greatest rivals.

On one occasion, I told Nipper that, since starting the book, McLintock's name had come up quite a few times. 'Every time we ask someone from the '70s, be it fan or player, to name a well-dressed player, Frank gets mentioned. Couldn't have a word with Neil, see if you can get us an interview with him? If I go through the proper channels, nothing will happen.'

Mark was keen for the interview to happen as well. McLintock had once been assistant manager at Millwall. 'Pretty good guy,' Mark told me. 'We won promotion with him to the old First Division. John Doherty was the manager. They did one season there, went to the top of the table like Portsmouth did. Then it went tits up. They couldn't keep it going. The next season we went down. They bought Paul Goddard from West Ham for £800,000 but he was crap, it was a panic buy. But that was the team – Teddy Sheringham and Tony Cascarino up front, Terry Hurlock with Les Briley in midfield, Jimmy Carter on the wings. He went to Arsenal. Peanuts Carter, we called him. Obviously. Nah, that was a great team and McLintock was the coach.'

One Friday night in late November 2003, Nipper came through on the phone. 'Neil's just called me,' he said. 'His dad is in a pub in Winchmore Hill. Says if we go up there now, he'll give you ten minutes.' I called Mark but there was no way he could get from his home in deep South to high North in time. Twenty minutes later, Nipper turned up and, an hour later, I was sitting with Frank McLintock.

In her book *Proud To Say That Name*, the writer Amy Lawrence says of McLintock, 'His quest for glory nagged him with the overwhelming intensity of a drug addict aching for a hit, and he searched, relentlessly, for ways to satisfy the craving.'

She reveals that every morning McLintock and trainer Don Howe would drive to training together, obsessively talking team tactics and selection in the car, working out what was best for the team. 'You could put a lot of Arsenal's success in that period down to Frank,' Lawrence quotes Howe as saying. 'He created this "we'll win this together" mentality. Frank was an outstanding captain, a

The Fashion of Football

wonderful leader of men, a wonderful presence in the dressing-room.'

In 1964, McLintock arrived at Arsenal from Leicester, for whom he had already played over 200 games. Three of those were Wembley Cup finals, none of which had him on the winning side. That hurt, big-time. In 1967, he was made Arsenal club captain and then in the next two seasons lost two more finals, one to lowly Swindon in the League Cup. That hurt even more. In 1969, a taste of success. Frank guided his team to their first trophy in 17 years when Arsenal beat Sporting Anderlecht in the Fairs Cup final, thus igniting what some refer to as the greatest party ever seen at Highbury.

The following season, with McLintock's drive and manager Bertie Mee's astute tactics, Arsenal finally caught up with Spurs and won both League and Cup. How sweet that Double must have tasted when it finally arrived; the cherry on top was Frank being named footballer of the year in 1971.

The following season, Frank took Arsenal back to Wembley for the Cup final but they lost to Leeds. The dream was nearly over. In June 1973, he was transferred to QPR, played with the mercurial Stan Bowles, and, four years later, hung up his boots and went into management at Leicester, Brentford and Millwall. Now, he earns his corn as a media pundit and he's good at it. On TV, McLintock is relaxed, intelligent, knowledgeable. He also hasn't changed much since his playing days. A bit of weight, bit of grey hair, but if the last time you had seen him was wearing a football shirt on a pitch, you would have no difficulty recognising him now.

I certainly didn't and, just as I expected from watching him on the box, he was attentive, courteous. When he told me that in one European game he had broken his nose twice through fisticuffs and *played on*, I found it hard to equate the polite, affable man talking to me with such actions. Then again, it's always the quiet ones you have to watch.

He couldn't stay for long, his wife had been a bit ill of late and he wanted to get home, make sure she was OK. But he was amused (and I think a little proud) that his name had kept cropping up in our research. 'It's very hard to think back all that time,' he said, settling down on the pub sofa, 'very hard.'

Frank McLintock was born in 1940, raised in Glasgow. His

family were working class and clothes played a major role in Frank's upbringing. At an early age, it was drummed into him that however much the family sweated for money, however hard times got, you always presented yourself to the world in the smartest way you could. You might be poor but you never showed it in public. That's because you had pride, pride in yourself, pride in your family.

For working-class kids of the post-war generation, your first suit represented a rite of passage. You usually received it when you turned 16, about to leave school and enter the world of men and work. Your father usually bought it. If your family could afford it, he took you to a tailor; if not, a gentlemen's outfitters. Your suit was sacred. You never wore it during the week but saved it for Sundays and special occasions.

'You had just the one suit because you couldn't afford two suits,' Frank recalls. 'So you had the one suit which you looked after and you always felt the business when you dressed in your one special suit. When we were 16, 17, the Italian suits came in for the first time. This was '56, '57. Then there were shiny suits, what was the name? Tonik, that was it. In fact, I just saw someone the other week with a three-button Tonik suit on and I thought, that was us 40 years ago. These things keep coming back all the time.'

Indeed they do.

'When I was 15, 16,' he continues, 'we had a thing called the full-back jacket. It had no splits in it, no double or single vents, it was a whole back. In Glasgow, it was called a full-back and if you had a full-back jacket on, you were the bee's knees.'

'You tend to forget how important these things were to you at the time,' he says with a grin. 'If you had a certain suit on, you were with the "in" crowd. Nowadays, I sometimes think, what are these kids going on about? But then you remember how you were at that age and you were so into music and so into the right suits, the right ties, the right shirts and the right haircuts.'

I ask him if turning pro allowed him the chance to fruitfully expand his wardrobe. He shakes his head.

'The modern-day players can buy the best gear, the best shoes,' he says. 'For us, the money wasn't that good. It was certainly more than what other people were earning but I was married at twenty-

The Fashion of Football

two as well, and I had four kids within seven years. But you would try and buy what you thought was the style at the time.'

Like so many players from the '70s, he is annoyed by the wages today's players earn. 'The modern-day player lives on a different planet,' he states. 'My wages weren't that high. It was mainly bonuses at Arsenal, but we didn't do well for four years and I was on the same money as I was on at Leicester. Even 10 years after I had finished, players were on £2,000 or £3,000 a week. To me, that seemed phenomenal because when I finished in 1977 my wages were £200 a week basic wage.'

At Arsenal, certain rules had to be adhered to. When Frank thinks of Arsenal manager Bertie Mee, he doesn't hear tactics or words of encouragement. Straight away, he hears his ex-manager's voice demanding, 'collar and tie, collar and tie'.

'It was always collar and tie, unbelievable. If Bertie Mee told you to go casual, you came in with a tie which was maybe a little bit undone. For Bertie Mee, that was casual. Clubs, as they do today, insisted on their players looking smart in public. Club suits were obligatory – blazer, shirt, tie and trousers. Long hair was frowned upon. So was casual dressing.

'Times change,' Frank says, reasonably. 'Casual clothes are big now. A lot of the players *want* to look scruffy with the cuts in the jeans in a certain place.' For the Arsenal team of the early '70s, the idea of a player appearing on billboards wearing nothing but a tight pair of Calvin Klein briefs would have been as unfathomable as sending an email. Footballers were celebrities but only within a certain section of society. They were back-page news, rarely front page. At the same time, clubs curbed any excess that resulted from their fame. They liked their players to be obedient, to stay rooted in a team image, avoid getting too big for their Puma Royal boots. They didn't want their stars associated with anything deemed to be subversive or edgy. They wanted them as teachers at school had their students – in uniform.

The only players to develop a more outlandish image were the highly talented, flamboyant ones – the Stan Bowleses, Frank Worthingtons and Charlie Georges: players who expressed their individualism through their football, their clothes, their lifestyles. They knew they could get away with it because their talent protected them. Yet, for Frank and many of his team, obeying strict dress rules was never a problem. They had been raised to know the importance of looking smart at all times. His fellow teammate George Graham, a Scot, was just the same.

'George was our clothes horse,' Frank reveals. 'I would put on a suit and it would look quite good, but when George put on a suit, he looked fantastic. He had an upright manner and clothes always looked great on George. And he is still, to this day, absolutely immaculate. It might not be everyone's style but it's a classic style and [they] last years and years. He never looks out of date.' He pauses, then adds, 'Although I'm sure most of his clothes are ten years old.'

'The worst dressed player of your time?' I ask.

'Gerry Francis,' Frank states unequivocally. 'Gerry Francis was a great player, a real nice guy but what a terrible dresser. Gerry's trousers were always two inches above his ankles, which used to crease us up but we never told him. He would wear the most outrageous gear, yet he was such a shy guy. No one could figure it out.'

He glances anxiously at his watch. 'You mustn't forget Charlie George and his Windsor knots and his flares,' he says. 'Charlie was a supporter who ended up with an Arsenal jersey on his back. The crowd loved him because he was one of them and, to this day, he goes to every Arsenal away match. He was the original Arsenal fan who became the Arsenal player and is still an Arsenal fan, which is unique.'

Time to go, he has to see his wife, make sure things are all right.

'Good luck with it all,' he says, shaking my hand and then he is gone, exiting the pub to a chorus of genuine goodbyes, dressed neatly in his white chinos, his blue top. Out of everyone, Frank McLintock knows that such things are still important.

The Fashion of Football

The Best a Man Can Get

In his gruff accent, he kept saying, 'Sorry to have dragged you so far out of town.' He said it a few times, in fact.

I just smiled. 'It's fine, not a problem,' I kept repeating. In truth, I was thinking, you're Mike Summerbee. I would have gone to John o' Groats to talk to you and I'm not even a City supporter.

Mike Summerbee is the legendary Manchester City player who opened up Edwardia with George Best in 1967. Summerbee stayed with George for a year and, with the money he earned from the venture, started his own shirt-making business. It is still thriving, 37 years later.

Naturally, his name came high on our list of people to meet. Through contacts, we got a number, a time to call him. He could meet us in Radlett, Hertfordshire, the following week. He had business there early Wednesday morning, we could meet elevenish at a café. I relayed the news to Mark. He screwed up his face.

'I can't swing that day from work,' he said, as a spark of disappointment streaked briefly across his eyes. 'We've got so much on, they won't stand for it.' Work wasn't going well. He had recently let it be known that he was writing a book and the reaction from some of his workmates had stung him. 'You? Writing a book? Having a laugh, aren't you?'

The attitude reminded me of a way of thinking that I hadn't encountered in years. Back in Woking, where I did most of my growing up, I had met a lot of people who were convinced that books were not for the likes of them, that they were for the highly educated, or those who were socially above them. The idea of Mark getting involved with something as fancy as a book amused them. And that hurt him. If he wasn't getting it from his 'superiors', his peers filled in for them. At least Mark wasn't the only one whose literary endeavours were misunderstood. When the writer Alan Sillitoe gave his dad a copy of his first novel, the brilliant *Saturday Night, Sunday Morning*, his father exclaimed, 'Why, Alan, a book! You'll never have to work again.'

'Sure you won't be able to make it?' I asked Mark. I knew what a buzz he got from meeting footballers, both past and present.

'I need my holidays,' he replied. 'Me and Lou are going to try to get married this year and are going to want a honeymoon. I'll have to leave it.' He had been with Lou a million years now, was aching to marry her. He couldn't let a book get in the way of their plans. I know. People are funny sometimes.

A week later, I caught the train to Radlett. On the way, I phoned a mutual acquaintance of mine and Mike Summerbee's, Paul McGuigan — ex-Oasis, my co-author on a Robin Friday biography, *The Greatest Footballer You Never Saw*, a book screaming out to be made into a film. When I rang, Guigs was in his home studio producing The Nazarites, a London band he had recently discovered. Such was the noise, he had to come outside to talk.

'Guigs,' I shouted, 'give us the low-down on Summerbee.'

'Mike Summerbee was known for a few things,' he shouted back. 'He was a winger who was a great crosser of the ball and he was also one of the hardest men on the pitch, which for a winger is going some. Mike didn't wear shin pads. I think there's a bit in the George Best book where Best says he kicked Mike and hurt himself. Mike actually started off as a centre-forward but he and Franny Lee switched halfway through the second season and that was it, they were off.' Mike Summerbee was a ghost of both our pasts. Who was it that said of them, 'With each passing season they appear stronger in our minds?' Actually, I did.

Mike Summerbee was a major player in the last great City team — the one from the late '60s, early '70s, which contained Franny Lee, Colin Bell, Glyn Pardoe, Mike Doyle and Tony Book, all names and faces I remembered from a thousand football annuals and a million issues of *Shoot* magazine. Man City were a good team, won many trophies, were always considered a force, but the team aged and success left town. Mike scored 67 goals for that team, moved on to Burnley, then Blackpool, and ended his career as player–manager for Stockport.

The Fashion of Football

Throughout that time, he maintained his shirt-making business. Still does today. He works hard at it, as well. Even now, Mike Summerbee will get up and drive from his Manchester home to wherever you are in the country, measure you and then provide the shirts you want exactly on time. He also works for Manchester City. They say he is a sales manager but I think it's more of a roving role they've given him – Mike is ready to do whatever is asked of him.

The day I met him was an important one for the club. Manchester City had an FA Cup replay against Leicester that night. Tottenham were next, if they got through. The omens didn't look good for City, though. Whispers, growing louder, said that manager Kevin Keegan had lost control of the dressing-room, that the team was bitterly divided. A story filled with these rumours took up the back page of the newspaper Mike was reading when I walked in and introduced myself. He looked fit, dressed in a nice polo-neck woollen jumper, good cords. His face was slightly ruddy, clean-shaven.

'What do you make of Keegan?' I asked him, nodding at the paper and sitting down, ordering coffee. I intended the question to be friendly but realised instantly that it was potentially inflammatory.

'Keegan's a good manager, as good as anyone,' he said a bit warily. 'You can only do so much. You've got enough players to win games but it's attitude, isn't it? I find it difficult to think that you have to motivate anyone when they're doing something that they really enjoy. You can only do it for a certain amount of time, so enjoy it while you can.'

He looked me straight in the eyes, saw my very real interest and mistook it for something sinister. 'You're not from *The Sun*, are you? One of them papers?' Mike asked. 'I won't talk if you are.'

'No, no,' I quickly assured him. 'This interview is for a book about football and fashion, I promise you. Ask Guigsy. You know him, don't you? I wrote that book about Robin Friday with him.'

Of course Mike knew the man. He had dealt with Oasis on many occasions; inevitable, really, given the rabid support for Man City that Noel, Liam and Guigsy had expressed over the years. Indisputably, one of the band's career highlights was playing the old Maine Road stadium in 1996. Nowhere to go but Knebworth after those shows.

'They came up to a game once,' Mike recalled, starting to settle down. 'We were playing Portsmouth and I had to bring them onto the pitch. I said to Liam, whatever you do, don't go down the Portsmouth end and cause any bother. We go out on the pitch and what's the first thing he does? He goes straight to the Portsmouth fans and starts winding them up. Then he comes back up the pitch and, as he does, the crowd start singing that song "Wonderwall". Unbelievable – 40,000-odd people singing at once. Unbelievable.'

His face assumed a look I remembered a lot from those heady, unsteady days of the mid-'90s. It was one of disbelief at what was occurring, even greater disbelief that you were lucky enough to be there to witness it.

'You sure you're not from *The Sun*?' he said, half-joking.

'No,' I replied. 'Honestly.'

'Well, when Liam was with Patsy Kensit,' he continued, pretty confident now that I wasn't the enemy, 'I came down to London on business. So I'm driving past this house in St Johns Wood and there's a crowd of people outside this house, and suddenly this guy comes running out and up to the car. It's Liam, so I pulled over and said jump in here. We went off for a drink. Mind you, he had to keep phoning Patsy to tell her where he was.'

Mike Summerbee was born on 15 December 1942, grew up in Preston. Football coursed strongly through the family blood. Mike's dad was a pro player, played for Preston as a wing-half, and Mike's son, Nicky, would also turn pro. Three generations of footballers – not many families can boast that fact. The Summerbees moved to Cheltenham, where Mike's father was appointed manager.

'It comes from my father,' he said of his close relationship with clothes. 'He was very clothes-conscious. He always had smart shoes, nice suits. Sometimes, he had his suits made at a tailor's in Preston called Percy Belberg. His shirts had to be perfect. My brother was the same, he was pretty clothes-conscious. I'm not talking about going out and being stupid and flashing it, I'm talking about clothes-conscious in the way I want to dress. I think it's important. My father always said to me, if you have clean shoes and a smart shirt on, clean cuffs, your suit can be rubbish. He influenced me mostly. You had one suit – you had a jacket and if you were lucky you had a couple of pairs of trousers.

'When I lived in Cheltenham, I always wore detached collars, my

The Fashion of Football

shoes were always from Saxone, which was a small shop then, and there was also a little shop called Famous, which sold Daks suits. In those days, Daks suits were top of the range. We weren't a rich family but what I had I looked after. Always cleaned my shoes, which was important.'

Mike's first suit was actually bought for him by Bert Head, his manager at Swindon. 'We asked for a rise, me and Ernie Hunt,' Mike recalled. 'Bert said, I can't afford it, so he went and bought us two suits from a 39-bob tailor.'

Despite the abolition of the maximum wage, Mike's wages at Swindon didn't extend to Savile Row-type extravagances. In 1965, his financial outlook changed when he was transferred to Manchester City. He was 20 years old at the time, the lone sheep about to enter the wolf's lair. 'I went to Manchester dressed in a tweed jacket and a pair of slacks [note how the man can recall what he was wearing 39 years ago] and all the other players were wearing mohair suits or Tonik suits, and shiny suits.'

He continued, 'Manchester had nightclubs and I'd never been in a nightclub. Swindon closed at half ten. I was staying in the Grand Hotel at the time and there were neon lights flashing over the road. One night, I went over to a nightclub called The Piccadilly Club. I went in and I had my tweed jacket on, spoke with a Wiltshire accent. Went in at about half ten, which was late for me, sat at the bar and finally a girl came over. I said, are you open? She said, yeah, so I said, you can't be doing much business. She said, this is a nightclub, it doesn't start until twelve o'clock at night.'

It was Mike's teammates, Matt Graham and Johnny Crossingham, who took him out, showed him the ropes, and fitted him up and out.

'Suits weren't expensive and I was on big money then. I was on thirty quid a week and you could get a suit for ten or fifteen quid. You could go out on a fiver in those days. Take a girl out, buy her a meal, have a few drinks, take her home, get your way and still have three quid left! Plus, when you went for training, you wore smart slacks, a nice sweater, a nice jacket. You never wore tracksuits, you never came to the ground in a tracksuit and went away in a tracksuit. You always looked smart,' he said.

Despite his new Manchester look, Mike considered the smartest players to be those operating in London. It made sense. The capital city contained areas such as Carnaby Street and Savile Row, shops such as the Ivy Shop, Lord John and Michael's, and stylists such as John Stephen, John Simon and John Pearse.

'Whenever the London players travelled to us, they always looked smart,' Mike continued. 'Whatever was out, they wore. Frank McLintock was always very smart. You look at Frank McLintock, he's never changed. He still looks the same, he hasn't put weight on.' I pull out an old football annual a friend lent me and show him a picture of the late Peter Knowles, the ex-Wolves footballer turned Jehovah's Witness. Knowles looks fantastic. He wears a light-brown jacket (three-button), a dark polo neck, pinstripe trousers and white shoes. His hair is cut *à la* Rod Stewart and he leans, arms crossed, against a sports car. Absolute class.

'He was a whippersnapper coming up,' Mike remembered. 'People weren't as loud as that then. Everyone dressed similar. Either a blazer or a suit or a jacket, but it was always smart. You wouldn't wear white trousers and a big, checked jacket.'

What team was the sharpest dressed? I wondered. He instantly said West Ham, instructing me to look at their haircuts around that time. 'They were the Mod team,' he stated. 'You'd finish the game and their hair would still be the same as when they started.' He was thinking of players such as Geoff Hurst, Martin Peters, Harry Redknapp but the epitome of that team's style was, of course, Bobby Moore. Again, Moore dressed how he played – stylishly, elegantly and with little apparent effort.

'Did you know Bobby Moore was involved in the leather business?' Mike asked. 'One time, when we played them, we got into London at lunch-time and Bobby met us at the hotel and he took all the team down to his warehouse. We went to the East End, Brick Lane, round there, and we all bought some full-length pigskin coats.

'We all looked like the pop groups. We looked the business. It was nice. You got a bit of discount off these beautiful coats and Bobby did well out of it. I think everybody supported each other then. If a footballer had a business in London, you would go there and buy a few things. And then when they came to Manchester, the same thing. Everybody scratched each other's back. There was a very close community then. I don't think there is now.'

Summerbee formed a good relationship with Moore. Both were drawn from the same well. They were neat, fastidious people, and cared deeply about their appearance. When Summerbee was picked for England, the two men roomed together.

'You wouldn't think anyone lived in the room,' he said smiling. 'Everything was immaculate and in its place. When you packed your case, you didn't throw it in, you *packed* your clothes. Today's players have thousands and thousands of suits but we only had a few suits, so we kept them tidy. You wouldn't come into Mooro's room and find a pair of trousers on the floor.'

A thought struck me. 'With all due respect, Moore was well known for breaking curfews laid down by England manager Alf Ramsay. You, too, liked a drink. What about when the pair of you got back at five in the morning and the ceiling is spinning wildly and so is your head. Were the clothes neatly hung up then?'

Summerbee leaned forward and sternly replied, 'Look, lad, it might have taken me half an hour to put my suit on a hanger but I would do it. That was it, and the same with Mooro. You looked after things because things were hard to come by. A pigskin coat or an antelope jacket, they cost £60 or £70 at John Michael.'

These were men raised during Britain's years of austerity, 1939–55, and, although they might have been earning a small fortune compared to their peers, they never forgot the value of things. This is another working-class ethic slowly draining away in a prosperous Britain where so much of value has no value any more.

'How did you get together with George Best?' I asked.

'In a coffee bar called The Can Can,' he replied. 'It was a lunch-time place we used to go to. In those days, the players from both sides would go and have lunch together. United lads would go there or to The Oxford Road, a pub that had a dining area, and we'd go in there sometimes as well, so there was quite a big bond, a big friendship. When Malcolm Allison had a housewarming party, all the United players were there, which was wonderful. Maurice Setters, Bill Foulkes and Denis Law were there.'

I was stunned. City and United, hated rivals, the cause of eternal division in Manchester, hanging out *together*? 'Sure,' he breezily replied. 'George Best was my best man when I got married. It never crossed my mind that because someone played for another team you couldn't be friends. Billy Bremner and Norman Hunter were good friends of mine. We used to kick lumps out of each other and then go to the bar afterwards, and that was it.'

I thought of that terrible day when Sol Campbell moved to Arsenal from Spurs, recalled that nasty, sick feeling that stayed in my stomach for days. I recalled the two weeks I endured with people cracking jokes at my expense – my next-door neighbour Paul, the local shopkeepers. I thought of my mate who showed up at my birthday with two bottles of *Sol* beer and two cans of *Campbell's* soup, and placed them in front of me with a smirk the size of Glen Hoddle's talent. Then I pictured the current Tottenham and Arsenal teams meeting up at a secret location, players drinking together at a bar, laughing, slapping one another's backs. It was horrendous.

Not all City players fraternised with the enemy, Summerbee reassured me. Mike Doyle for one. 'He was so anti-United,' Mike went on, 'that when a United fan moved into his street, he sold his house and moved away. Others had families to attend to. Not Mike. He was a single man, free as a bird, darting around from here to there.'

When Mike met George, the latter was living in lodgings with the famed Mrs Fullaway. A local businessman by the name of Malcolm Mooney (who later died in a car accident) was behind the deal. Mike couldn't recall who thought up the name Edwardia but it was probably Mooney, looking for a title that suggested something exotic.

'It was a nice shop in a good area, right in the centre of Manchester, right by the taxation building,' Mike recalled. 'It was called the Village. There was a hairdressing shop which Malcom Wagner ran. He was a friend of George's and mine, very close to George, and then we had the shop Edwardia. It was a good release for us. Both George and I had a lot of spare time. With Bestie there, he was a magnet for women. We actually had a unique situation. We got the sole rights to sell Ravel shoes in Manchester. We really let that go. We had the opportunity there to make a lot of money.' You can tell he still ruminates over that lost financial bonanza, like strikers do over a missed goal.

So, what did they sell? 'Suits, shirts, ties. I think the suits came in from Italy. Malcolm Mooney ran the business for us and he knew what he wanted to do. People would come in not necessarily to buy

The Fashion of Football

clothes, but get them through the door and you've got a chance of selling them something.'

Although Summerbee had a penchant for clothes, you surmise he had little input into choosing the shop's stock. His and George's job was to visit the shop after training and draw in the punters. It was said that the mirrors in the shop's changing-rooms reflected more than just men trying on the latest fashions. They also showed George and Mike performing moves more associated with a boudoir than a football pitch. 'I think I got my money back, I'm not sure, but I had a good time!' said Mike. So did George.

Not so for Malcolm Mooney. For a shop fronted by a national phenomenon who still created absolute mania wherever he went, Edwardia didn't make half as much money as it should have done. The reason was simple: it attracted more women than men.

About a year after the shop opened, Mike moved into the bespoke-shirt business. He did so because of a man he had met named Frank Rostram. He suggested they create a shirt-making business.

I asked if Mike sold mainly to footballers at first. 'No way,' he answered. 'They don't like paying, do they?' I laughed out loud at that one. I was really warming to this man. The only player Mike dealt with was his friend Bobby Moore. Moore offered Mike's company work but as we have seen, they didn't have the manpower to keep up production. 'They used to measure the people up and we made the shirts. But we didn't have enough machinists,' Mike explained.

Still, Mike's business expanded, did well. It was he who supplied the shirts for that terrible football film *Escape To Victory*. 'I did Michael Caine, Max Von Sydow, Sylvester Stallone . . .'

'What about Pele?' I said, interrupting him.

'I left Pele alone,' Mike responded. It figured. Summerbee knew how to treat the masters – they come to you, not you to them.

He moved on, told me that the style of today's footballers leaves him cold. He recalled how he recently went to a football function wearing a collar and tie. Stuck out like a true stylist amongst all the designer labels, the open, wide-necked shirts, the sockless feet. 'They all thought I was a bank manager,' he says sadly. 'But I've always worn a collar and a tie.'

He had a journey to make, driving back to Manchester and home, so one final question: any idea who made Bobby Moore's suits?

'He had them made by Dougie Hayward. Famous tailor, he's in Mount Street. You should go in and ask for him. Tell him Mike Summerbee sent you.' He stood, shook my hand and then added, 'Tell Dougie that I still make the finest shirts.'

And give the best interviews.

The Fashion of Football

■■■
The Mexican Job

On the train back to London from Radlett and Mike Summerbee, I decided we should pay Mr Dougie Hayward a visit. I phoned Mark and arranged to meet him at Bond Street station after he had finished work. Naturally, he arrived before me. 'Where we going?' he asked when I greeted him. 'What you thinking, you little tinker?'

'We are going to visit Bobby Moore's tailor,' I replied.

'Really? Who would that be then?'

'Doug Hayward on Mount Street.'

'I've been past there a few times,' Mark cautioned, 'but it doesn't seem the sort of place you can just stroll into.'

'It is today,' I replied.

Five minutes later, a bell above us was ringing as we pushed through the door of Hayward's. The front of the shop was cosy, designed for clients. There were sofas gathered around a table upon which books and magazines had been placed. At the back, you could see two men at a long desk, busy with chalk and scissors, and long ropes of measuring tape. There was also a woman standing near them and it was she who came to meet us. Her name was Audie.

'Can I help you?' she said pleasantly.

'Yes,' I said. 'We're writing a book about football and fashion and we have just interviewed Mike Summerbee.'

'Oh, I know Mike,' Audie said. 'How is he?'

'He's very well and he sends his regards.'

'How sweet,' she noted. 'Nice man.'

'It was Mike who told us that Doug Hayward made suits for Bobby Moore and we were just wondering if we could grab a quick interview.'

'I don't see why not,' Audie said. Then she turned and said loudly, 'Doug, can you come here a minute?'

An elderly man, impeccable in a brown three-piece suit, came forward. He looked like the headmaster of a public school. We would later discover that he was, in fact, a lively pupil, to say the least. 'Hello,' he said in an accent I took for upper-middle class. He looked to Audie for clarification.

'These gentlemen . . . I'm sorry, I don't know your names,' Audie said.

'This is Mark, I'm Paolo.'

'Well, Mark and Paolo are writing a book about football and fashion and wanted to talk to you about Bobby Moore. You can spare them five minutes, can't you?'

'Sure,' said Doug Hayward. He sat carefully on the leather chair by his desk. I noted his stylish socks, green stripes to go with his brown suit. I perched on one of the sofas, held the tape recorder in front of him. From nowhere, a small dog leapt up onto my lap. I love animals, so I couldn't resist stroking it. Mistake. It wouldn't let me be.

'Oh, get off him, Jack,' Audie said. 'He's such a nuisance sometimes. Would you boys care for tea?'

We would. I switched on the tape recorder and, as I gently pushed the eager Jack away for the tenth time, Doug said, 'You want to know about Bobby Moore? He could have stepped into any job, Bobby, but he was never guided. He would get involved in some suede-clothing business and lose money. Very disappointing.'

'When he came to you, did Bobby have strict ideas about his suits?'

'He had an idea but it was mainly a very classic look, not outrageous clothes. He was very neat, very tidy, the way he played football, in fact.'

I surmised from this insight that Hayward was no stranger to footballers. Indeed, he informed us, he had made suits for George Best, Geoff Hurst, Alan Hudson, many others. I said to Doug, 'Clothes were so important for such players. They acted as an important part of their working-class culture. The suit in particular.'

'They had suits that they pressed within an inch of their life,' said Doug, agreeing. 'That began when you were kids. All these people working on the roads in their mucky clothes but on a Friday night they would come out looking absolutely immaculate. Clean, polished shiny faces and very smart clothes.'

'I know who else we did,' Audie said, coming back to place down a tray containing tea cups. 'Dave Webb. He was a delightful man.'

'Dave Webb?' Doug said dismissively. 'He still owes me money.'

'What about the other David?' I enquired, wondering what he made of Mr Beckham's style.

'It only takes one to have good taste and then he'll make all the others go,' Doug replied. 'Footballers don't really give a bugger about how they look but now there is so much attention on them, they stop the traffic when they walk down the street. Now, they all dress like each other. Beckham looks smart.'

'He does it right, he gets it right,' Audie offered. Such was her obvious closeness to Doug, I took her for his wife.

'He's doing all right over there, isn't he?' Doug said of Beckham's role in the Real Madrid team. 'I always thought he was a bit of a luxury player.'

I asked if he followed the game. He did, although he didn't support a team as such, he explained, because he felt that prevented you from fully appreciating the beauty of football. 'I like to go and watch a match,' he explained. 'Nowadays, no one actually goes to *watch* a match, they go to see their team win, so if they are 2–0 down by the second half, they get pissed off and start going home.' He admitted that, come Saturday afternoon, he looked for Fulham's result first, Arsenal's second. 'When the Arsenal get it right, they are the most beautiful team to watch. Don't you think?' he asked me. I grimaced.

'Ah, a Spurs supporter then,' Doug noted straight away. 'I think United will win the League and Arsenal will come second and win the Cup. But to watch them the other night, when they won 4–1 (against Inter Milan in the Champions League, 2003), just a joy to watch. That's how football should be played.'

Doug should know; he nearly made the grade himself. He had been raised in the East End and developed a major talent for football. In the mid-'50s, Chelsea gave him a trial, that's how good he was. He recalled he had a great game as well that day, scored two goals. Future West Ham player and manager Ron Greenwood was playing alongside him. After the game, the scout who had brought him in told Doug he would drop him a note. Doug went home and waited and waited and waited but no letter came. Finally, he said *c'est la vie* and went into tailoring, serving his apprenticeship on Savile Row, his footballing dreams now laid aside for ever. About a year later, he bumped into the Chelsea scout. He demanded to know why Doug hadn't been in touch.

'You didn't write to me,' Doug replied. 'I assumed you didn't want me.'

'But we did,' said the scout. 'We sent you a letter.'

'Never got it.'

'But you could have phoned us.'

'Didn't think you wanted me.' The letter had obviously got lost in the post.

'Jesus,' I say, amazed, 'if that letter had arrived, your whole life would have been completely and utterly different to what it is today.'

'Yes,' Doug wryly replied. 'I'd be earning £14 a week now.'

Audie interrupted, asking him to tell us about a film he had made. But Doug waved his hand impatiently. 'Nothing, nothing, of no consequence,' he said.

'Oh, go on,' Audie said. 'It was about the 1970 World Cup,' she confided.

Doug sighed, then began his tale. Back in the days when he was young and so was the world, he and friends, such as the photographer Terry O'Neill and actor John Alderton, formed a park football team. They called themselves the Mount Street Marchers, played every Thursday night in Hyde Park. At that point in his life, Doug was a well-known man of the cloth. His clients were star names that hailed from both Britain and abroad. In London, he attended to Terence Stamp, Michael Parkinson, Jackie Stewart and Peter Sellers – Michael Caine's great suits in *The Italian Job* were Doug's. From America came the likes of Tony Curtis and Kirk Douglas. Hayward was a major success, a name around town. In Nik Cohn's 1971 book *Today There Are No Gentlemen* he is described as a 'very fair tailor, and bright and funny and quite un-pompous'.

In Michael Caine's biography, the great actor calls him 'the official tailor of the '60s, and a lifelong friend who has made my suits ever since . . . Doug became such a star in his own field that he now makes Ralph Lauren's suits.'

In the winter months of early 1970, Doug and his friends hatched an audacious plot. They decided to make a follow-up film to the Rank documentary on the 1966 World Cup. Using his contacts, Doug got the likes of Tony Curtis, Sean Connery and Kirk Douglas to write letters asking the production company to provide cameras, flights and hotels in Mexico for Doug and his football team so that they could document the 1970 World Cup tournament.

Rank agreed. They gave Doug and his mates a budget of £20,000. The boys then looked around for sponsorship. Rothmans came through, gave them 40,000 cigarettes. None of them smoked, so they sold them and bought a lorryload of vodka instead. Off, then, to Mexico.

'Hang on a minute,' I said. 'I want to get this right. You got Rank Films to pay for you and your mates to go to Mexico to film the World Cup with a lorryload of vodka, all expenses paid?'

'That's right,' Doug said softly, smiling.

'Don't forget the 12 models you took as well,' Audie said.

'Oh, yes,' said Doug absent-mindedly. 'Forgot about them.'

They named the film *Today Mexico, Tomorrow the World*. 'Nothing to do with the tournament, of course,' Doug explained. 'We just shot ourselves playing football against a Mexican park team. Once in a while, we put in a shot of Gordon Banks making a save or Bobby Moore tackling somebody.'

'I've got the film on tape, if you want to borrow it,' Audie said. We certainly did.

Mention of the photographer Terry O'Neill's involvement in this outlandish exercise had served to spark Mark's interest even further. He was a huge admirer of the East End cameraman's work.

'Oh, you just missed him,' Doug said. 'He was a dirty sod at football, he was. Very good player but no nonsense with him. Anyone got past him – wallop!'

'I'll ring him for you,' Audie said. She picked up the phone, dialled his number. After a brief conversation, she held the receiver to her hand and said, 'He says he can see you here tomorrow morning at eleven, if that's OK? Is that OK for you boys?'

I didn't have to look at Mark to know he wasn't going to let work get in the way of that appointment. We said we'd be there. We thanked both Doug and Audie for their huge kindness, said we'd see them the following day.

Afterwards, we went for a quick drink in a nearby pub. It was becoming something of a routine for us, this drinking after an interview. We would start off saying, just one each and then we'll leave it. But one became two became three became four and then, as the alcohol bit into me, I would say to Mark, 'Come on, one for the road.'

'Fucking long road you live on,' he'd reply, shaking his head.

He brought the drinks back to the table and we commented on what a fantastic day it had been. 'Definitely,' I said, 'but that dog was worrying me. Wouldn't leave me alone.'

'Don't know about Dougie Hayward, more like Doggie Hayward,' chuckled Mark.

Mark called later that night, after looking on the Internet and through his books. He'd dug up a little info on Doug, the most interesting being the man's membership of a club called 'The Mayfair Orphans'. This gang consisted of Michael Caine, Terry O'Neill, Philip Kingsley, Johnny Gold and, later on, Mickie Most. They were all working-class boys *done good* who were now without their parents. They met once a month on a Thursday and tore it up at Langan's. 'Its great how they've all stuck together as friends,' Mark said. 'It's like a hidden network. Proper.' He loved this idea of these names meeting up, forming a secret society almost. It was romance and the '60s and cool stardom all rolled into one.

The next day we returned to Doug's, sat on the sofa with Jack all over me again and Terry O'Neill to my left. As we explained to him about the book, the door opened. In came Jackie Stewart wearing a chalk-grey suit, white shirt, red tie. He looked great, slim, beautiful. He greeted Terry cheerfully, looked at Mark and me. Doug then walked over, shook his hand. The racing driver greeted his tailor and then turned to O'Neill. 'Terry,' he growled in his inimitable Scottish brogue, 'don't tell me things are so bad now you've got to use this as an office.'

Before he could reply, Doug Hayward interrupted, 'Tell me about it – everyone comes in here but no fucker buys as much as a tie!'

He then strolled magnificently to the back, where he started work on another Dougie Hayward suit, cost somewhere around two and a half grand.

Terry O'Neill couldn't have been more helpful. He said that when

The Fashion of Football

George Best relaxing at his fashion boutique, 1967. (© Empics)

Scotland's Jim Baxter looking relaxed in the days leading up to the Home International Championship match, Scotland v. Wales, 1965. (© Empics)

Malcolm Allison in the famous fedora, mid-'70s. (photo by Terry O'Neill)

Left to right: Terry Mancini, David Webb, Geoff
Hurst, Alan Ball, Alan Hudson, Terry Venables
and Rodney Marsh. (photo by Terry O'Neill)

The Casual band The Accent, who played at Stamford Bridge,
featuring 'Ginger' Mick Robinson. (© Tony Mottram)

Bobby Moore with his first wife, Tina, in one of Bobby's
England shirts, late '60s. (photo by Terry O'Neill)

A Mod, a Skin, a Suede . . . he's Peter Knowles it all, 1968. (courtesy West Ham George)

Steve Perryman in 1970 sporting the haircut that got the Tottenham Skinheads on the terraces declaring 'He's one of us.' (courtesy Keith Palmer)

A United Front: (left to right): **George Best**: bottle-green velvet suit by Lincroft, white cotton shirt from Austin Reed, Paisley-print tie from The Village Gate; **Denis Law**: Beige gabardine double-breasted suit from Take Six, beige voile shirt with tiny brown print and silk tie, both by Cassidy from The Village Gate, lace-up shoes from Bata; **Willie Morgan**: brown double-breasted wool suit with faint chalk stripe by Lincroft from The Village Gate, white rayon tie and silk hankie, both from Austin Reed, brown and white spot shirt by Mr. Harry; **Sammy McIlroy**: pink shadow-design shirt by Pancaldi, grey double-breasted suit with faint chalk stripe by Lincroft, pink silk hankie from Simpson, brogue shoes from Ravel. (source: *Club* magazine)

Keith Weller and Alan Hudson modelling for *Club* magazine. Keith (left) is wearing a long-sleeved cotton-jersey vest by Highlight from Take Six, £3.00; velvet top-stitched jeans from Mr. Freedom, £6.95. Alan is wearing a cotton polka-dot shirt with red patch-pocket from Mr. Freedom, £4.75; cotton-jersey vest by Highlight from Take Six, £2.50; velvet top-stitched jeans from Mr. Freedom, £6.95. (source: *Club* magazine)

Mike Summerbee holding one of his handmade shirts in 1974. (photo by Terry O'Neill)

Leeds United's £18 million new signing, Rio Ferdinand (left), is
paraded before the home fans by chairman Peter Ridsdale.
FA Carling Premiership, Leeds United v. Arsenal, 2000. (© Empics)

David Beckham, now at
Real Madrid, seen here
wearing a suit by tailor
William Hunt. (© Empics)

he first started working for Fleet Street, his main assignment was footballers – Cyril Knowles with a model draped over him, that kind of thing.

'I love that shot from the early '70s, the one you took of Hudson and the chaps around a table with cigars and brandies,' enthused Mark. 'Got to tell you, that shot is amazing.'

'I shot that at San Lorenzo's in the Kings Road, as I recall.'

'Great photo, but then so is a lot of your stuff.' Mark wasn't going to let this opportunity to pass on his best to the best slip by.

'Thank you,' Terry said, graciously. He promised he would look into his archive, sort us out a few snaps for the book. I expressed my fears that our budget might not stretch to his majestic images. He waved my consideration aside. 'Give me a drink and the printing costs and they're yours.'

As we walked down the street, Mark said, 'That place is amazing. Every time we go into Hayward's something great happens and I come out buzzing. Jackie Stewart, Terry O'Neill sorting us out on the snaps front – it's incredible.'

'It's like this amazing social club for all these great names,' I exclaimed, and pointed out that back in the day, tailors had assumed that very function – men would spend hours lounging and socialising in them, many of the early ones even running brothels upstairs. A man could be measured up many times visiting such establishments.

A week later, I went to pick up the tape of Dougie's film, played it when I got home. The film lasted just under an hour. It began with scenes of some kids playing street football, then it switched to Michael Parkinson sitting at a desk. He introduced the film and supplied the narration. It then moved to Doug's team playing in Hyde Park, then you saw them boarding a plane to Mexico, the start of a drive to bring 'the beauty of park football to the rest of the world'.

You saw the chaps, including Doug, O'Neill and John Alderton, at their hotel 'training', the game they play against a local Mexico side (the Marchers win) and brief snippets of the World Cup itself. It's a bit of a one-joke film but fascinating, especially when you tried to imagine the expression of the Rank executives who bankrolled it. 'Erm, guys, we kind of wanted a documentary about the England football team, not the park side you guys play in.'

The next day, I took the tape back to Hayward's, thanked Audie for lending it to us.

'Enjoy it?' asked Doug.

'Certainly did,' I replied. Then I shook their hands and left. As I walked out, a silver-haired man brushed past me. Michael Parkinson.

Just another day at Dougie the tailor's, then.

■■■

Footballers' Lives

I am on the phone again to the Guigs, my co-author on the Robin
Friday biography, a book *still* screaming out from the shelves to be
made into a film. I'm halfway through telling him about this book
when he makes a statement that is typical of his insightful nature
when it comes to football. 'You know the difference between
footballers and musicians?' he asks.

'Go on,' I say.

'You don't want to be mates with a footballer. You do with
musicians. A lot of them you think, I'd love to hang out with you,
see what makes you tick. But footballers? Not really. What footballer
would you want to hang out with today? Beckham? Owen?
Rooney?'

The man was right on the button. Most players who duly trooped
in front of the camera every Saturday didn't exactly excite you or
intrigue with clever answers, witty replies or force of personality.
They answered their questions competently, they answered without
a hint of controversy or challenge, and then they were beamed back
up to Planet Premiership.

'In fact,' the Guigs continued, 'the last batch of players you
would have wanted to know were guys like Alan Hudson, Stan
Bowles, Frank Worthington, Robin Friday.'

'Get all four of them out for the night and your drinking,
gambling, womanising and drug-taking instincts would be
splendidly accounted for,' I replied.

'You wouldn't get out alive,' Guigsy chuckled back.

The conversation finished but, later that day, Guigsy's quote
about footballers came to mind. Of late, I had been thinking about
two players – Manchester United's Willie Morgan and Arsenal's
Peter Marinello. Both men had been sold to the public as 'the new

George Best' but neither lived up to the billing. How could they? Just because they had been blessed with dark hair and good looks – replacing Georgie was never going to be an option.

Especially Marinello. He had come to Arsenal from Hibernian in January 1970, as a winger with enormous potential. The fee for his services had been £100,000, pretty substantial money for those days. Soon after his move to London, the process to make him as popular as a pop star began. Within months, Marinello was involved in all kinds of capers. These included a ghosted column for the *Daily Express*, advertising, and cutting a pop disc but the majority of his work involved modelling clothes, which is why a substantial amount of Freeman's catalogues dating back to the early '70s are filled with the shy, well-intentioned boy, modelling suits, shirts, trousers and overcoats.

Unsurprisingly, he could not live up to the hype generated around him. His time at Arsenal was not particularly productive for either player or club and he returned to Scotland a year later.

Marinello's innocent, clean-boy image stood firmly at odds with his badly behaved contemporaries who defined that era. I started thinking that maybe this was when the footballer replaced the musician as the true rebel. The space was certainly there at the time. By the early '70s, the bands that had kicked up the '60s and challenged the authorities to a fight had either split up (The Beatles), turned inward (Dylan) or become flamboyantly decadent (The Stones).

The biggest selling album of the '70s, after all, was Pink Floyd's introspective *Dark Side of the Moon*, hardly a rallying cry for all street-fighting men.

The footballers who emerged in the late '60s and early '70s had no such cultural baggage. They were different. They were the first generation to enthusiastically take up the George Best route, to throw themselves into the public spotlight, to seek out and surround themselves with glamour. The famous photograph Terry O'Neill took of Hudson, Marsh, Hurst, Venables et al. could never have been taken ten years previously. Bill Nicholson would never have allowed it. Nor Shankly, Busby or Cullis.

The rise of the individual who aggressively courted the spotlight was not to the clubs' likings. This period of football history is splattered with rows erupting between club and player, country and player, the player storming out of the ground, the manager or chairman publicly castigating him, the handshake a few days later and then a brief interlude before round two. In such a manner, football mirrored the wider world: the continual clashes between government and workers, events such as the three-day working week and the miners bringing down Prime Minister Edward Heath.

In 1979, the inauguration of Margaret Thatcher put a stop to such nonsense. Her removal from society of all values that pertained to left-wing principles and her crazed drive to create a money-centred society brought forth the rise of the bland footballer. One only has to think of Glen Hoddle and Chris Waddle on *Top of the Pops* with mullet haircuts, terrible voices and the sleeves of their designer jackets rolled up to the elbow. Another one that springs to mind is Kevin Keegan, whose eagerness to sell himself beyond football included modelling clothes, sporting a terrible perm haircut and making very dodgy records.

Fashion in the '80s reflected this new money-conscious ethos. The designer, once confined to the world of haute couture, stepped out of the pages of *Vogue* and destroyed the notion that clothes shops were the main providers of fashion. The young and the wealthy were to be found in designer shops now. Take Six, Lord John, Michael's — all of them began to fade away. Designer labels triumphed in the '80s, and are still doing so now.

The worlds of football and brands were finally brought together at the 1996 FA Cup final when the Liverpool team walked out onto the pitch wearing brilliant-white Armani suits. It is still spoken about today, and usually in disparaging terms, yet at least the action created a debate. The '80s and the '90s, in terms of footballers' fashions, were in no way as interesting as the previous decades had been. The really interesting developments, as we will see, took place on the terraces. That said, there were a few spots of interest worth noting. One was Arsenal's Charlie Nicholas.

One of the few players to ever grace the cover of the *NME*, Nicholas was a Glaswegian who joined Celtic at the age of 15, scored a ridiculous number of goals for them and then moved to Arsenal. His early style of dress strongly suggested that every morning he awoke, he reached for the phone to ask U2 singer Bono what he should wear that day. Unfortunately, not only did Bono give him the advice he sought, sending him out into the world in a style which echoed punk-goth, he also neglected to tell him that mullet hairstyles weren't, and never would be, a good idea.

Nicholas, like the young Scottish player Pat Nevin later, was of interest to the music press because he at least professed musical leanings towards rock music, often citing bands such as U2, The Alarm, Sade, Psychedelic Furs and Depeche Mode as his fave raves.

Another Arsenal player, but in a very different vein, was the striker Ian Wright, whose flamboyant skills on the pitch were matched by his dress sense off it. Wright's use of jewellery in particular placed him firmly in hip-hop culture, a tradition that included rappers such as LL Cool J, who combined striking sportswear with conspicuous quantities of gold. (The rapper once said to an uncomprehending *NME* journalist as they drove down Wall Street, 'Look at those guys with the briefcases and the Brooks Brother suits. They've got an expensive uniform, so why shouldn't I?') Later on, this penchant for jewellery would fuel what we today call 'bling-bling' culture.

Over at Chelsea, the club's love affair with Italian players such as Roberto De Matteo and Gianluca Vialli brought a Mediterranean influence to the scene. Dennis Wise vividly recalls Gianluca Vialli walking into the Chelsea dressing-room for the first time dressed in an Armani cashmere sweater, smart designer trousers and brown brogues. Within minutes, players were asking him where he got his clothes. Within days, they were wearing them.

Players such as Ray Wilkins and David Platt returned from playing in Italy sporting a similar style but Liverpool's Ian Rush did not. He felt that playing in Italy was 'like playing in a foreign country'.

In 1990, Thatcher went. Seven years later, so did Prime Minister John Major and, with him, eighteen years of Tory rule. When Tony Blair took the hot seat in 1997, the Premiership was five years old. At the time of writing, it is twelve years old, a huge moneymaking beast that occupies a central position in the life of Britain today.

Football, the working man's ballet, as Alan Hudson once memorably called it, is now the national dance. And so today's players experience football in ways their turbulent predecessors could never imagine. The fashion world cottoned on to this fact in the mid-'90s. Giorgio Armani asked goalkeeper David James to model his clothes on the catwalk in 1995 and then went on to work for Newcastle United and Chelsea, the latter opting to work with Dunhill last season. David Ginola has also donated his sportsman's body and classic good looks to various advertisers, as has Arsenal's Freddie Ljungberg, who is now to be found on the side of London buses posing naked except for a skimpy pair of Calvin Klein shorts.

The latest development in this world has seen designer Dirk Birkemberg launch a range of T-shirts featuring front covers of the Italian football paper *La Gazzetta dello Sport*. Time, then, for Mark and I to talk to Terence Parris.

* * *

He remembers those days well, him and John Barnes, the future Liverpool and England winger, 15 years old and going to Crackers dressed in Gabicci tops, Farah slacks, Bass Weejun loafers. Terence Parris was from round John's way, up there in Watford, and they were Soulboys. Crackers on a Friday afternoon, 100 Club Saturday afternoon, The Lacey Lady in Ilford Saturday night. Barnes dressed a lot better than he would later on in life when, as a celebrity, he decided for some inexplicable reason that garish jackets were the thing to wear on national TV.

Terence Parris would also make his own mark in the football world. Puma, the company he markets, were behind the innovative kit designs that the Cameroon team adopted during the World Cup in 2002 and the African Cup of Nations in 2004. The first was a sleeveless top, the second an all-in-one body outfit. For the latter, the country were docked World Cup qualifying points and given a hefty fine by Sepp Blatter's FIFA.

They would not have got away with such an audacious plan in the Premiership. Terence's friends are footballers. One of his closest acquaintances is Jimmy Floyd Hasselbaink. 'He's huge on Dolce & Gabbana stuff,' he told Mark and I in a café near the Puma office, just off Carnaby Street, 'but he has huge thighs so he has clothing issues.'

Parris has worked amongst footballers for years and knows their general mindset. That's why we went to talk to him.

'One of the things that is true about footballers right across the board,' he states, 'is that they are almost lemming-like. That's because, in their world, doing anything out of the norm gets you absolutely slated. Whatever tends to be the trend, everyone will go into it. For example, every players' lounge you go into today, 50 per cent of them will have Louis Vuitton toiletry bags, they're massive at the moment.' Without looking at each other, Mark and I instantly flash back to Matt Elliott walking into Alan Birchenall's office clutching such a bag and smile inwardly. It's a good moment between us.

'It's where they keep their bits – their phone, their wallet, their watch,' Terence continued. 'You don't have to take anything to a game now, it's all there for you now. If you look at players now, it's Prada, Gucci. It was only when certain people started to be a bit lairy then other people started to be a bit bolder and bite the bullet. If you wore Katharine Hamnett or Comme des Garçons, which were a bit avant-garde, you would have got slated.'

It was a point of view Mark and I had come to as the book had progressed. The majority of players today seemed more than content to *follow* trends, not *make* them, or indeed reflect them. It was as if their contracts had clauses saying that they must train five times a week and shop wherever David Beckham favoured at the time.

'If you bought a house,' Parris explained, 'and you had an unlimited bank account, you would go in and buy everything in one fell swoop, which is fine but you haven't created anything with imagination. With clothes, those of us who have to hustle a buck and work for a living, we always end up making our own little look. You might wear a white Burberry mac with a trilby hat. The style might fit into a general genre but it will have a bit of you in there.

'Footballers tend to buy in bulk and therefore they don't have to think about style. Sociologists say the middle and upper classes have this mentality of deferred gratification. It's all about putting money aside for a rainy day, whereas the working class want to have it now. The danger with football is that it gives you too much opportunity to have it now. It all comes in one hit with no thought or imagination really.'

I told Terence that of late we had been looking at '80s and '90s players, finding precious little to get excited about. Mark mentioned the exceptions, the likes of Ian Wright and Gianluca Vialli, and Terence agreed on their importance.

'What Ian typified was the increasing influence of urban black culture on society as a whole,' he stated. 'He was very indicative of the bling-bling culture and probably made little white kids buy into it. It almost stopped it being a race issue and I think he was right at the forefront of that. Vialli's reign almost coincided with classic tailoring becoming popular in mainstream fashion. So, designers like Ozwald Boateng became quite mainstream around the time Vialli was on TV wearing browns and blues together. That was a look that people wouldn't go anywhere near at the time but now they would be quite comfortable with that. Tailoring became quite a strong route for players to go down and, to some extent, that's still very much the case. You've got people like Ozwald Boateng and Richard James.'

Was there anyone now who caught his eye?

There was – Rio Ferdinand. 'I think Rio's importance is that he is one of the few people who hold their hands up and say, I really like fashion and I really want to influence things. Rather than that lemming-like scenario, he is saying, I want to be the leader of this pack. But you know the best people to ask, don't you? The footballers themselves.'

Mark smiled. 'If you saw the amount of paper we've got turning down our requests for interviews, you could build a bonfire.'

But Parris was right. We needed a player's perspective.

* * *

Had to be a Millwall player. With Mark directing the book's traffic, there was no other choice, really. That said, Mark had been talking about Darren Ward a lot that season, as both a player and a fashion man, and although at the time the Millwall faithful had yet to be convinced by their centre-half, Mark thought differently.

'I reckon he's a confidence player,' he told me in Bar Italia one dinnertime, 'and you probably don't need telling but the crowd at Millwall can destroy anyone's confidence, especially if they put in a dodgy game or two. I mean, the verbals I've had with some of the guys around me about Ward. They've been slaughtering him. Of course, his barnet don't help.'

'What's it like?' I asked.

'It's like a blond mullet with a twist, a bit like Beckham about a year ago with lumps and bumps sticking out all over the place. That's what the local papers and the crowd call him, 'the Peckham Beckham', plus he drives a Harley Davidson pick-up, same car as our man in Madrid. But I think he's a good player and I also think he's really into his clothes. About a year ago, I saw him on Bond Street, bags and bags of Gucci, Vuitton, Prada gear. I think he's worth a punt.'

By the time Mark had fixed up an interview, Ward had won over the notoriously hard-to-please (actually, isn't every football crowd notoriously hard to please?) Millwall faithful. His confidence was flowing, his defensive talents drawing applause and they had even stopped using the Peckham Beckham title to insult him.

I couldn't make the interview because of a prior engagement but Mark and his partner Lou (who supports Chelsea and has a thing for Millwall's manager Dennis Wise that borders on the insane) trooped down to Millwall's training ground in Bromley in mid-February.

Prior to his arrival, the Millwall PR, Deano Standing, called Mark, told him that although Ward would love to talk about the subject, he wanted Mark checked out. He was suspicious that the interview might be a wind-up by his teammates. Ward had taken a lot of verbal for his dress sense in the changing-room and was a touch sensitive.

Even when the player met Mark and Lou, he acted in a shifty manner, constantly looking for signs of his teammates lurking nearby. Finally, satisfied that the interview was indeed kosher, Ward took Mark and Lou to the dining-room area. The following transcript is a record of their conversation.

Mark Baxter: Darren, thanks for agreeing to speak to us.
Darren Ward: No problem.
MB: Can we get a bit of background on you, footballwise?
DW: Yeah, I started playing in park football, really, Sunday teams and all that. Got scouted by Coventry and was there for a while, wasn't really working out, got approached by Watford and went there at 13 or 14, and signed as Schoolboy, YTS, and then I became a pro and came up through the ranks to the first team. Played in the Premiership for a couple of games when Watford were last in there. Anyway, Mark McGhee came in for me and I was happy to sign for Millwall.
MB: How about clothes, always an interest?
DW: Oh, yeah, always have been into fashion. Always into my gear.

When I was younger, I was mainly into labels — Armani, DKNY, Gucci. As you get older, you find your style and I've got into the hip-hop look, all baggy and that. Hip hop is ruling the world, really, if you look around, with all the music, cars and fashions. I'm into some of it but with a bit of a twist. Stamping my own take on it.

MB: How about more formal wear, suits etc.?

DW: Yeah, had a couple made and have bought off-the-peg. Boss, Armani, typical footballers' wear, but to be honest [looks around], here at Millwall I'm on my own fashionwise. Some of the stuff I was wearing when I first came here is now being worn by some and I haven't worn it for ages. It's almost like I had to wear it first and then it got accepted. The amount of stick I've got over the years hasn't really bothered me, it's what I'm into, so be it.

When I was at Watford and Vialli came in, he got us all suited up, Italian cut, smart, but not really me, too smart. They love a label, a certain make, I prefer a mix-and-match look, a street look.

It's like the Christmas do here. I wore 508 really baggy jeans, Converse trainers, a funky Goofy top, a suit jacket and a beenie hat. That's normal for me, dressed down, in fact, in some ways. Some took the right piss. A month or two later, they sort of come up to you and say 'You know that gear you were wearing, where d'ya get it?' I told them, 'Go find it yourself, I ain't telling you.' Half the gear I've got, I wouldn't wear it here.

MB: I think you are quite brave in a way, to walk into a dressing-room with 30 geezers in it, wearing something a bit different.

DW: Yeah, I took some verbals but I can give it back and they get used to you after a while.

MB: Where do you shop? Where do you go?

DW: I go up Bond Street, Covent Garden. I like the shop Rokit at the moment. A lot of it is second-hand. Imported from the States.

MB: Where do get your fashion ideas? Magazines, telly?

DW: Off the streets, really. My brothers are well into fashion as well and we keep each other informed. I've got one brother at West Ham, one on trial at Wycombe and the youngest is at Watford. I'm not really into a certain brand.

MB: Can I ask you about Beckham? We've asked everyone we've interviewed so far what they think of him.

DW: I think he is top man.

MB: You ain't got his number, have ya? [Laughter all round]

DW: Mate, I probably could get it, Wilkins [Ray, Millwall's assistant manager] knows his assistant really well. The way he handles it all, outside of football, terrific really. I think he sets the tone. He's clued up to the max. People think I'm copying him with my hair and all that, but I ain't really, I've just got similar tastes.

MB: Where do you get that cut?

DW: It's at a place called Artisan, near Harrow. It's cut by my brother's girlfriend actually.

MB: That's handy, cheaper that way.

DW: Nah, she's good, mate.

MB: Well, it certainly is a work of art. All geometric. That's what first made me think of approaching you for an interview. With a barnet like that, you must be into your fashions.

DW: It's all about having the balls to do something different sometimes. But you still have to know what's what.

MB: Are there any other players out there you admire?

DW: Dichio [Danny, Millwall centre-forward] here, he ain't bad.

MB: He liked an interesting barnet back in his QPR days, didn't he?

DW: At this level, there ain't too many. I liked what Scott Parker wore when he signed for Chelsea the other day. Suit jacket and ripped jeans.

MB: Do you buy stuff regular?

DW: Two or three times a month, I'll buy something but I'm getting into the whole lifestyle thing now. Interior design, motors, a nice kitchen and all that. Me and my missus are doing our flat up, the whole package. I'm quite creative really. I don't stand still, I like to move on. If I change anything, clothes or what have you, I like to upgrade, get something different, better, each time.

MB: You're going well on the pitch this season as well.

DW: Ta, I've knuckled down, stopped going out, got a few early nights in. I can't go out and about, and play at my best. It's all about growing up, really. I expect the stick from the crowd if I ain't performing well. It's like you today, if you mess this up, you're gonna get stick, ain't you?

MB: Oh, yeah, not half. You haven't met Paolo, have you?

DW: Anyway, I feel it's going well this year for me. I want to have a good season.

The Fashion of Football

Prophetic last words. Darren Ward, the Peckham Beckham, was in 2004 voted Millwall's player of the year . . . by the fans.

* * *

It was Sunday morning and I was a-lying in bed, wondering if she would change at all whilst I just sat there and read. I turned over the page of a Sunday supplement and read that a magazine dedicated to footballers and fashion was going to hit the shops the very next day. I panicked. All writers do when they see their idea thrown into the public arena by a different source. I called Mark straight away.

'Have you seen this?' I demanded. 'They're doing a magazine on football and fashion.'

'You're joking,' Mark replied.

'I wish I bloody was.' I read the article out to Mark.

'It doesn't say if it's weekly or monthly or what,' he said when I had finished. 'Look, I'll see what I can find out tomorrow.'

I spent the rest of the day fretting.

Mark did get the magazine. It was big, it was glossy and it featured pictures of my very good friend Sol Campbell wearing Farhi, Burberry and Hermès. Elsewhere, Sir Paul Smith spoke to Andy Cole, Andy Cole spoke to Giorgio Armani and Kevin Sampson wrote a very brief history of style and football. Its very existence confirmed the exalted position of today's footballers. This was the kind of venture that musicians were once approached for. Not any more.

The footballer is now a permanent fixture in the fashion world. He walks on the catwalks, sponsors and advertises certain labels in magazines, beds the models, poses half-naked on the sides of buses and accepts that clothes are a vital part of his armoury.

Some, like Nigel Quashie at Portsmouth, fully embrace this development. Quashie, the son of a clothes-conscious father, only shops at William Hunt, won't go anywhere else. Like Darren Ward, at first his style was mocked by his colleagues. Now, he's seen as a man of individuality in a world where conformity is very much the safest option. But footballers need leaders. They also need tailors.

■■■

The Tale of the Tailor

Before we parted company, Terence Parris had told us about Tony 'the
Tailor'. 'He's got a business where he goes round the clubs and designs
suits for footballers,' Parris said. 'He's been doing it for years.'

He gave us Tony's number. The next day I called and after I
explained what we were doing, Tony agreed to a lunch-time meet in
Muswell Hill. Mark couldn't make the interview, which was a shame
– he and Tony would have got on.

Tony was well dressed, funny, self-deprecating; a man with the
gravelliest voice I have heard in a long time. He hailed from the East
End, grew up in Leyton, in what he termed 'David Beckham
territory'. His father was a neat dresser who valued clothes a great
deal. Tony was given his first suit aged nine and by fifteen he was a
Mod, stepping out in mohair. He left school at sixteen, the rag trade
the only place in which he was going to go and prosper.

He joined the clothing company Moss Bros, worked his way up
the ladder. By the early '70s, his brief at the company was enviable.
Anyone rich and famous who came into contact with Moss Bros
went through Tony. A wide range of names and faces appeared
before him: The Osmonds, Larry Hagman and Robert Wagner, along
with African kings and millionaires.

He enjoyed his work but there was one type of celebrity he found
himself drawn to above all others – the footballer. An Arsenal fan,
he was thrilled to bits when, through his work, he found himself
shooting the breeze with the likes of George Graham, Paul Mariner,
Bob Wilson and Brian Talbot, all Arsenal players at the time.

'Footballers needed a lot of guidance in those days,' he recalls.
'They are a lot more tuned in now because things such as fashion
magazines have grown [in popularity]. In those days, there was
nothing.'

The Fashion of Football

The Arsenal players were different. Bertie Mee, the Arsenal manager during the late '60s and early '70s, insisted players wear a shirt and tie at all times and many gladly did so. After all, they had been raised to dress smart, present themselves to the world in a neat and tidy manner.

'George Graham is the type of person that makes sure that before he leaves the front door, he looks immaculate,' Tony says of the ex-Arsenal player and manager. 'Nothing will be out of place. It was that generation. Their fathers were brought up to have made-to-measure suits even if they didn't have the money; they would save up and George followed that through. A lot of the players from that era were the same.'

I told Tony I had been to see Frank McLintock so I knew exactly what he was talking about. Tony knew Frank, he had played in celebrity games with him for charity. It was at one of these games that Tony suffered a bad injury to his cruciate. Through his Arsenal connections, he was given treatment by the club physio. Pretty soon, Tony was a regular Highbury visitor and on first-name terms with all the players, supplying them with any clothes they cared to order.

'They would buy loads of jeans from me,' he explained, 'and sweatshirts and T-shirts and casual tops and jackets and, through them, my relationship expanded very quickly. I'd take them to the players I knew and they would introduce me to other players.'

It was at this juncture that Tony decided to take a gamble. He quit his job at Moss Bros, opened up a small clothes shop in the East End and started supplying clothes to the players. It was a good time to make such a move.

Just as he did so, Sky TV started putting millions into the game and, in doing so, changed it forever. 'When I first saw the reaction the media and the public were giving players when they wore their lairy suits,' Tony states, 'that's when I realised how powerful the medium was going to be. I saw that the association between football and Sky was going to be absolutely key in terms of fashion. The players didn't know it at the time but I saw there was potential for a brand associated with footballers and sport stars, more so footballers because [they] are icons, unlike any other icons.'

'More than pop stars these days?' I ask.

'Absolutely. Music has always been there but footballers are now the new pop stars.'

Tony's business expanded. At first, it was all London traffic. From Arsenal, he went to Spurs, then QPR, Crystal Palace and West Ham. Some players he measured up for suits, others he provided with designer-label clothing. 'Footballers have moved on since the money has come in,' he points out, 'and they find it harder to go to general shops.'

West Ham approached him, requesting a new club suit – was he up to the job? 'For the players, money is no object, they can buy the Armanis and the Versaces, so to wear a corporate uniform isn't very good,' he explains. 'I thought I'd be creative and I created a classic three-button suit and, in the inside of the jacket, I put a West Ham lining. It was a navy-blue suit but inside was claret with the West Ham logo across the lining.'

How did manager and ex-Mod Harry Redknapp react to that? I wondered.

'Harry liked it,' Tony replied, 'but it was noticed more by Paolo Di Canio because he was appreciative of design and thought. You tended to find that most players just wanted to know what brand it was, whereas players like Paolo and Ian Wright looked at the suit as a suit and saw the thought processes that had gone into it.'

After West Ham, a commission from Wimbledon, and then an old client called him up. It was Kevin Campbell, formerly of Arsenal, now at Everton. He wasn't happy. He had just seen the club suit he would have to wear on match day. 'Kevin called and said, can you come up? We have these club suits which are crap,' Tony recalls. 'He introduced me to the manager and that's how we ended up doing their suits. Logistically, it was a nightmare. You try making made-to-measure clothes for people 200 miles away.'

At the same time, clubs started looking to Europe for players. Dennis Bergkamp was an early recruit, so were Gianluca Vialli and Gianfranco Zola, who came to Chelsea. Their presence immediately caused waves. 'The foreign players arrived, number one being the Italians,' Tony recalls. 'The smarter, more coordinated look rubbed off on the British players. No longer were they into wearing jeans with holes in them but the suit came in and was used in a more general way, not just special occasions.'

The Fashion of Football

Accordingly, Tony's business boomed. He sold up the shop and moved into what he jokingly refers to as 'my new home'. It's his car. His company has a staff of one – himself. All day, he drives here, he drives there, meeting his favourite kind of people, putting them into his favourite kind of clothes.

At the end of season 2003–04, he will launch his own range of clothing specifically aimed at footballers and sportsmen. It will be called Q'aja Couture.

'It's a range of tailoring but tailoring taken to a different level,' he says. 'A much higher level, plus a designer range of leather and cashmere for which we've signed a world-famous designer who has become part of the company now.'

Who are the stylish players today? I ask Tony, changing subjects. Surprisingly, Beckham's name doesn't get an airing. Tony fixes on Di Canio, Ian Wright, Andy Cole, Gary Lineker, Michael Owen, and then he thinks of Paul Gascoigne, and has a little laugh. Tony used to dress Gascoigne, had done so ever since Venables brought him to White Hart Lane in 1988 and asked Tony to help with his protégé's wardrobe.

Tony and Gazza got on well together and when Gazza was transferred to the Italian club Lazio in 1991, Tony designed a special number for his very first press conference. 'We made him a purple suit because he was going to the home of fashion and it was a colour the Italians appreciate,' he recalls. 'All the media picked it up. In fact, the first question at the conference was "Where did you get your suit from?" Unfortunately, Gazza replied, "I got it from my rag-and-bone man." Obviously, us boys from London can understand what a rag-and-bone man is but the Italians just smiled and said, "What is this rag-and-bone man?"'

You can imagine Tony sitting there, one minute expecting to have his name trumpeted to the entire world, thinking of the orders that would deluge him and the millions he would make; next minute his dream sinking into the ground thanks to Gazza's 'joke'.

'I said to him, Gaz, what's with the rag-and-bone man? Oh, I thought it was funny, he said. I said, yeah, it was funny but I could have had endless phone calls coming through saying we want to use you.' Tony looks up at me, smiles and ruefully adds, 'I've had to work for a living since then.'

■■■
The Continental Drift

Not too long ago, I had dinner with Dave Mackay, the legendary former Tottenham player. In Mackay's case, that overworked epithet 'legendary' is, for once, applicable. Dave Mackay was the highly skilful midfielder whose talent and immense drive helped Spurs to the famous, groundbreaking 1961 Double, the European Cup-Winners' Cup and two further FA Cups.

But Mackay also has a further and deeper significance. Simply by existing, he reminds us of a time when football carried deeper and better values, from top to bottom. Money was not God, the players were not untouchable, the crowd was not to be callously betrayed.

Some aspects of that era are to be located and pondered upon in Mackay's recent biography, *The Real Mackay*, which I got the great man to read from at the literary night I host at the Islington pub Filthy McNasty's. Acting on the principle that he could only turn me down, I had rung Dave's publishers to see if there was any chance he could come to London for a reading. Two days later, much to my astonishment, Dave Mackay was on *my* phone in *my* house, agreeing to *my* request. This was truly something.

'Dave, I have got to tell you, it is such a great honour to talk to you.'

'Yeah, never mind that,' he said. 'Now, what time you want me there?'

Like I said, different times, different values.

As I owed fellow Spurs man Keith Palmer for setting up an interview with Steve Perryman, I phoned and invited him along to meet the great man at Euston train station. I think Keith's first words to him were, 'I'll take that Mr Mackay,' as he picked up his suitcase. Mackay was clean-shaven, suited up and wearing highly polished brogues. We left the station and a local Pizza Express drew us in. We settled at a table in the half-empty restaurant and ordered. As we ate, I couldn't help thinking, Jesus, I'm eating pizza with Dave Mackay.

I also couldn't help peppering the man with questions about Spurs manager Bill Nicholson. Nicholson had died in November 2004 and I badly wanted to write his official biography. If I was going to get the job, I'd need a lot more information on the man. Who did Bill vote for? What was his general outlook on life? Did he like The Beatles, for example? Or was he a jazz man? Did he like other sports? These and many more questions I kept firing until Mackay turned to me and said, 'Look, strange as it may seem in this day and age, I never really knew Bill. I only spoke football with him. He was the manager, I was the player. In fact, I went to his office two times in my life. Once to sign with Spurs and once to tell him I was leaving. That was it. We never sat down and spoke like this.'

Of course − silly me. That's how it worked back then. Football was a different world. Managers were figures of authority. Their word was sacrosanct. No one challenged their authority. No one went to the papers and criticised them for not recognising their God-given talent. No one spilled the beans or went public. A hierarchy was adhered to. Managers managed, players played.

Fashion-wise, this translated into two distinct looks. The players wore regulation club blazers and ties; and the managers kept to a fixed wardrobe consisting of two combinations: suit, tie and shirt, or smart jacket, trousers, tie and shirt. The managers, the great illustrious names such as Bill Nicholson, Bill Shankly, Matt Busby and Jock Stein, might as well have shared the same wardrobe. Apart from little oddities such as Brian Clough's bright-green jumper, there were no variations on this theme; not until Malcolm Allison came along and took centre stage.

A former centre-half for West Ham and Charlton, Allison had gone into management in 1964 at Plymouth. Such was his impact there (League Cup semi-final in his first season), he was soon appointed right-hand man to the Manchester City manager, Joe Mercer. Over the next five years, he would help coach and guide the Blues to the Second Division title, the League championship, the FA Cup, the League Cup and the European Cup-Winners' Cup.

But playing second fiddle was never going to be enough to satisfy

Allison's expanding ego. On 31 March 1973, Malcolm was appointed Crystal Palace manager. Within two years, he had overseen his team relegated not once but twice. Failure was now his constant companion. Yet it was at precisely this period that Allison's clothes seemed to increase in outlandishness. Think Allison and one instantly thinks of large fur coats and fedora hats, usually accompanied by the man waving magnum-size bottles of champagne and rather large fuck-off cigars in the air. Such is the power of clothing. Dress for success, talk success and at some point people will think you are a success, despite the facts. No other manager understood this principle better than Malcolm Allison.

In his third season as Palace manger, Allison completely restructured the side and the decline was halted. In fact, the 1975–76 season was Malcolm's most successful at Selhurst Park. He guided his side to an FA Cup semi-final appearance, masterminding brilliant victories against higher-league opposition such as Leeds United, Chelsea and Sunderland. Unfortunately, he couldn't find a way past eventual winners Southampton. Yet such was the impact of Palace's Cup exploits, that season the club shop sold up to 4,000 Allison-style fedora hats.

With his ego spectacularly lifting itself into the stratosphere, Allison made his big mistake. One day, he divested himself of his flash clothing and jumped stark naked into the Crystal Palace bath after a training session. Which was fine, except the bath not only contained most of his players but a porn star by the name of Fiona Richmond. Predictable outrage engulfed the manager and Malcolm resigned in May of 1976. Despite two successive relegations, Allison is still remembered fondly by Palace supporters, who no doubt cannot look at a fedora hat without feeling twinges of warm nostalgia.

Allison returned to Manchester City in 1979. He was now the club's 'coaching overlord'. On being questioned by the press about this appointment, he stated: 'I am not just a coach, I am a scientist and, like all good scientists, I can make things work.' We should not be surprised at Allison's self-belief. After all, this was a man who had previously published a book cheekily entitled *Soccer For Thinkers*. Unfortunately, this period was not a success and chairman Peter Swales dismissed him in October 1980.

Sadly for style observers, the Allison look did not find favour with his contemporaries. To this day, managers have mainly stuck to the uniform described previously. The exceptions have all been foreigners and they have all settled at Chelsea.

First, there was Gianluca Vialli, with his classic and ever-influential Italian style. In Italy, clothes carry far more significance, retain a deeper cultural value, than they do in many other countries. In Italia, clothes announce to the watching world who you are and what your status is. The better the clothes, the better the person. Vialli's style was timeless, mainly consisting of smart V-neck jumpers, worsted trousers and brown brogues. Not that he needed to impress anyone. Vialli's playing credentials included memorable stints with Cremonese, Sampdoria and Juventus, as well as helping Italia to third place in the 1990 World Cup. He became Chelsea player-manager in 1998 before giving way to the second part of the Chelsea Style Trinity, Claudio Ranieri. Ranieri sported quite dull suits but made up for it occasionally in darkest winter with a number of stylish three-quarter-length jackets.

Of course, the final part of the Chelsea Trinity again settles around an outdoor coat.

For the British press, José Mourinho's long grey overcoat is evidence of the man's innate Mediterranean style. Most of us think that assessment is simply wrong-headed. The coat, with its soft shoulders and drab colour, does the man no favours, except acting as some kind of lucky totem. Certainly, up against the standard set in Italy by the Roberto Mancini's of this world, Mourinho wouldn't stand a chance. And that's even with his Russian benefactor's millions behind him.

Meanwhile, managers earn a fortune but seem to spend little of it at the tailor's or the fancy clothes outlets, preferring to stay anonymous. Apart form the welcome mavericks such as Allison, they seem to regard clothes in the same way they regard the press — a necessary evil that's simply part of the job.

■ ■ ■

PS Actually, It Seemed Like
a Good Idea at the Time . . .

In the 1960s, the Tottenham Hotspur captain, Dave Mackay, was approached by a shop owner. For a one-off payment, could he use Mackay's name for a tie shop he wished to open on White Hart Lane? Mackay took the money and the shop is still there, 40 years later, trading under his name and doing good business.

Terry Venables was always going to expand outside football. His drive to make money has been a constant throughout his career. One of his earliest ventures was a business partnership with Chelsea teammates George Graham and Ron Harris, along with the football writer Ken Jones. The men set up a tailoring business in Old Compton Street, Soho, looking to attract the show-business people who came to Chelsea games.

'Unfortunately, they were less than enthusiastic about paying their bills,' Venables recalls in his biography, going on to say:

> Norman Wisdom was one of our celebrity clients and I had been a huge fan of his as a child, but his patronage was a very double-edged sword. The fact that we clothed him wasn't necessarily the best endorsement for our goods. When I told some people that we made Wisdom's suits, they said, 'Well, that's not much of an advert for a tailoring business,' and walked out of the shop. I only realised after they had left that they thought I meant the crumpled ones, two sizes too small, that he wore on stage. The tailoring business did not survive for long.

Venables and Graham then turned their attention to a new invention, the Thingummywig, which was a hat with a wig attached, aimed at women who could use it to hide their curlers if they had to go out. Surprisingly, the venture failed.

The Fashion of Football

PART TWO

■■■■■■■■■■■■

HALF-TIME

From Beau to Burro – A Kickabout with the History of Fashion

■ ■ ■

A Tale of Two Streets

Before Prada, before Gucci, before designers, British male fashion in London had two major centres. One was Savile Row and the other was Carnaby Street. One was posh, the other young; one was inward, the other outgoing.

Savile Row does not take kindly to strangers, never has, never will. This is a street of tradition, of permanence, a space built on cast-iron values of Englishness, of skill, quality and tradition, its roots located in the highest strata of class-ridden England. Its first inhabitants were nobility, then the military and afterwards the medical profession. The original land 'belonged' to a Lord Burlington. In 1695, he signed a development lease allowing for streets to be built on his property. Asked for a name for this particular passage, he donated his wife's surname, Lady Dorothy Savile.

For years, the lords and their ladies bade good morning to their military and medical neighbours. Then came Beau Brummell. Born George Bryan in 1778, Beau was the most famous of the dashing young men of the regency. He was not of aristocratic birth – his grandfather was a shopkeeper in St James's Parish – but to earn extra corn, his grandfather would rent rooms to aristocratic gentlemen. Beau became obsessed with the well-to-do, constantly studied them, how they behaved, how they dressed, their manners, their ways. He yearned to live as they did, developed a very real passion for their clothes, their style. He understood such things instinctively. He once stated that the well-dressed man never drew attention to himself, passed by as if invisible.

Brummell was educated at Eton, his nickname there, Buck. He was a popular student, drew attention and admiration from his peers. He had literary talent and wit. At a dinner once, where the champagne served was of an inferior quality, Brummell waited for a pause in the conversation before loudly shouting to the waiter, 'John, bring me some more of that cider, will you?'

A wit then, but deeply intelligent as well. At Eton, Brummell was placed second for the prestigious Newdigate Prize and through his humour and charisma created a ripple. Word of his individual character reached the Prince Regent and soon Beau had been granted a military commission. He worked his way quickly through the ranks, became a captain of the Tenth Hussars. He was overjoyed. Now he could wear a fancy uniform every day of the week. He became a confidant of the young Prince Regent, the future George IV. George liked Beau's wit and style, his individual streak. Beau took hours to dress himself and he also bathed, cleansing oneself being a revolutionary idea at the time. Soon Brummell's individual ways allowed him to assume a position as the oracle on matters related to dress and etiquette.

He resigned his commission just as the Napoleonic Wars were beginning and, soon after, inherited £30,000 from his family. Can't help if he's lucky. He bought an elegant abode in Mayfair, London, and set about placing himself at the absolute centre of London society.

At the same time, in 1806, the first tailor had been established on Savile Row, although tailoring did not in fact originate there. The art is French, *tailler* in French translating into 'to cut'. Brummell began frequenting Savile Row and many others followed his lead. Soon, tailoring shops opened up one after the other to cope with the demand. If Brummell had a passion – clothes – he also had a flaw – gambling. When the money he inherited ran out, so did his high-placed friends. In 1816, with huge debts on his shoulders, Brummell left England for France to escape the debtors' prison. He was only staving off the inevitable, however, and ended up incarcerated in a French debtors' prison. His passion had been obliterated by his addiction. He became slovenly and unclean, unrecognisable from his sparkling youthful days.

He finished his life in the Asylum du Bon Sauveur, a hospital in Caen for the insane. Part of his legacy was that by 1838, Savile Row was a street known for tailors, their names rich in suggestion – Henry Poole & Co., Anderson & Sheppard, Turnbull & Asser. Royalty now came to them, unable to resist, bestowing on the street

The Fashion of Football

enormous prestige, creating a reputation of excellence that travelled worldwide, and which persists to this day.

But the wheel turns, always turns. Come the twentieth century, the monarchy's sway on the public began to falter. New kings came to take their place – they were American, from Hollywood, men made famous by the invention of cinema, and with whom old royalty could never compete. For unlike royalty, Hollywood never ages.

Kilgour, French & Stanbury made clothes for Fred Astaire; Gieves & Hawkes did business with Charles Laughton. Later, Gary Cooper, Cary Grant, Clark Gable, Bing Crosby, Dean Martin, Frank Sinatra, Robert Mitchum and a million other gods came to the street to be suited and booted. There were beautiful Brits standing in front of long Savile Row mirrors as well, tapes around their bodies and legs: Noel Coward, John Gielgud, Paul McCartney, Terence Stamp, Tommy Steele, Michael Caine, Michael Parkinson, Jackie Stewart. There was also Terence Young. He directed the first James Bond film and took the film's young star, Sean Connery, to Anthony Sinclair, his tailor. Young had in mind Brummell's philosophy. He wanted Bond well dressed but to move unnoticed through the crowd. Sinclair came up trumps, single-handedly creating the Conduit Cut. Bond took to the screen, suave as you like, in a lightweight suit, the jacket slimline and single-breasted with two buttons.

Then came Tommy Nutter, 'the Savile Row Rogue', who in the late '60s turned the street upside down. Nutter's name in the tapestry of Savile Row's history is crucial. He was a Londoner, born in 1943, and was attracted to design, the shape of things, from the off. He studied plumbing at Willesden Tech but soon switched to architecture. He got bored of this discipline quickly and so answered an advert for a salesman's position with the Savile Row tailors G. Ward and Co., working for their Burlington Arcade outlet. Sometime in the mid- to late '60s, he fell in with Peter Brown. Brown worked for the biggest and best band in the world – The Beatles. They had just formed a company called Apple and had taken offices at 3 Savile Row.

With Brown's backing and with money thrown in by John Lennon and Yoko Ono (her surname being whispered every time she stepped up to a microphone), Nutter opened up at 19 Savile Row.

There was a discreet gasp when the established tailors heard the news today, oh boy. Nutter was not a tailor as such – he hadn't spent years and years apprenticing – Nutter was a fashion designer. He cut your suit to his own design. He didn't just offer the classic Savile Row suit, he offered the trendy rich a way to get with it. His first client was John Lennon, who bought six of his numbers straight away. Others followed. Later, the cover of their famous *Abbey Road* album depicts three Beatles in Nutter suits. His young apprentices included John Galliano, Ozwald Boateng and Timothy Everest. Not a bad line-up. Nutter left the company in 1976 and joined Kilgour, French & Stanbury. Later on, he launched a ready-to-wear collection under the Austin Reed label. Nutter was the first man to break with Savile Row tradition, an action that took great character and style. Recently, *GQ* placed Tommy Nutter at number 11 in their '50 best-dressed British men of all time' poll.

Mark Powell, the Soho tailor of today, cites Nutter as a huge influence on his career and believes he is responsible for opening Savile Row up to life and colour. 'The climax of it all, the Nutter suit I always think of,' Powell told me, 'is the brown one Elton John was wearing round about the time of "Don't Go Breaking my Heart", which I think was 1974. If you look at that suit [brown with huge checks, flared trousers], that is the classic Tommy Nutter suit.' Nutter's name and reputation established, the Savile Row Rogue died of Aids in 1992, aged 49.

The Row's modern-day representative, Carlo Brandelli of Kilgour, French & Stanbury, is a man who feels it is important to preserve the long-held traditions of the street. Carlo is young, Italian, an Inter Milan man, but he is also an expert at keeping his cards very close to his chest. Carlo (his clients might like to know) is very discreet, very Savile Row.

For 200 years, the street has kept to its own traditions, its own way of doing things. It haughtily ignored developments outside of its environs, especially '60s Carnaby Street, which was invaded single-handedly by a man of Scottish persuasion and made famous the world over.

Carnaby Street owes John Stephen. Without him, it would have remained anonymous. Stephen came to London as a young man with a taste for clothes. He found himself a job with Moss Bros but soon got disillusioned with the hours, the pay, the boring staff around him. Salvation came with the opening of London's first male boutique, called Vince, on Newburgh Street.

Vince was established by the photographer Bill Green. He started off concentrating in specialised stage portraiture. After the Second World War, he began to capture muscle men and wrestlers on film, and changed his name to Vince. Many of his shots were of naked men, something to be deemed perilous in an economically and spiritually depressed British society. To help himself, Green designed a range of skimpy briefs to satisfy the moral police. In 1950, he advertised these shorts in the *Daily Mirror*. The ad ran on the Saturday; by Monday he had orders totalling £200. Green immediately started a mail-order business and put the photography aside.

Whilst on holiday in France, a further development: Green, with his photographer's eye, is fascinated by the black clothing of the emerging existentialist young around him. On his return, Green starts to import French clothing into the country, which, with his briefs, creates a catalogue that proves highly successful. This in turn allows him the financial muscle to open a shop in Newburgh Street, which instantly draws a very theatrical clientele. 'The only shop where they measure your inside leg each time you buy a tie,' the jazz singer and writer George Melly once said.

A male model the shop often uses for publicity purposes is named Sean Connery. Stephen is delighted by Green's success. He engineers a move from Moss Bros to Vince and works there, albeit not particularly successfully, until he has saved up £300. Stephen resigns and takes over premises in Beak Street, which he turns into a shop named His Clothes. It is just down the road from Vince. There, he sells and designs clothes; his business partner, a Mr Bill Franks. As the shop gathers custom, Stephen starts dreaming of owning Carnaby Street, just around the corner from him.

Centuries before, Carnaby Street was made up of grass, used for hunting purposes, the riders shouting, 'Soho!' as they galloped off, hence the name applied to the heart of London. Over hundreds and hundreds of years, Carnaby Street developed and gradually took shape.

The Carnaby Street Stephen knows is a gloomy passageway, its shops made up mainly of tailors specialising in alterations. Located between them are a tobacconist, an ironmonger, a couple of cafés and a huge building which contains several London Electricity Board generators. This building dominates the street, casting a gloomy light over all its neighbours. It would be Stephen's triumph to dispel this dark, to bring life and colour to Carnaby Street, and turn it into the most fashionable street in London.

Stephen triumphed through his unique energy and vision. He rented his first premises on Carnaby Street for a massive £7 a week, and placed bright colours and lights and clothes in the front window. Soon, word of mouth swept the capital and the shop's success allowed Stephen to rent more premises. Before long, Carnaby Street was full of his shops, which he bestowed with names such as Lord John and Male West One.

Stephen designed for the teenage young, and the teenage young alone. They were a new invention from America. When the films of Marlon Brando and James Dean, and the records of Elvis Presley hit Britain, the English youth follow their example. They, too, want to build their own culture, away from their stuffy, 'square' parents. And Stephen was the man to dress them for such a purpose, giving them bright colours and striking designs to separate them from the grey mass of British society.

All around, change is in the air. In America, Cassius Clay and John F. Kennedy; in Britain, the contraceptive pill and The Beatles. The young will inherit the earth and Stephen knows it all too well. He employs the young to staff his shops, has them play pop music all day long. You only get silence and attitude in stuffy department stores.

By 1966, Stephen owns the majority of shops on Carnaby Street. His neighbours know him well. Ben Sherman has an office opposite one of Stephen's shops and if you are lucky enough, you can often catch the Small Faces disappearing into manager Don Arden's office at number 52–55. At the La Caretta restaurant, the first topless waitresses are introduced into London by a Sicilian (who else?). His name is Paul Inga. He started La Caretta in 1966 and that December employed three waitresses to serve there. A national scandal followed: MPs expressed outrage in the House, the news was reported all over the world. The restaurant survived and prospered until a fire brought it to its knees in 1969.

If fire destroyed La Caretta, it is success that does for Carnaby Street. The young are fickle, the young are restless. They are also highly disdainful of the world outside. With Carnaby Street's name known across the world, the young look for change.

The Mod Casual look championed by Stephen is replaced by the dandy, psychedelia-inspired designs of craftsmen such as John Pearse at the shop Granny Takes A Trip, which is located on the Kings Road. LSD, not speed, is the drug of choice and its effects are starting to show up everywhere − in music, in films, in the consciousness of the clothes designer. The wheel turns, the focus shifts to west London. Meanwhile, Savile Row just keeps tending to its own, forever buried in a past which pays for its present.

■ ■ ■
Designer Gear

Stoned Island

At first, the message from Stone Island seemed absolutely surreal. No, the company would not talk to us because they did not want to be associated in any way with football. Company policy. Thank you, and goodnight.

Incredible, but true. I don't think the word flabbergasted sums up how Mark and I felt. This was a company whose famous insignia can be seen at every football match in the land, a motif that is absolutely synonymous with terrace culture. Stone Island clothing fills row after row in stadiums across the land. At every game I have attended in this country these past few years, be that in London or Cardiff or Manchester, or even Woking, their jackets are everywhere. I once quipped to Mark that such was their popularity they should change their name to Clone Island!

As ever, an Italian was to blame. The Bologna-born Massimo Osti created both the CP Company and Stone Island. His utility jacket in particular found instant favour with the young football crowd, eliciting from Osti the humorous aside, 'Even though they're hooligans, evidently they are able to make some good choices.'

They certainly did. In the early '90s, Stone Island took off in a massive way. Their famous insignia invaded first the streets, then football grounds everywhere. The clothes flew out, the money poured in. Yet the company wanted nothing to do with the game or its culture? This we discovered when Mark phoned Stone Island to see if anyone would talk to us.

Mark was put through to a Gino Da Prato and explained what we were doing. It was a book about the link between fashion and football, the history of the relationship that took in both the players and fans. He added that, as a Millwall season-ticket holder and football aficionado himself, he knew how big the label was, saw it every other Saturday in fact down the New Den. He also mentioned the Stone Island pirate badges he had recently seen on eBay. These replicated the Stone Island logo but left a space so you could insert your own club's name.

Gino testily replied that the company knew about these badges and they were dealing with them right now. He was also acting very cagily with Mark and we found out why later. The week before, *Front* magazine had run a lengthy piece on football violence which clearly linked hooligans to the label. This was not the kind of publicity the company were seeking. Questions had been asked at the highest level. People had been taken into offices and answers demanded. This explained Gino's wariness. The man had a job to protect.

He told Mark he would get back to him about an interview. Which he did, informing us that he could not speak publicly but instead we should email the company's PR department and explain what we were doing. Maybe they could supply someone we could talk to. Mark asked me to write the email but I was too busy at the time. 'You do it,' I said blithely. 'You'll be fine.' Mark sent the standard email – it's a football and fashion book . . . majority of fans who wear their stuff do not commit any kind of violence . . . violent disturbances at games are a thing of the past thanks to the Premiership, bada bing, bada bing . . .

A day later, the PR people replied.

> Dear Mark,
> Can you let us know some more about the book, if it is purely fashion-based and who are the other confirmed fashion participants and celebrities involved? Will there be any reference to football violence being related to any particular brands?
> Thank you,
> Sophie

Mark called me up. 'Look, I think you should write to them, bruv. I've got a horrible feeling I've scared them off.'

'Scared them off? How do you mean?' I replied.

'Look at that last sentence in the email. I've told them a million times the book has got nothing to do with football violence and still they're on about it.'

'They're just being careful,' I replied.

Mark shook his head. He had his doubts, his suspicions. 'Nah, when I spoke to that Gino, I let go I was a Millwall supporter. They ain't going to like that. Also, there's my accent — people run a mile when they hear it. Millwall season-ticket holder, voice like mine, they probably think I'm some kind of psycho.'

'A psycho in pinstripe,' I replied, admiring his three-quarter-length jacket with black velvet collar. 'You're just being paranoid. They'll talk to us.'

'God knows what they think,' Mark said. 'It's your fault.'

'My fault?'

'Yeah, if you hadn't been so busy writing that other stuff, you could have handled this. This is all new territory for me, talking to these kind of people. Does my nut in sometimes.' Despite the Blair-speak, the hopeful view that somehow we live in a classless society, Mark knew different. All his life, he'd been judged on his accent, just as I had during my time in the music press.

'OK, OK, calm down. I'll write to them,' I said, reassuring him.

And I did, that very night. I gave them the idea — clothes and football, nothing else, I swear. Absolutely no violence. Plus, I added, all their competitors had agreed to talk to us. Surely such a great company as Stone Island wouldn't want to be left out in the cold?

The next morning I got my answer.

Dear Paolo,
Thank you for your email. The main concern we have, other than Mark originally saying that there would be some reference to football violence in context, is that the other brands that are so far confirmed: Ben Sherman, Fred Perry, Lacoste, Ted Baker and Duffer of St George, are not on the same level or price-point as Stone Island, therefore we would have to decline I'm afraid.

  Yours sincerely,
  Sophie

I was furious. I rushed to my computer, spent ten minutes composing a letter full of vitriol and anger. Halfway through, I suddenly stopped, thought, no, steady on — look at the damage you've caused yourself in the past, wading in with all guns blazing. Stone Island are crucial to the project. Start again. I deleted the email, began again. Look, I know you have problems with football, I wrote, understandable, but not everyone who goes to a game is a hooligan, quite the contrary, in fact. Since the advent of the Premiership, violence has decreased considerably. Plus, we're not bothered with that side of it. We're into clothes, the history of. We're into football, the beauty of. We just want to put the two together in a book. Please reconsider.

Next day, the final reply.

> With regards to Stone Island's involvement with your fashion and football book, and as explained when you initially contacted us, the brand owners of Stone Island (our clients) have instructed us to decline any involvement in projects associated with football. It sounds like an interesting book but unfortunately and, as explained by Gino Da Prato, we are unable to get involved.
> Sophie

'They're not having it,' I told Mark over the phone. 'Unbelievable.'

Mark took this defeat personally. In terms of the book, he had appointed himself midfield general, determined to direct the play without a hitch. I was the striker upfront, being fed people he thought were of interest. Stone Island's refusal to play meant he had just lost the midfield and gone a goal down. He didn't like that feeling.

'Fuck 'em,' he said. 'Let's get onto the other ones.'

We decided to approach as many of the main players in British fashion as we could. We reasoned that even if they had nothing to say about football, their testimony about clothes would be just as important and would help us build up a history of British fashion, stretching from the '60s to the present.

Mark went to this task in a fervour. He drew up a long list of clothes people and started contacting them, requesting their time. Every three days or so, Mark would ring and tell me he had arranged another interview. Again, we would meet at his 'office', drink a latte or an orange juice, marvel at how their prices had gone up yet again, talk about football, music, clothes, the book, football, relationships, clothes and football. Then we would move off, questions and tape recorder in hand. First, we went to see Geoff Garet, who works for John Simon in Covent Garden.

Top of the Ivy League

In British street fashion, John Simon is a legend. As a young kid in the East End, Simon became obsessed with the Ivy League look and as a young man dedicated himself to promoting the style in Britain. It became a lifetime's work. He started his career as a window-dresser, working for all the key names – Cecil Gee, Austin's – before striking out on his own and starting his first enterprise, Clothesville, with his partner, Jeff Kwintner. Clothesville's success allowed the pair to take over premises in Richmond and open the Ivy Shop.

Simon and Kwintner's aim was to attract British executives and dress them in the same manner as their American counterparts. Instead, their shop was overrun by young, working-class Mods who adored the smart American clothing, the crème de la crème as far as quality and style were concerned. The Ivy stayed in business for years and, such was its success, allowed the two men to move into the centre of London and open up another venture, the Squire Shop in London's Brewer Street. Soon after, Kwintner and Simon argued (Simon refuses to say why) and they split up. Simon stayed at the Ivy Shop, Kwintner moved on, opening up a succession of well-regarded shops with names such as The Village Gate or Thackeray. Meanwhile, the Ivy Shop lasted until the early '80s and then Simon moved his operation to Covent Garden, where he works today.

Whilst we were talking to him about this book one day, Simon mentioned that one of his assistants, Geoff, was not only a dedicated clothes man but a major football-head. He arranged for us to meet at the shop. Geoff wore a green roll-neck jumper, chino trousers,

The Fashion of Football

brown loafers. I complimented him on his look. During the interview, he told me that, years ago, the tailor Sam Arkus in Berwick Street had made him a wonderful mohair suit. It cost 33 guineas, a small fortune at the time. In fact, so beautiful was this suit, Geoff could never bring himself to wear it out. It was that beautiful. 'I gave it away in the end,' he confessed.

His team were Spurs, first saw them in 1953, a time when sons dressed as their fathers, a time when youth was still bereft of individuality. Geoff remembered the Spurs team wearing gabardine macs, Harris tweed jackets, waistcoats and, of course, shirts and ties. 'You never went out without a tie at that time,' Geoff said. 'Even if you went to the discotheque, you always had a tie.'

In 1958, Geoff saw his first button-down shirt in Austin's, which was situated where the Trocadero is today on Shaftesbury Avenue. He hasn't worn any other kind of shirt since. His favourite Spurs man was Danny Blanchflower, although he also admired the way Jimmy Greaves looked as a 17 year old. 'A slip of a man but with a short crew cut,' he enthused. 'Did you know Jimmy once owned a clothes shop?'

We didn't.

'It was in the late '70s. I used to be in wholesale then and he used to come in and buy from us. It was all smart-casual stuff. I rang him once, told him we had some stuff in.' Geoff said. Jimmy bought the lot, worth £500. 'He signed a cheque [and] I said, Jim this is really ironic. I stood outside White Hart Lane asking for your autograph for ten years and you used to tell me to fuck off, and now you sign a cheque over to me for £500.'

Despite Geoff's fervent support for Spurs, he could not in all conscience nominate them as *the* London fashion team. That accolade went to the West Ham of Moore, Redknapp, Peters, Hurst. 'Tottenham looked like an old-boys team compared to them,' Geoff mused. 'The West Ham team, players like Hurst and Peters, all had short college-boy haircuts.' The only Spurs players with a similar style being Cliff Jones and Johnny Brooks. Geoff also remembered Eddie Coleman, a Busby Babe who dressed like Elvis Presley and was mercilessly ribbed by his teammates for doing so.

He regretted the status of footballers today, their remoteness from the fans. In his time, players were far more accessible. More often than not on away games, the team would travel back on the same train as the fans and mix with them. (Although, given the season Spurs were having, it was probably best they travelled separately. Most of them would be slaughtered by the time they got home.)

How did he view today's footballers? Had they any style? He screwed his face up in displeasure. 'The players of today dress expensively, but with no style at all,' he commented. He recalled the late '70s, the time of Kevin Keegan, and again he expressed his displeasure. 'They looked horrible with their long sideboards and flared trousers, kipper ties.'

He looked at his watch. The shop was opening, time to start work.

Eddie, Steady, Go

Onwards. Next on the list was Mr Eddie, a tailor who had been operating out of Berwick Street since the '50s. We met him at his shop. A nice man, he told us that he had made some suits for footballers but couldn't remember their names. He recalled how in the early '60s everyone at 16 years of age either bought a suit from Burton's or had it tailor-made, cost round about £20. 'Even if you went to the pub on a Sunday morning, you wore a suit and a tie,' he stated. 'You never dreamed of going out not dressed in your suit and tie.'

He vaguely gestured to the street outside. London, at this point, he stated, was home to hundreds of tailors. 'I mean this street, Berwick Street, had five tailoring shops. There were probably three in Old Compton Street, two in Wardour Street. It was a huge business in those days.'

The birth of the teenager and the rise of Carnaby Street, propelled by designers such as John Stephen, helped to slowly smother the trade. The arrival of designer labels such as Armani in the '80s dealt it further critical blows. Today, there are just three tailors on Berwick Street.

After Mr Eddie, Mark and I went for a drink. Mr Eddie's talk of 'Sunday best' suits and Sunday lunch pubs had sent Mark's mind spinning backwards to his youth and he wanted to share the images in his mind. Some of his fondest memories, he explained, settling down with his customary vodka and Diet Coke, brown cigar in hand, were bound up with this ritual – Mark and his father dressing up to the nines on Sunday morning and then strolling down to the local pub; Mark hanging out with his mates as their fathers relaxed

The Fashion of Football

nearby and took sweet alcohol, discussing the previous day's game at Millwall, other results, then their work, their play and what had been happening in the neighbourhood. Then it was home for Sunday roast and snoozing in front of the fire before heading back to the pub at seven. Happy days.

'What I remember the most, apart from the stories you would hear, was how well my dad and his friends were all turned out,' Mark recalled. 'They'd all had a suit made at 15 or 16 and most of them at that age were doing manual labour. Most of them worked in a factory but they all wanted to get on the dust or the print. Those were jobs for life back then. But they'd get the money for their suit somehow.'

Mark often spoke about his father in such a fond manner. He had died four years earlier and sometimes it seemed that for Mark and his family it was only yesterday. I did not know my father – still don't to this day – so when Mark spoke of his and I glimpsed the deep sorrow he felt at his passing, I could never quite work out whether I felt glad that I would never know such tragedy or sad that I would never know what it is to be fathered.

Change of subject. 'Where did your people go to have their suits made?' I asked Mark.

'They had them made locally,' he replied. 'At places like Levy's at the Elephant and Castle, Ben Bebers on the Old Kent Road or Albie Harris in The Cut.'

'Where did they get the material?'

'Nicked, wasn't it? Someone would stroll in a pub with a roll of material under their arm and sell it to whoever fancied it. A couple of them would go halves on the cost and hope the cloth would stretch to two suits. Off to the tailors on Saturday and, as long as he didn't say that's my bleeding roll of cloth, you'd be away.'

We laughed, moved on.

Gentleman Georgie

One Saturday morning, Mark went to talk to his tailor, George Dyer, about the history of his craft at his Threadneedleman shop on Walworth Road. 'He's never dressed a footballer as such but he might have some nuggets,' Mark explained over the phone.

The next day, Mark rang again, told me that George's story was worth noting if only for one detail.

At school, the budding tailor had gone through the usual route from Mod to Skin to Suedehead before settling on the Soulboy style. In 1972, he entered the cloth trade. George first worked on Berwick Street then went to Brixton, where he recalls a lot of youths with Caribbean roots ordering the Rude Boy look – that was a suit made out of Tonik material, a three-button jacket, the trousers short enough to show off the socks and a pork-pie hat perched on top.

'Interestingly,' George had noted, 'the Brixton boys would have side vents on their jackets but the Peckham boys would have a centre vent. So, when they went out to a blues or a party they would be able to identify each other. A small but very important detail. Lots of rivalry and very creative tailoring!'

The Jolly Boy Mod

We moved on, went to see Fred Harris, an ex-Mod who owns a shoe shop named Men's Traditional Shoes on Camberwell Road. Fred was a member of the original Jolly Boys, a title the writer John Sullivan had used in his brilliant *Only Fools and Horses* TV show.

Fred spoke of his Mod days, of suits and scooters, of clubs and RnB, of a life lived in detail. He still kept the faith. On the day we met, he was wearing a smart grey top, black trousers, brogue shoes, and his shop was filled with boxes that had legendary labels such as Loakes and Bass Weejun printed on them. This is the strength of the culture. Forty years after turning Mod, he was still wearing the clothes, still trying to persuade others through the shoes he sold.

The Tailor Takes a Trip

We moved on – to John Pearse's stylish shop in Meard Street, Soho. Mark thought Pearse would be good to talk to. He was what happened after Mod faded, when fashion went colourful. Amongst his many achievements was his role at Granny Takes A Trip on the Kings Road. It symbolised the shift in popularity from Mod to psychedelia in the mid-'60s, from Carnaby Street to the Kings Road.

John had grown up in working-class Paddington, attended one of Britain's first comprehensive schools. His mother was a milliner, hence the interest in clothes. At 15, he left school wanting nothing more from life than a mohair suit, and figured the best place to get such an item was Savile Row. Pearse brazenly walked into Henry

Poole's premises and asked for a job. He was told to sit and wait. Five minutes later, the actor David Niven walked in. This is the life for me, Pearse thought.

Poole had no vacancies but an assistant told him to approach Hall & Curtis around the corner in Dover Street. They took him on and Pearse worked there as an apprentice for two and a half years, studied well and also watched luminaries such as the Duke of Edinburgh, Frank Sinatra, Donald Sinden and Peter O'Toole pass through the door.

At 18, such spectacles were no longer of interest. Pearse took a sudden U-turn and decided to follow his growing beatnik impulses. He quit work, found employment on a building site, saved up for a month and then travelled to St Tropez with friends. It was the '60s. You did that kind of thing then.

On his return to London, Pearse met an artist called Nigel Weymouth. Weymouth and his girlfriend had been buying up old frock coats with a mind to redesigning and selling them. Pearse showed them the proper way of customising clothes and, two weeks later, was asked by the couple to become a partner in their venture, a shop to be called Granny Takes A Trip.

Pearse worked there for three years, designing clothes that were distinguished by their great tailoring and exquisite art nouveau-influenced patterns. His timing was good, his dandy and colourful creations arriving just at the moment the drug LSD hit London. The priests of the new hip – The Beatles, The Stones, Hendrix and a thousand other London names – tripped through the door at Granny at some point or other. As did hip Americans Andy Warhol and Dennis Hopper.

Then John woke up one day to find himself burnt out. 'So I went to Italy,' he says. 'Started acting with Federico and Marcello.'

'You mean Federico Fellini and Marcello Mastroianni?' I blurted out. These were two very big names in my book.

'Yes.'

'*Maron*! You just went off to Italy and hooked up with two of the biggest names in Italian cinema?' I said.

'Sure,' Pearse said with a thin smile. 'Why not?'

I thought about his answer for a moment, then thought, 'Why not, indeed?'

After Italia, Pearse returned to Britain. At the time, he wasn't really thinking about clothes or tailoring, he says, but then he went to a Led Zeppelin concert, saw a 'sea of disgusting denim' and decided to take up the scissors again. That decision led him to where we were that day, in Meard Street, Soho.

After the interview, Mark and I went for our customary quick drink. Some nights, we were good, managed to keep it at just two drinks, other nights, not so good. 'One more for the road' was now my catchphrase.

'It's a very long road where you're concerned, isn't it, son?' was Mark's.

This night had a two-glass limit. Mark had plans that I would not be allowed to disrupt on any account. 'Going out with the missus for a meal tonight. Can't let her down,' Mark stated as he handed me a pint.

'Amazing man,' I said of Pearse.

'Told you,' Mark replied.

'The only thing is he didn't mention football once. He never dressed a player, never went to games, I don't know how we are going to fit him into the book.'

'Yeah, bit of a choker that,' Mark replied, dipping his slender cigar into his drink. 'Still, bit of a brain, ain't you? I'm sure you'll find a way around that.'

The Suaveheads

Onwards to Eddie Prendergast, one of the founding members of Duffer of St George. Duffer have been dressing the trendy young since the early '80s and are a pivotal shop in the history of contemporary British menswear, always receptive to the nuances on the street outside. Their success had been built on anticipation, not reaction. They saw what was coming and then moved quickly, got in first.

The shop started in Camden in 1984. There were four of them: Eddie, Cliff, Marco and Barrie. The boys sold second-hand gear but only of a certain kind. It had to be the right kind of blazer, the right kind of shoe. 'It was through the stuff we eliminated that we got our style,' Eddie reveals.

The Camden branch did well enough to fund premises on London's famous Portobello Road. Then they moved into Soho.

Finance was partly supplied by Barrie K. Sharpe's ground-breaking rare-groove club Cat in the Hat, another example of their street smarts, although Barrie would leave in 1994, Cliff having jumped ship four years earlier.

'We kept Duffer pure,' Eddie states of this time. 'We didn't try to exploit it. And then a German partner joined us and we moved into properly doing collections. So, up until then, we were self-financed. We still had the street-market head with the street-market money.'

Duffer proved themselves swift in the penalty box. They'd bring in a line, sell out quickly and, before other shops could follow suit, Duffer would be on to the next thing. They soon got noticed, style mags and the fashion press running large articles eulogising the shop's ability to clue into the mood on the street.

Duffer sold Mod, acid jazz, acid house, hip hop and then in 1990 they put on sale the famous Burro top proclaiming 'Non Alla Violenza'. It was Italia '90 time. Again, the boys had seen what was coming. 'As soon as Duffer became well known, the footballer bought into us,' Eddie recalls. 'If you're celebsville, people buy into it.'

He named a few players who have since passed through their doors: Ryan Giggs, Patrick Viera, Paul Ince, Andy Cole, Chris Powell, 'a whole list upon list,' Eddie says.

Duffer then moved from their famous D'Arblay Street premises to Covent Garden, before taking on the big one – Savile Row. Eddie says he took no notice of the snobbery around him, just got on with doing business. But Duffer in Savile Row? It didn't feel quite right, a bit like imagining Roy Keane at a sedate dinner party.

The shop shut down in 2002. Eddie said the lease was up, so they moved. I suspect it may have been for other reasons. No matter. Eddie and Marco now operate out of a large Shoreditch building, head of a global brand that is the London dream realised: from market stall to marketing giants.

Eddie thinks that the footballer of today has come full circle from his initial rise to prominence in the late '60s. 'At that time, they started hanging out with models, driving E-types, living large on the Kings Road,' he points out. 'Well, that's what they do now. It's just that, in between, they've forgotten how to dress and left the clothes bit out. Now designers want to dress them because they're the new style icons.'

It was a phrase we kept hearing, the footballer as style icon. Personally, I didn't agree – the majority of footballers were designer fashionable, not stylish, not creative in their look.

The Dundee Pistol

Onwards to see designer Kenneth Mackenzie in his Shoreditch office where he runs his 6876 company, named after the date 'Anarchy in the UK' by the Sex Pistols was released. Mackenzie had worked for Duffer of St George but in the early '90s left to go solo. His clothes have yet to dominate mainstream British fashion but his designs reach a trendy, cultish audience and are revered within it. Furthermore, Mackenzie was once a handy footballer for the Shamrock Boys, a club in his home town of Dundee.

The first thing Mackenzie told us when we met him was that he didn't really have much to say on the matter. Then he spoke for about an hour and a half. The book made total sense to him.

He revealed that football was now infiltrating the fashion world at the highest levels. The other day, his wife, who is a stylist, was sat at an Armani show when suddenly she felt that intangible rush of excitement that occurs when a major celebrity walks into a room. At first, she thought it was Beyoncé or Madonna or Di Caprio. She swivelled round and saw instead a man she was told was the Real Madrid centre-forward Ronaldo. Didn't know who the fuck he was but if proof that the footballer was now the new rock star was needed . . .

Had Kenneth worked with any footballers himself?

'I've had stuff borrowed for shoots and things like that but not really. I mean it's interesting with Freddie Ljungberg doing the Calvin Klein shoot and all that kind of stuff, but I also think there's a bit of a backlash coming. Like this rape thing that is going on. [A 17-year-old girl had recently alleged that a number of Premiership footballers, the majority Newcastle players, had gang-raped her in a hotel.] I think it's a total crisis. You've got Bobby Robson [Newcastle manager, sacked by the club in August 2004] in charge of a bunch of total reprobates and he's an old man who's out of touch with that side of it.'

Mark brought up the Stone Island story, both of us expressing our amazement at their attitude. Kenneth wasn't that surprised. He said,

'Up in Scotland, the St Johnstone fans were singing about Armani and he was completely mortified. Absolutely mortified. My mate Taft and my dad go, they told me about it. The fans there are really into the Casual, golfy kind of tip. They like Pringle, Aquascutum, Burberry, stuff like that. For them, Armani is totally superb, so they all started singing, "Armani, Armani, Armani," and he found out about it and he was saying, this is disgusting, I don't want it.'

Designer labels had recently become a major talking point in Scotland. Doormen working the bars of Aberdeen had started refusing entry to anyone wearing Burberry. David Cook, a security boss, had stated, 'Obviously not everyone who wears the label can be called a troublemaker but we have to be careful.' Very careful, it seems. The ban had come to light when a married woman carrying a Burberry handbag and umbrella was stopped entering Aberdeen's Filling Station bar. 'I was wearing my best clothes,' she later told the press. 'I look nothing like a soccer Casual.' Her handbag might have backed up her claim that night, given that most soccer Casuals don't carry them these days.

A few months after, it was reported that Burberry's profits had risen again for 2004, yet not one mention was made in any of the reports of the company's massive popularity with football fans. Then in August that same year, it was announced that police and publicans were compiling a list of upmarket manufacturers, including Burberry, Stone Island, Aquascutum and Henri Lloyd, with a view to banning anyone wearing those labels from city centres. It was a joint attempt to try to stem the rise of alcohol-fuelled violence. Whether this ban also extended to the Prime Minister Tony Blair, who was photographed on holiday wearing a Burberry polo shirt, was not made clear. Still, the reasons behind the reticence of Stone Island and their ilk to publicly link themselves with football were becoming vividly clearer to us.

I Can't Believe It's Not Burro

Onwards to Covent Garden on a winter Tuesday morning to talk to the Burro boys, Tim and Olaf. They were the last people we spoke to about designer gear but had been the first on our list after Charlton Athletic (the team the two boys had supported since they were kids of four and five) had appointed them to design their new range of club merchandise. Not surprisingly, the brothers were thrilled to bits at the commission. It was their dream assignment and they had handled it well. Their first range of shirts were already a huge hit, in particular the print of Charlton legend Derek Hales which they had designed to echo the famous '70s picture of the Cuban revolutionary Che Guevara. We met the brothers at their Covent Garden premises, went for coffee and panini. This is what they had to say.

Paolo Hewitt: Were you brought up around Charlton?

Tim Burro: Yeah, that's where our family comes from, up there. South-east London basically.

PH: And when did you start going to football matches?

TB: Our dad took us when we were four or five. He was saying the other day, 'Do you know why I used to take you when you were four?' It was more to get us out of the way of our mum. It would have been 1962.

PH: And Charlton were in the what, First, Second Division?

Olaf Burro: First Division.

PH: When did you first become aware of, say, fashion or style, either for yourselves and for what you do or on the terraces?

OB: It was mostly old men in flat hats, though, really, wasn't it? Later on, we got into punk, leather jackets, drainpipe trousers.

Mark Baxter: What sort of crowds were you getting in them days?

TB: About 4,000 to 5,000, something like that.

MB: I'm a Millwall season-ticket holder. I know exactly what you're saying.

PH: So, after the punk, what did you get into then?

OB: I think we went through sort of all the natural things then. It was like the sort of New Romanticy thing to some extent, the zoot suits. I can remember when we were sharing with Palace, which would have been mid-'80s to the end of the '80s. I would have been at college, and I can remember walking in and there was someone documenting the style of football fans and I thought, 'What do you want to take a picture of me for?' Afterwards, I realised that it was because I looked like a freak. I was wearing a tweed jacket, sort of skinny jeans, brogues, my school scarf, which was like a black-and-white-striped scarf, and, you know, those Duffer hats that were like the Italian flag?

It just must have looked so out of step. Then I thought, 'Oh, yeah. I get it.'

MB: You were a bit of an unusual looking fella?

OB: You didn't think about it. That's what you wore.

PH: So, wearing a tweed jacket suggests to me a kind of Casual thing.

OB: No, not at all. There was the deerstalkery thing and all that stuff but it wasn't my thing.

MB: Did you get any grief for what you wore at the football?

OB: There were a couple of times I remember going to away matches and someone giving me a bit of stick, you know. We've just always been interested in fashion and had our own style. In fact, we had a sample sale once in the shop when we were in Floral Street and a whole load of blokes came in and said, 'This the shop run by the two weird twins that go down Charlton, innit?' And so I think we did stand out a little bit. Especially when the crowd was smaller, you know. We looked a bit different, you know.

PH: How did you get into the fashion game? How did that come about?

TB: We were both always interested in fashion and my brother went into clothing and textiles, and I was in advertising. And, in 1986, you [Olaf] did some T-shirts, didn't you? Some T-shirt designs.

OB: I was still at college, so it was a way of making a couple of quid, you know, print some T-shirts up.

PH: And they . . .

TB: . . . went down really well.

OB: Yeah, they sold well, you know, we made some stuff.

PH: And what kind of T-shirts were they?

TB: So, it was like, it was the Jules Rimet trophy done in a sort of freehandy sort of style printed in gold. So that's just very, very simple.

PH: For the '86 World Cup?

OB: For the '86 World Cup.

TB: And in 1990, I said . . .

OB: Well, a lot of his mates thought because he was in a proper job he had some money. So I said, 'Let's do it again,' you know. 'Let's come up with some ideas for T-shirts and try . . . Let's see what we can do.'

TB: Duffer was the first that we went to. They loved them . . .

PH: These were the 'Non Alla Violenza' tops?

OB: It went absolutely crazy and what was interesting was that this was the first time that there was any sort of football fashion link-up to that sort of higher independent designery kind of area.

TB: Through them, we got into all the independents, which was brilliant. Because people like Woodies [main shop for Cardiff and Wales Casuals] and those kind of people all across the country made a few quid. So, when the World Cup ended, we just thought, 'Well, shall we? This is really easy, the fashion business.'

OB: Exactly, yeah. 'We're gonna be rich in no time.'

TB: It was literally, 'If we get all the money in that we're owed, we've got this pot of three or four grand each and we can carry on with it.' We were thinking, 'We'll just do a bit more and see what happens.'

OB: You know, a few calculations on the back of an envelope with a pencil.

TB: Looked easy.

PH: Right. And how did you start then, where did you start?

OB: The World Cup ended in the summer and then we thought, let's do some knitwear.

TB: We had a little studio in Deptford.

PH: Had you given up your job?

TB: I gave up my job then to do this. Highly paid advertising job. What a bloody idiot!

PH: Think where you could be now.

TB: Yeah, exactly.

OB: So, when Tim joined sort of proper full time, that's when it became a bit more serious.

PH: How do you divide the work between you?

TB: He designs with his partner, Sue; I do the business side. Lately, we've been working with Charlton. I don't know if you know what we're doing . . .

MB: I saw a piece in *The Times*.

OB: Yeah, there was something.

TB: We haven't got any samples here but it's on, I'll show you the website. They've just put it up.

PH: Before we move on to that, what about the past? Any footballer you can think of that was stylish?

The Fashion of Football

OB: There's that great film with George Best, the early film when he opened his boutique and all that. He was quite amazing.

TB: I think the trouble is, it is very easy to look back and say that it was much more stylish because people wore suits and all that kind of thing. But it's not really until, what, the '70s, I suppose, that footballers had any sort of style beyond what they were told to wear almost, because things were so rigid, weren't they?

PH: Well, you had Bobby Moore.

OB: You did, you did.

PH: I mean, I keep on saying this, and Mark's probably bored of me saying it, but it always fascinates me that the British working-class youth are the leaders in this field, it's always them who are coming up with things like Skinheads or Casuals. Yet, if you take the footballers who are all from that class, most of them haven't got a clue.

OB: Well, that's what I was going to say. There is the footballer's style, whether it be that classic mullet thing in the '80s or the sort of Italiany Gucci style that they're really into. They always seem to be slightly, you know, slightly naff and they always get it slightly wrong.

TB: There are some styles, though – Paolo Di Canio. He came on to be introduced to the crowd and he was wearing the tightest suit you've ever seen and it was such a contrast to everyone else. And he was really, really trying.

MB: We spoke to Dennis Wise who was at Chelsea and, before Vialli turned up, they were pretty much wearing Next suits. Vialli walks in and it was like, 'Jesus Christ. What is he wearing?' And a week or two later they're all wearing it.

TB: That was when that Italiany style first came here.

MB: Yeah, after that it went really big. They have got something, you know. There's something different . . .

OB: Yeah, because if you go to Italy, the tiniest town has got really stylish people.

PH: Even the old men, 75, 80 years old . . .

TB: It is quite amazing. They are just far more interested in clothes.

TB: Who's that Italian club who play in pink? It's like a Prince of Wales check and its got a dog's-tooth check kind of thing? [Probably referring to Palermo] It's amazing. But you can't imagine Millwall having that. They should, though, it would be great. Especially all the fans wearing it.

MB: Yeah, all the fat blokes. [Laughing] Wish I could carry it off!

OB: The thing with that Italian style is that the rules are very, very, very rigid. It's like, they don't really get dressing down. Same in France. It's like the women dress fantastically because they follow these set rules. And blokes are the same, you know.

PH: Yeah, that is true.

MB: The stuff that you've done for Charlton. How has it gone down with the fans in the shop? Has it sold well?

TB: Amazing.

OB: When we went in there, the merchandising company didn't know what we were going to come up with at all. They didn't know who we were, what it was about or anything.

TB: So they didn't know what to expect, which is the great thing. And they just went, 'Wow!' you know. 'Great idea.'

MB: Millwall! Do Millwall, please. I'm fed up with the merchandise there.

PH: This is obviously something you want to pursue?

OB: I don't think we want to do it too much.

TB: We didn't even think about the money.

PH: This must be the first time a major football club has . . .

TB: Worked with somebody like us? I think so. I mean, you have had the things like Paul Smith doing the England team suits and stuff like that but, as far as I'm aware, for a club to be working with an independent . . .

OB: Well, I did a bit of research on some of the websites and I looked on the Chelsea website and they've got, I think they've got Pringle but . . .

MB: They have, yeah.

OB: But it's a bit different.

MB: It's almost like Casual stuff. They got a few ravers in there, ain't they? But I agree, when I read about your link with Charlton I had to read it twice because it's such a brave thing for a club to do.

OB: We're talking to someone else as well which kind of ties in with what you're doing but it's not official yet. Tacchini re-released a load of those '80s-style classics which sold brilliantly in the shop, so we got in touch with them. We had a meeting a

The Fashion of Football

few days ago and we're gonna hook up with Sergio Tacchini.

TB: They're flying Olaf out to Milan to go through all the archives.

OB: I can't wait. It's gonna be fantastic.

PH: Carry your bags, sir? I'll come with you.

OB: But the great thing is, we're sitting there having this meeting and we didn't know what the meeting was about. We just knew what we wanted to do. And it turned out that what we thought would be really good for us to do is exactly what they think they want us to do for them.

TB: And he said that, you know. 'We really want to do this but it's not gonna work unless you let us use your name on it,' you know. 'Every time Sergio is in town, he always comes, he loves your shop, he always comes into your shop.' And I'm going, 'Really? Christ.'

OB: But it was very difficult not to go 'Wow! Fantastic!' you know.

TB: We kept our cool, just about. But he is connected with the football thing.

PH: Do Tacchini understand they are connected to the football thing?

TB: Well, I think the UK people understand but the Italians, they think they're a tennis company.

MB: We spoke to Lacoste and it was like, 'We don't do football. We do tennis.' I was like, 'Yeah, I know that but . . .'

PH: Stone Island won't go anywhere near us.

TB: I know what you mean. We spoke to Fred Perry and someone there was saying, 'We don't want nothing whatsoever to do with football. We want to distance ourselves as far as we can.' And I was like, 'Really? Why?' And you know, we felt slightly nervous, didn't we, with the thing at Charlton and having our name on it. It was like, 'Would it be good or bad?'

OB: You first felt nervous, I never. I didn't feel nervous at all.

TB: I felt nervous about it.

PH: And why would you feel slightly nervous?

TB: I suppose because of that connection of, like, aggression.

OB: I think the other thing was the sort of partisan nature. It's like everyone's got their team and it's like, if you're associated with one team, then maybe you alienate other people? But the great thing about being a Charlton fan is that there's no one really who majorly dislikes Charlton.

MB: I was just about to say that.

TB: Even Millwall like us! I don't know what happened and how we did it but to be in the Premier League and not really have any sort of proper enemies, it's amazing.

OB: I think it's because we're not a threat in any way.

TB: I think we've got probably four or five seasons of doing well before people start to turn.

MB: No one's really got any problem with Charlton supporters, whereas I get slaughtered. Everywhere I go, I get slaughtered.

TB: I don't know what you can do about that really.

MB: I've been going since '69. I'm 41, so I've been going since I was a kid. Always gone. I mean, I've seen all the ups and downs. Seen terrible things on the terraces but I actually go for the football, just like you do. To me, that's dedication. To keep going and see the team really struggling.

PH: What's your parentage? Because Olaf is . . .

OB: No, it's a nickname.

TB: Our parents lived in south-east London.

OB: It's a nickname from roughly the time when we first started going to Charlton.

PH: Right. And how did you get it?

OB: Do you remember that TV programme, *Noggin the Nog*?

MB: Yeah, I do, yeah.

OB: Sort of funny cut-out kids. It's like, anyway, there's a character in it called Olaf and my name is Oliver. So Tim started calling me it.

TB: I used to torture him. He was about five and I was four, and it's stuck since then.

PH: It's not a bad name, though, is it?

OB: It's all right, but it does confuse people.

MB: Look on the bright side, it could have been Noggin, couldn't it?

OB: Exactly.

PH: Whatever your name, thanks. That was great. Do you want to get the bill then, Mark?

MB: Fuck off, Noggin.

PART THREE
■■■■■■■■■■■■

SECOND HALF

Terrace Ghosts –
The Fashion Fans

■ ■ ■
The Skinhead's Dressing-room, 1970

Shirt is by Ben Sherman, a company founded in 1962, operating at first out of Hove, near Brighton, Ben's home town. Ben himself, bit of a character. Born in 1925, he finds himself leaving home age 20 to travel to America; a big move in that age of non-travel. For many people, the world was far too big to imagine. Ben travels to the States, works his way to Los Angeles, chews up two wives along the way.

In Los Angeles, he meets Ruth Minken on a beach, feels that familiar fire stir. They marry, have three sons. Ben starts work for Ruth's father, Aaron, a clothes manufacturer, swimwear and shirts a speciality. Lancia is the name of the shirt company. They specialise in classic Ivy League-style shirts (a quick recap – that is button-down collar numbers in conservative colours and styles). Ben's fascinated by the style but in his mind's eye can see how to improve the product, take it much further. Lancia are having none of Ben's ideas. They say to him, 'We do what we do, and nothing more.' To Ben, that kind of thinking is so non-fabulous.

A restlessness sets in. Then his mother falls ill. Perfect opportunity. Ben moves the family back to Brighton, buys a factory and starts making button-down shirts but in his own style. He uses colours not associated with men – the pinks and the pale blues, for example. He uses only Oxford cloth material from America. It gives the shirt a classy look and mums adore it because, after washing one of Ben's shirts, ironing is not necessary. He makes the collars big. There is a top left-hand pocket and, at the back of the collar, he puts a button that serves no purpose whatsoever. A large pleat running down the back of the shirt is accompanied on its journey by two lines of stitching.

By 1971, Ben Sherman is receiving 40,000 orders a week. They can only make 35,000. In step his competitors Brutus and Jaytex to mop up the crumbs and make their money. Ben eventually sells up, moves to Australia. In 1987, his fearsome temper does for him. He rows with the porter from his building and his heart gives out. He is 62.

The jeans are by Levi.

The shoes are by Dr. Martens. Dr Klaus Maerten is your man, here. In 1945, this German soldier broke his foot in a skiing accident. As he recuperated, he started imagining a shoe that would offer real protection to the foot. The idea of an air-cushioned sole appears before him.

Along with a friend, the wonderfully named Dr Funck, Maerten sets about bringing the idea to fruition. The resulting item sold so well in Germany that Dr. Maertens (as they were then known) expanded worldwide. In April 1960, a new style of boot, bearing the code 1460, rolled off the presses, along with the Anglicization of Dr. Maerten. Eight years later, it entered Skinhead folklore.

A British firm, the Griggs Company, distributes Dr. Martens in Britain. They are based in Northampton. The company makes a fortune and the chairman, Max Griggs, decides to spend his money on football. In 1992, he buys up, then combines, two local teams – Rushden Town and Irthlingborough Diamonds – to create Rushden and Diamonds Football Club. At the same time, he builds his team a stadium opposite his huge Dr. Martens factory. The club starts its ascent. It takes them ten years to rise from non-League football to the Second Division.

Meanwhile, Griggs has literally taken his eye off the ball. As the Diamonds sparkle, sales of Dr. Martens slump worldwide. Griggs closes his factory and, at the time of writing, the club's future remains shrouded in doubt.

■ ■ ■

Palmer, Pinheads and Peanuts

When football took hold of the nation's soul – a process which started with the drama of Italia '90, the birth of the Premiership and the subsequent interest in the game from a much wider section of society – football writing in this country raised its game considerably. The craft is now exemplary, the majority of articles in newspapers and magazines filled with depth and knowledge.

The writers, however, are not so good on one area of the game – the fan. Fans are their Achilles' heel, a condition that may arise from simple logistics or simple prejudice. At the games they report on, football journalists sit in press-boxes, separate from the crowd. Afterwards, they mix with players and management, always absorbing and reflecting their point of view. Fans are rarely spoken to, their way of thinking rarely made public. When Spurs fans continually booed Sol Campbell's return to White Hart Lane after his controversial move to Arsenal, the press were outraged – they still are. In an article in *The Observer* in June 2004, Andrew Anthony wrote 'the invective aimed at Campbell was disturbingly primal'. He failed to mention that, the year before his move, Spurs had turned down a £25 million offer from Manchester United, certain that Campbell would make his plans clear before he could go on a free transfer. Instead, Campbell played out his final season, firmly refusing to negotiate or reveal his plans until the season's end. He then demanded a wage rise so exorbitant people laughed, before joining Spurs' biggest rivals on a huge salary, made possible by his free transfer. This was greed and disloyalty on a huge scale and a slap in the face of the fans who had placed so much trust in him. Their reaction was hardly going to be the most welcoming and in truth little of the opprobrium aimed at Campbell during the game deserved that 'primal' title. The effigy of the man hung outside

White Hart Lane certainly did but that was the work of a very small minority. The rest of us were left trying to remove the bitter taste of his underhand behaviour from our mouths.

When Alan Smith went from Leeds to Manchester United, the press singled out his 'bravery' for joining Leeds' hated rivals and castigated any fans that thought differently. The writers seemed to view the move with the same indifference they might apply to an employee moving from Marks & Spencer to Woolworths, their words unable to comprehend the fans' public disgust, their howl of anger at a friend's betrayal.

I use the word 'friend' knowingly. Fans give players their money, their love, their applause, their anger, their humour, just as they do their family or their mates. They expect those emotions to be at least respected. When Campbell jumped ship to Arsenal, the Spurs faithful felt as if everything they had given the man had just been thrown back in their faces.

Football scribes see the world differently. To them, Campbell had every right to move to Arsenal. Spurs were going nowhere and if the man wanted to win trophies, what better place than Highbury? It's an argument that is hard to pull apart if there are no emotional ties to consider. Which is probably why football fanzines have come to such prominence in the last few years.

Fanzines are self-published projects, a space to discuss topics as fans, without interference. One of the most famous and influential fanzines of the past few years was *The End*, started by Peter Hooton and his friends. Hooton sang with a Liverpool band called The Farm and *The End* represented his and his mates' passions – music, football and terrace culture. (Or to paraphrase Irvine Welsh, 'All the boring things that make our lives so great.')

Feeney at Ben Sherman lent me three issues of this now-defunct fanzine. One carried a huge interview with the ex-con and author Jimmy Boyle; another had Alexei Sayle on the cover; the third a piece by playwright Mick Mahoney on clothes. It was dubbed 'the voice of the scally' and symbolised how football in the '90s had assumed an importance in youth culture that was easily on a par with music, the traditional creator and shaper of youth culture. It also inspired a rash of publications.

Mark sent some of them over to me. The most striking was called

The Fashion of Football

Ultra, started in 1996 by a Scot, a Hearts/Chelsea, clothes-obsessed man called Gavin Anderson. The first article I read was called 'War on the Terraces'. In a dispassionate manner, it detailed the violence at various games around the country. Much writing on football violence assumes such a tone, as if the writer is simply reading out the results on a Saturday afternoon. Spurs: six men down; Manchester United: retreated; Chelsea: stabbed one; West Ham: caught in an ambush.

In future issues, *Ultra* contained detailed lists of clothing. In Issue Four, there was the birth and rise of the Portsmouth Skinheads, how they first wore 'studded Army boots with steel toe-caps which were then discarded in favour of monkey boots when the "steelies" were outlawed by the police. However, monkey boots were soon given up in favour of Dr. Martens . . .'

In Issue Five, the 'Style Wars' page railed against the proliferation of replica shirts that heavily dotted the terraces of all Premiership clubs. The writer pointed out that, in contrast, clubs from lower divisions attracted 'a lot of traditional working-class football fans and, as a result, the percentage of Stone Island, Burberry and other decent labels is far higher than at the big clubs where the "Football is Coming Home" brigade have made replica shirts almost compulsory.'

In Issue Six, there was a summary of the clothes worn down the years at Wigan Athletic's ground. It began with original Ben Sherman shirts and ended with the designer labels Valentino and Massimo Osti. In between, there came Tonik trousers, Crombies and Harringtons, Budgie jackets (worn by Adam Faith in the '70s series of the same name), silk scarves tied around the wrists and Oxford bags ('70s-style flared trousers), before entering the era of Lacoste, Ellesse, Fila, etc.

Music also played its part. There were pages where the names Primal Scream, Flowered Up, Oasis, Paul Weller, reggae and Northern Soul emerged as the fans' favoured and flavoured sounds.

Beat About the Bush, a Queens Park Rangers fanzine started by John Wild, detailed similar concerns – football, clothes, fan behaviour. In Issue Four, amidst the jibes at Spurs and the article on the avant-garde composer Michael Nyman meeting Stan Bowles, came another story on Skinheads. I wasn't surprised by the amount written about this cult. Skinhead was the first working-class fashion to be heavily linked with football. Since then, the major fashion developments of the last 30 years have basically emanated from the football fan. It was not always thus.

* * *

Ready Steady Go! was a live music show that was first transmitted in 1963. It was filmed in a London studio (on a street called Kingsway, in Holborn, to be precise) and showed bands playing live to a young 'with-it' audience. This crowd, picked from hip West End clubs such as The Flamingo, transmitted the latest London Mod fashions to the rest of the country.

By 1965, this once-elitist cult had turned itself into a national phenomenon, as Mods fought rockers in seaside towns and took over the front pages of the national newspapers. The following year, England won the World Cup and, in doing so, triggered a huge explosion of interest in the game. The next season, attendances reached an all-time high. At the same time, an improved British infrastructure based around motorways that linked cities allowed fans to travel the country and follow their team.

Just as *Ready Steady Go!* had spread fashion nationwide, the London football fan now took over the role, taking his clothes and style to all the major cities. The illustrator Jim Ferguson, a Leicester fan, clearly remembers Skinhead Chelsea fans arriving at Filbert Street for a game in 1968. A week later, the first Leicester Skinheads were spotted on the terraces.

By 1969, Skinheads had become a national cult. Those involved did not relate to or find anything of value in rock culture. In fact, they hated it. It is no coincidence that the first reports of Skinhead crowds causing trouble occurred at two rock festivals – The Stones in Hyde Park in 1968 and the Isle of Wight Festival in 1969. The battle lines had been set. It was the short-haired versus the long-haired.

The Skinhead's gestation may be traced in part to John Simon. When Simon opened the Ivy Shop in Richmond, his stock of American clothing was bought by many young, working-class kids. Some of these customers would come to be known as 'hard Mods', a

The Fashion of Football

term applied to those who desired a return to a much sharper style. One of the distinguishing features of the hard Mods was the severe haircut, known as a crop. In the past, this look was assumed to have been a reaction to the emergence of the long hairstyle favoured by the hippy. Not so. It was a radical stylistic development which happened to become far more threatening to the authorities than the long hair worn by others.

Skinheads filled the football stadiums and their presence alone created a climate of violence. However, Mod principles still applied. Wearing expensive American clothing to football matches, where the risk of ruining them was high, was simply not on. A much more functional style was required, hence the Skinhead's gradual adoption of the work boot (made by Dr. Martens or Tuf), Levi jeans, braces, Harrington jackets, etc. It was this look which dominated the terraces in the late '60s. At White Hart Lane, one of the style's earliest proponents was one Keith Palmer, who had responded to an ad Mark had placed on the Internet requesting information.

Keith's testimony began at the start of the '60s. 'Everybody wore suits to football in those days,' he wrote. 'Even kids marooned in the backstreets of SW8, where I lived, turned out in pristine best school uniform just for the day.' Keith supported Spurs and for him the club became everything. 'Jimmy Greaves, Pat Jennings, Alan Gilzean, I knew more about their lives than those of my own parents.'

The majority of the fans wore black suits with obligatory skinny black ties. I couldn't help thinking how the crowds of my childhood resembled huge, mobile penguin colonies, with their jet-black plumage and preened white chests for public show.

'I'll never forget it as long as I live, the day that changed my sense of dress forever. It was a school day and two mates had invited me to a Church youth club to "listen to a few bands". We wandered down to a backstreet doorway somewhere in South London, entered and just listened. Young lads and adolescents all around donned regulation waist-length hair, some played air guitar with playful aggression, others danced and let out the frustrations of youth. I simply hated it.

'I wanted to scream, to let them all know that I felt highly uncomfortable in what was tantamount to a few hundred skinny, pimply kids innocently enjoying themselves. The "music" was awful and, despite that burst of uncharacteristic inward logic, I escaped via a toilet window, went home early to recuperate and rose at the crack of dawn intent to change my life for good. Yet the biggest irony was never lost on me: they were letting out their social anger in their beloved rock music, I was letting out mine in my hatred for it . . .

'Perched in the huge, black barber's chair, with the sound of shears whirring in my ear, I worried about the reaction of my parents, especially Dad. For all their inevitable words and outrage, my one consolation was that they couldn't stick the hair back on me, although knowing my father, I was sure he'd try.

'Still, the haircut felt smart, with its single-tramline parting whistling its way across my head like a new, purpose-built express route, and pointing due south to the prominent pleat in my new, pristine Ben Sherman shirt.

'The more I thought about it, the more I had utter disdain for the "hairies" who followed the underground rock movement which I had grown to hate so much. Nothing in my previous life had made me feel this smart or elite, and it wasn't long before I'd attained a full set of Skinhead attire.

'Skinhead clothes had a magical effect on you. They made you feel good, clean and proud of yourself. It was a cult that shaped my future life, a cult that had a profound effect on its members and probably its enemies too. To the outside world, we were all thugs and hooligans which, in some cases, was partially true; to the like-minded, it was the sharpest and most enduring cult that ever roamed the earth. Yet there was more to it than ever met the public eye.

'Saturdays were purely and simply football days. A chance to play peacock, and a day to show the world we were a force not to be taken lightly, be it a day spent in brogues, a Fred Perry and Sta-Prest whites, or a day enveloped in Levi's, Doc Martens and a Ben Sherman.

'Getting from South to North London and back on a football day was now becoming a headache. South London was gripped with Chelsea fever and I supported their hated "norf of the river" rivals who had deigned to beat them in the 1967 FA Cup final.

'Pre-political correctness, Spurs fans had inherited an

intentionally derisive term ['Yid'] from rival supporters. This was due to the convergence of a large Jewish contingent in that part of town (it is a term that was eventually to be parodied by Spurs fans the world over). Despite my chosen attire, admitting to an allegiance to the perceived enemy was tantamount to donning a skullcap and long white beard in certain parts of the capital in those days. And to be honest, I don't think things have changed very much to this day. To the Chelsea fans, I may not have been totally kosher, but was seen as easy meat being so heavily outnumbered and with such obviously dubious taste.

'The bus to Tooting Broadway was now too dangerous to chance. As it flew through Streatham on the way to the Tube station, it was packed to the rafters with Shed End Chelsea fans adorned in various Skinhead attire, and only too pleased to teach a stray Tottenham fan the time of day. There'd be Skins in Ben Sherman and Brutus shirts, Sta-Prest trousers with half-inch turn-ups held up by coloured braces, some in cherry-red boots and others wearing what had become known as "granddad shirts". These resembled the two- or three-buttoned shirts that British grandfathers wore in the '30s and '40s, although I never got to the bottom of why they adopted them.

'I was clearly a Skinhead and yet had to cover up my allegiances till out of "their" manor. The Broadway soon became a meeting place for large numbers of the Chelsea firm in those days and, I promise you, they weren't a pretty sight. Imagine it – you've made the station in one piece but to enter it you have to run the gauntlet of, say, 400 baying Chelsea fans dressed in bleached jeans and braces with shaven heads [and in some cases mohican haircuts], a sea of blue-and-white scarves hanging down from midriffs and hell-bent on tribal confrontation. Feeling brave?

'Despite what the media said, and says, Skinheads were nobody's fools. I soon learned that I had to delay my departure between the arrival of certain mobs if I wanted to survive. I had to learn to be streetwise, then buswise, then Tubewise before the terms had been invented. Many memories come flooding back of those exceedingly violent, yet strangely exciting times. Like the time I got trapped in a train with 20 Chelsea fans, maniacally chanting "Yid, yid, yid" directly at me. Like the time I went home minus two teeth for wearing the wrong colours in South London. Like the time I was

Second Half

159

chased home by bikers, and merely for the "crime" of following the hated Skinhead enemy. Unluckily, they'd just been beaten up by "my kind" around the corner and, in their hurry to flee the scene of the crime, bumped headlong into yours truly.

'What was unfortunate for me was a godsend for the family dentist. Bikers and Skinheads became deadly enemies, and more so if one of the "bar stewards" had rearranged your teeth like Stonehenge.

'We all imagine our own football club to be unique but Spurs was a truly amazing place to be in those times. It seemed to be everybody's favourite day out amongst the away fans, and a meeting place for all of life's characters. My early hormonal recollections were of a group of young ladies known locally as the Tottenham Skinhead girls. Boy, were they sexy, and how many times did I try to hang around them in any one of a dozen local watering holes? Then, one day, the flamboyantly dressed infiltrator seized his chance and asked one of them out. Result? Much the same as his earlier encounter with the Bikers. Me wandering down the High Road, head in hands, bicuspids in the gutter!

'The Tottenham Skinhead girls were a legend. There were about 25 of them, all with the latest Skin gear, and all sporting those little corkscrew bits of hair that twisted provocatively in front of their ears. Short skirts, Ben Sherman shirts, black fishnet tights. I was in love, and may even have missed a treasured game or two given the chance to get to know them a little better. Needless to say, I never was, but my most endearing, naughty thoughts go out to a group of gorgeous girls standing on the corner of the Park Lane End of the ground, dressed to kill, and with the assets to kill. Their perfume alone could have driven a man wild, their make-up and sexiness appropriately applied, adorned with enough sheepskin to have covered a generation of second-hand car dealers.

'So that was the original Skinheads, minus the stigmatic violence that always seemed to follow their name around. Forgive me for not dwelling on it but this is all about the fashions of the time and the enduring memories that we will all take to the grave with us. Of course, the Skinhead image was latterly replicated and too many people remember us for negativity and the heinous racism that later Skinheads perpetrated and attached themselves to. I would seriously like to point out – that wasn't us, or what we were all about. In fact, quite the opposite.

'I just hope that if the cult ever comes around again, it would be more like its first coming rather than its dubious heirs and that the new generation of Skinheads enjoy it as much as we did. And so it comes to the time for an ex-Skin to delve into the memory bank and leave you with a list. Big, deep breath, large intake of air, here goes: button-down Ben Sherman and Brutus shirts, skinny braces (which persistently snapped and hit you in the face), Sta-Prest trousers with half-inch turn-ups, SX200 Scooters, green American flying jackets, jean jackets (normally bleached light blue), buffed, cherry-red boots of varying height, anything with the Dr. Martens logo on it, pork-pie hats, Fred Perry shirts (especially those ones with lines around the collars and sleeves), cardigans (yes, cardigans!) normally worn with Ben Shermans, football scarves skilfully tied round your neck with club crest showing and tucked inside a jumper, Trevira skirts (if a young lady), Ivy brogues, tassled shoes, moccasins, smooths [brogues without their distinctive pattern], red woollen socks, Harrington jackets (named after a character in *Peyton Place*), sheepskin coats, Crombies, 'beanie' hats (rolled three or four times, making your head look like a woolly penis), two-tone mohair suits, coloured hankies for the top pockets (with pearl studs holding in the hanky), long sideburns, jeans so tight it looked like your testicles would explode (this also applied to the Tottenham girls), tramline partings in your hair, a stolen dab of your dad's Brut, butcher's coats adorned with the names of your favourite players, guys who lived the *Clockwork Orange* cult and the omnipresent football badge showing off your proud allegiance.'

■■■
He's One of Us!

In June 1979, I had my first music review published in a national newspaper. Since then, I have interviewed a considerable number of major musicians including (he said not a little proudly) Marvin Gaye, Smokey Robinson, Stevie Wonder and Nina Simone.

Through my job, I have travelled the world, met hundreds of interesting and funny and charming and inspirational and extremely obnoxious people. I've had some amazing experiences. I have written 11 books, been on TV countless times, same with radio. But when Steve Perryman came through the door of the City wine bar Mark and I were sitting in, I was rendered speechless. It was . . . Steve Perryman.

I began supporting Spurs in 1967. I was nine years old. Steve Perryman joined Spurs the very same year. He was seventeen years old and would become an essential part of a Spurs team that in the '70s and early '80s would win two FA Cups, two League Cups and two UEFA Cups.

Perryman was the spirit of the team. By his own admission, he was not a Gazza or a Hoddle, outrageously talented footballers, but his commitment just couldn't be faulted. Actually, scrap that last sentence. It implies the man was a journeyman footballer, a blood, sweat and tears guy but without talent. Not so, not so at all. Steve Perryman was a tenacious, defensive midfielder with fine passing skills and a sharp football brain. He drove the Spurs team forward relentlessly and did so with strength and imagination. That's why Perryman would feature in most people's all-time Spurs 11, including mine. Perryman put as much into the game as any fan on the terraces. He was as exultant in victory as we were, and similarly as crushed by the punch of defeat. In 1981, the club's centenary year, this is what he had to say about Tottenham: 'I enjoy Spurs because at this club everyone, from the humblest backroom boy to the highest paid player, is treated with equal respect. They're all equally important to our success. That's what makes Tottenham Hotspur a great football club.'

So sad that such sentiments are almost unrecognisable today, yet the words say much about the man dubbed 'the Baby-faced Assassin' a million years before the same title was bestowed upon Manchester United's Ole Gunnar Solskjaer. (In fact, Perryman discovered the young Solskjaer in Norway when the boy was just 18. He automatically rang Spurs. 'You got to sign this boy, he's amazing,' he told the powers that be – this was during the Alan Sugar and Gerry Francis era. They ignored him. Just as they ignored Dennis Bergkamp when he became available. Foreign players? Having a laugh, aren't you? Bunch of bloody Carlos Kickabouts.)

Keith Palmer had arranged the interview. He knew Perryman, said he would persuade him to come for a chat. 'The day he came out onto the pitch with a Skinhead cut is legendary,' Keith told us. 'We were Skinheads and he looked like one of us. For that reason alone, you have got to talk to him. I'll phone him. I'm meeting him next week. We can hook it up then.'

Both Mark and I said that would be great but privately never thought it would happen. 'Can't see it myself,' Mark said over the phone. We had heard a lot of promises throughout this journey and Mark in particular had been taken aback by people's flaky attitudes. As far as he was concerned, if you said you were going to do something, you did it. Full stop. If you can't do it, don't lie.

Lying, conniving and cheating upset Mark's sense of graceful living. However, Keith was as good on his word as Perryman was in a Spurs shirt. Two weeks later, he phoned and told us to be in a certain bar at a certain time. We arrived and, a few minutes later, he walked in with Perryman.

For five minutes as we sat around the table, I just looked at my glass and let Mark do all the talking. He could explain to Perryman what the book was about. I couldn't. I just kept thinking to myself, it's . . . Steve Perryman, the man who played over 800 games for Spurs, who scored twice against AC Milan in 1972's UEFA Cup semi-final first leg, the man who played with his sleeves rolled up, the perfect symbol of his absolute commitment to the Tottenham cause.

Although he had filled out a little, Perryman still looked the same, still had that little-boy face, the short, dark hair I remembered so vividly from his playing days.

'So, son,' Mark said, finally. 'We going to put the tape recorder on? Ask a few questions, maybe?' Mark knew what I was going through, knew what Perryman was doing to my head at that precise moment in time. I needed a question to buy me a bit of time.

'Yeah, Steve,' I said, putting on the tape recorder, 'thought we could start with a bit of background,' I said.

'No problem,' he said kindly. Steve Perryman was brought up in Northolt, London with two elder brothers who played football. 'Because of them,' Perryman explained, 'I was always playing football with people older than myself and therefore it became very easy when I played with my own age group. It was soon obvious that I was better than my age group. I was playing with the fourth-year team in second year.

'My school was particularly football-minded. They'd have six-a-side competitions before it was normal to do that. So I'd get pulled out of my classroom. I was like a star but without wanting to be one. I played for the district team early and ended up going to a grammar school.'

Unfortunately, the school had made basketball their main sporting activity. 'They'd had problems playing the competitive games, fighting with other schools, so they decided to give up football.'

Fortunately, a new sports head teacher was appointed and the imbalance was corrected. 'He said, we have some good players here, and got six of us into the Under-15s district team, Ealing District,' Perryman related. 'I played my first game against Harrow. We won 9–1. That was on a Saturday. The Sunday, Charlie Faulker, the chief scout of Spurs, knocks on the door, come for a trial.'

The Perryman family knew of Faulker. Steve's brother had written to him a year earlier alerting him to Steve's talents. Faulker, then a scout for QPR, never replied. At the Perryman household, the family gave him an earful for his negligence and then persuaded Steve to start training at Spurs.

'We went training Tuesday and Thursday nights,' Perryman recalled. 'My schoolwork went completely downhill. I could only ever see football from that moment onwards. Fulham got interested

The Fashion of Football

but I didn't sign with Fulham because of my brother's influence. Signed on for Tottenham really for the honesty of the manager, Bill Nicholson.

'Other people, like Tommy Docherty at Chelsea, were saying like, we're in the Cup final [Spurs v. Chelsea 1967]. We'll pick you up in a limousine – your mum, dad, brothers, fucking uncles, aunts, they can all come. Then there's the after-match do. Just join us. And Bill Nick would say, are you going to sign for us or not? Because if you're not, I'll give your ticket to someone else. Forget the limousine. Forget the treatment. Just absolutely to the point. Which is lovely. And so I went for that sort of approach. Liked that. That was a long way from where I lived in west London and so it was taking me two hours a day to get there and two hours home again. Eventually, got in the team, when I was 17.'

That must have been an incredible experience, I suggest. Perryman shrugs his shoulders. Like all '70s footballers, the excitement of their achievements is now tempered by the wish to have been born 20 years later. What they could do with the money today's players are pulling.

'We certainly weren't overpaid,' he stated. 'I mean, I earned eighteen quid a week in the first team. End of the year, Bill Nicholson pulled you in. You sat in a little seat below him. He's up there and you're down here. And he'd just tap his fingers like that and he's offering you a score [£20], which I suppose is a percentage increase from eighteen quid to a score, but I said to Bill, those shoes cost fifteen quid. You didn't play for Tottenham for the money, that's for sure. Of course, I was earning more than people of my own age and I had more money than them but it was not like today. If you get in the team now, you get a five-year contract and, by the time you finish, you've got mega money.'

Keith now joined in, bringing up that day when Perryman ran onto the White Hart Lane pitch with a short-back-and-sides and a razored parting. The reaction was palpable and felt across the whole ground. He's one of us, the fans said and, in that very moment, player and fan became as one. Such is the power of football.

Perryman smiles. 'I remember Keith talking about my haircut. My haircut was down to one particular barber who was the barber of all the local boxers. Not that I was a boxer but I used to go to him and, of course, boxers have their hair cut short because that's what you do. It was really following the boxing fraternity rather than what some people thought, a Skinhead or whatever. It appeared to be the same thing but it wasn't meant to be.'

'It went right round the terraces,' Keith commented. 'I mean, you could hear it. Everyone's going, he's one of us.'

Steve shook his head in gentle amazement. 'That's a surprise to me. I wouldn't even believe that you could have that effect.'

'Everybody looked at each other,' Keith continued, 'and went, they've got a Skinhead on the team. You could hear it right across the terraces. And then everyone naturally assumed that you'd had it done because we had had it done on the terraces.'

Steve smiled wider now, and ruefully too. 'That would have been clever if it was that way but it weren't. That was too clever for me.'

As for clothes, Perryman claimed he felt happiest wearing suits, had worn them since the '60s, could remember when you had a suit made for Sunday best. Steve's were made by a tailor in Mill Lane, Acton; shiny mohair numbers and (nice touch, this) he always ordered two of the same trousers. 'Travelling on coaches ruined the crease,' he explained, thus a spare pair always came in handy. With the suits, he wore Oxford brogues and clothes that were a mix of Mod, Skin and Suedehead. Put that with a college-boy haircut and 100 per cent devotion to the cause, no wonder Steve was a player whose relationship with the fans is both deep and lasting.

His next brush with fashion came with the Steve Perryman sports shops, a business venture he and his brothers embarked upon. 'My second brother, Bill, had the wheeler-dealer silk cap,' Perryman says, smiling again. 'We were in a cup final or whatever [if only today's Spurs players could be so blasé about cup finals] and he said, crap sports shops around here, we can't ever buy anything we want, let's open one. I thought, yeah, go on then. We'll have a bit of that.

'We started in Hayes and ended up with seven shops, all run by him. We'd go to like a trade fair in London and see Pringle sweaters and think they're nice, rather than they're fashionable – that they're good. So we were sort of on it, about six months before anyone else. Fred Perry was round the corner from Tottenham, factory there in one of them sort of side streets. We could always go in and pick it all up and see the stuff. It didn't help, though, because it came again 20 years later. Which is fine but it didn't happen when we were trading.'

It is only recently that the Perryman family sold the last lease. 'It was never our way to borrow half a million from a bank and open up 30 shops,' Perryman states. 'We literally wanted to keep it small, family-run and manageable.'

When I asked him who he considered the best-dressed player at Spurs throughout his time there, Perryman selected the full-back Joe Kinnear: 'Big ties, the flares, long hair, flowing locks.'

What did Bill Nicholson have to say about long hair? I wondered. 'He didn't like it,' replied Steve.

'I bet he didn't,' Keith said.

Perryman laughed. 'When I had my hair a lot longer, he used to sometimes get hold of my head and say, think you look good? You think you look good like that? Because you fucking don't. Actually, my older brother was more of an influence. He used to sort of say the same thing. How can you run about? That fucking hair's in your eyes.'

I interjected here. 'Must have been a bit easier than Ralph Coates's hair, though,' thinking of the long strands of hair that continually flapped across that man's face as he hared down the wing. Memories of Coates and Kinnear brought to mind the other greats, the Chiverses, the Gilzeans, the Greaveses, the Peterses, the Archibalds, the Ardileses, the Hoddles, the Gazzas . . .

So, what did Perryman make of Spurs these days? 'It's the blind leading the blind,' he said, screwing his face up in annoyance and disgust. He still felt for the club in a huge manner. Since quitting as a player, Perryman had gone into management. His most notable spell was in Japan coaching Shimizu S-Pulse with friend and fellow legend Ossie Ardiles. In 1999, Shimizu lost the J League play-off final on penalties to Jubilo Iwate. Strangely, the game was played in Dubai. Prior to the kick-off, Perryman was offered a bribe, a good bung, to throw the game. He refused and lost anyway.

'I'll tell you this story before I have to dash off,' he said, and it was a story that confirmed his enduring loyalty to Tottenham. Perryman knew that by his team Shimizu reaching those play-off finals, his success would generate a lot of British media interest. He persuaded his club to arrange a press conference. It was the mid-'90s. Perryman walked into the conference, sat down and the first thing he did was to start lambasting Spurs' chairman, Alan Sugar. Many Spurs fans still believe that Sugar was the man responsible for Tottenham's woes in the '90s. Perryman was one of them.

'I knew that everything I said would go right back to him via the back pages,' he said, gleefully. And it did. The next day, Perryman got a phone call from a furious Sugar and the two men argued for hours. And that was Steve Perryman. Twenty years on and he was still defending his club to the last. When Perryman stood up, shook our hands and left, I had a glow inside of me. Mark and I had another drink, then we too made tracks. As we walked through the London cold, Mark announced, 'I clocked you at the start. You couldn't say a word, could you, son?'

'Mark,' I said, 'it was . . . Steve Perryman.'

'I know, son,' he said kindly. 'I know.'

■ ■ ■
The Suedehead's
Dressing-room, 1972

Shirt is by Ben Sherman, trousers are by Levi. They are called Sta-Prest, the first ever 'wrinkle-free product', according to Levi who launched them in 1965.

Next to them hang a pair of Tonik trousers from Dormeuil, a company started by Jules Dormeuil in 1842. His idea is to sell English cloth to French customers. Jules and his brothers, Alfred and Auguste, do just that, and do well. The business starts in France and by the early 1880s has offices in New York. Forty years later, they establish a women's shop and then create their flagship building on Regent Street in London. In 1960, they launch the first ready-to-wear range, thus assaulting a slumbering textile industry. The company motto is 'Domus amica, domus optima' (The friendly house, the best house).

His coat is a Crombie, named after a woollen cloth created by J. & J. Crombie in 1805. This wool provides the basis for a single-breasted, three-quarter-length, navy wool overcoat. At the time of the French Revolution, the English aristocracy started adding black velvet collars to these coats to show sympathy for their Gallic counterparts, who were being murdered by their thousands.

His shoes are brogues, an early Highland shoe that was developed when Scottish clans first came together to form the Highland regiment. The word 'brogue' either derives from the Huguenots, who settled in Ireland and began manufacturing shoes, or from the Gaelic word for shoes, bròg.

These shoes have been manufactured in Northampton for over a century. The soil there is some of the most fertile in the country and creates higher quality leather from the cows that eat the local grass. This is why Northampton remains the centre of shoe-making in Britain.

On the shelf opposite, the smell of working-class youth – a bottle of Brut aftershave, created by Fabergé and launched in 1964.

■■■

The Curator

When writing a book, a domino effect is created. You talk to one person, they tell you to talk to this person who then puts you onto another person, and so on and so forth. During his interview, *GQ* editor Dylan Jones put us onto a man called David Rosen. 'He's really into clothes, really into football,' he told us. 'You should definitely meet him.'

Although I had never met Rosen, funnily enough our paths had already crossed. A friend of mine had told me about a man from his neighbourhood he had recently got talking to who revealed he had kept his original clothing from the '60s, early '70s. He had in his collection Royals shoes, Sta-Prest trousers and Ben Sherman shirts, all in pristine condition. He told my friend he could come round and view them if he so desired. His original idea was to pass these jewels on to his children, that's how much he still valued them. I would later discover that this man was, in fact, David Rosen.

Rosen works in property, charged with finding unique and unusual buildings for wealthy clients. He is obviously very good at what he does – the view from his large Savile Row office is breathtaking. Suitably, he came across as a very self-assured man, exuded a quiet but unbreakable confidence in himself.

I saw him as part of a very small clique that worked around this money-sodden area, a new breed of entrepreneur (I was also thinking of people such as the tailor Carlo Brandelli at Kilgour, French & Stanbury) who are all in their 30s, early 40s, all very successful. They absolutely respect the past but their drive is to shape the future.

Rosen is an Arsenal fan, had been watching them since forever. When I first called him, we spent half an hour really slagging off each other's team. I liked him instantly.

Furthermore, he was a clothes connoisseur, a lover of the street fashions he had worn as a kid. Mod was at the heart of his style. Rosen was a Skinhead first, a Suedehead later and perfect for our purposes.

Dylan passed on his number and during a Bar Italia meeting with Mark, I called Rosen, arranged to chat. His address was 25 Savile Row, just around the corner from where Mark worked. We met at three o'clock and were shown into Rosen's spacious office. His desk was large, tidy and he wore a lovely Prince of Wales suit, red John Smedley top and Bass Weejun loafers. I opened up by asking him about his life as a Suedehead.

'That whole period – 1969 to 1972 – just before the Budgie jacket came in and all of that, was absolutely a wonderful period,' he stated. 'It wasn't Mod,' he stopped, corrected himself. 'Of course, it came out of the Mod thing but it was its own thing. It actually went more back to Modernism than Mod, the whole Suedehead look. It was a fantastic look, the Suedehead look.'

As he spoke so enthusiastically, I thought it amazing how the impact of this style – the button-down shirt, the Sta-Prest, the brogues, the Harrington, the Crombie – should still be so alive today. Although it was three in the afternoon and the phones were ringing non-stop outside, you could tell that this was a man who was at his happiest when talking about clothes and football. 'They're the two most important things in life,' he confided. 'But for God's sake don't tell the wife and kids,' he joked. I think.

Rosen then turned to Mark. 'I know you, don't I? I used to see you around. You always had these really nice Lonsdale bags with you.'

Mark was astonished. In 1997, he had left the printing game and opened up his own clothes shop in South London. He called it Clobber and filled it full of Soul Stylist clothes, from Mod to Casual. His adventure lasted three years.

Mark's main wholesalers were situated in Great Portland Street and, every once in a while, Mark would take two big Lonsdale bags there, fill them up with stock. Then he would march back home.

'Jesus,' Mark exclaimed, 'That was about six or seven years ago, and you remember me? Not that ugly, am I?'

Rosen laughed. 'C'mon, you know the score. You see someone on the street with nice clothes or accessories, you always remember them. You don't see many like that any more; the ones you do, they stay with you.'

I could feel Mark's elation from where I was sitting. I knew how much he prided himself on his dress sense.

'Did you see my article in *Arena*, by the way?' Rosen asked.

He had co-written a piece with Dylan Jones for the magazine called 'Saturday Boys'. In the article, he had put together a family tree of great London shops, made the connection between Cecil Gee and Austin's in the '50s, Richard James in the '90s. 'It was the whole family tree of Saturday boys,' he explained. 'Who had worked for whom. It started with Austin's in Shaftesbury Avenue and went right the way through to today. I spoke to everybody because everybody worked for somebody. I spoke to Eddie at Duffer's, John Simon, Ashley Lloyd Jennings, it was all about shopping on Saturday mornings then being on the terraces in the afternoon. South-west boys would go to the Ivy Shop then on to Chelsea; north-west London would go to the Squire Shop in Brewer Street or Quincy then on to Arsenal or Tottenham. You pretty much wore what you had just bought.'

The article highlighted key London shops, a list very much worth preserving, for in its own way it presented the reader with a real history of street style, from the late '50s to the present day. Rosen nominated Austin's, Stanley Adams, Lloyd Jennings, Clothesville, Cecil Gee, Just Men, the Ivy Shop, the Squire Shop, the Village Gate, Quincy, Browns, J Simons, Paul Smith, Woodhouse, Piero Di Monzi, Crolla, The Library, Jones, Hackett, Duffer of St George, Browns, Ted Baker and Richard James.

As far as football was concerned, in Rosen's world that means the Arsenal and one player in particular – Charlie George, the kingpin of style, the fashion icon par excellence in his time. 'Of course, there's no question,' he stated unequivocally. 'The suits he wore from the Squire Shop, later on Quincy. He had the whole look because he was straight off the North Bank. He knew about Royals, Gibson smooths, loafers, fringe and buckle, the lot. He literally came off the North Bank wearing a Harrington, probably with steel-toed Doc Martens, and then he matured into that whole Squire and Quincy shop look. I've got a pic somewhere.'

He darted over to a filing cabinet. 'This is Charlie wearing a window-pane mohair suit from Squire,' he said proudly, pulling out an 8 x 8 glossy pic.

'Looks great,' I averred.

Mark said, 'There's another one of your mob who keeps coming up, Frank McLintock.'

Rosen nodded his head approvingly. 'He was doing that Bobby Moore thing – very clean, very straightforward but it was always with the Mod look,' he explained. 'Funnily enough, Alex Ferguson was doing the same thing. If you see early pics of Ferguson you'll see what he was doing.'

How did he view Bobby Moore? 'In a sense, he was the kingpin of London. He would take all his gear off, fold it up neatly, hang his suit up. He set the tone for the whole look in London. He had a big influence on all the clubs and their players.'

Rosen had a lot of time for ex-Chelsea man Alan Hudson as well. 'The only footballer in the '70s who had a feel for that Tommy Nutter thing would have been Alan Hudson. Not Osgood, he was more of a Bobby Moore. Hudson was the Charlie George of Chelsea.'

Any footballers outside of the capital? He shook his head. 'They didn't have a clue. It was only the London boys and then it was only the real London boys.'

He acknowledged that football has now taken over from music as the premier cultural force in this country. A Beckham haircut is as avidly copied now as a Bowie one was back in the '70s.

'Beckham is The Beatles of today,' he said, slipping into a cliché from that day's newspaper. 'I think he's great. He's like a modern-day Bobby Moore. He's got integrity, kids love him, the grandparents love him.'

What about his clothes? 'Ah!' his brief word translating as a sign of disapproval.

A call came through, he had to take it. A client had arrived, business was business, he had to go.

'Look, boys, anything I can do to help out, be glad to help. I mean, if you want to take photos of my Royals or Sta-Prest, come round, be no problem.'

One last question. 'David, do you think your children are actually going to value your old clothes when you pass them on? Aren't they just going to go, Dad, what the hell are these?'

'Oh, my kids will get it,' he said confidently. 'One day, one beautiful day, they will get it.'

The Soulboy's Dressing-room, 1973

His shoes are made of plastic. Here's why. At the end of the Second World War, Europe suffered a leather shortage. It was then that a Monsieur Jean Dauphant, with the aid of his children, hit upon the idea of making shoes from PVC material. The family set up the Sarraizienne company, named after their home town, and produced the world's first plastic sandals, or jellies as they came to be known. In the '50s and '60s, these T-bar plastic sandals became popular school wear for children in Europe and Australia. In the '70s, the Soulboy made them an integral part of his style. Another shoe designer who began manufacturing this type of sandal was Manolo Blahnik, who settled in London in the early 1970s. His shoes, the Zapata, were 'fiendishly expensive' but considered 'must-haves' by the leading fashion faces of the day.

His jumper is mohair, first made available in this country at the shop Let It Rock on the Kings Road. The shop was owned by Trevor Miles, a man who loved American clothing. All stylists do.

The trousers are by South Sea Bubble, bought from the shop Acme Attractions on the Kings Road. In Mod tradition, the owner has customised them, splitting the seam and inserting a wedge of brocade, almost chintzy material, to flare them out.

There is also a pair of peg trousers, which are worn with three belts and which the owner has again tampered with, tapering the trouser leg so as to puff out the top half of the trouser.

The Casual's Dressing-room, 1982

The shirt is by Lacoste. You can tell by the crocodile label, its inventor a man who would exercise his brilliant imagination in many fields. Before Fred Perry, Henri Lacoste, born in Paris in 1904, designed the first-ever sportswear shirt.

Lacoste was a tennis player of immense talent, nicknamed 'the Crocodile' for the ruthless and patient manner in which he beat his opponents. He won Wimbledon and the US Open twice, along with three French titles, and also took time out to invent the ball machine. This invention mechanically fired balls at you and thus allowed players to improve their overall game. He retired suddenly in 1929 and three years later launched the first Lacoste shirt, named the Izod. It was so successful that it was worn both on and off the court. Still is today, thanks to its stiff collar. In 1967, aged 63, he produced the first-ever steel tennis racquet and 20 years later was as busy as ever, designing a new form of tennis ball.

The jumper is by Pringle, a company formed in 1815 by Robert Pringle. The firm, the first to introduce knitwear as outerwear in the early 1900s, is branded by its distinctive, diamond-patterned jumpers. The company is also held responsible for the invention of the twinset, worn by both men and women.

The jeans are by Lois, a Spanish company that since its inception have only used the Saez Marino denim mill for their products.

The trainers are by Adidas, a German company borne out of fury and revenge. Adi and Rudi Dassler were brothers who, in the 1920s, successfully ran a company producing sportswear. It was wearing their shoes that the black American runner Jesse Owens ran to victory at the famous 1936 Berlin Olympics and made a mockery of Hitler's views on white superiority.

Then came the Second World War and an argument so deep, so vicious, that Adi and Rudi never spoke again. The nature of the argument remains a mystery, the brothers' actions do not. Taking up buildings on opposite sides of the Aurach River, Adi started Adidas, his brother a sports shoe company he named Puma. Battle commenced, both companies hitting incredible highs and lows as they slugged it out with each other.

■ ■ ■

A Tribe Called Dressed

Bar Italia, again.

Although I had often used the place in the past, it had never been to this degree. The staff now greeted me as a real regular. They said, 'Ciao!', smiled pleasantly, parried my and Mark's jokes about their ever-changing prices. 'What do you mean the price change? Uh? You don't change ever?' It was getting to be a home from home.

As usual, Mark was waiting for me at the back when I arrived. I greeted him, sat down, told him he looked a bit peaky.

'Tell me about it,' he said.

He had been working hard of late, burrowing away, bringing up info on the Casuals. He had finished his research now. Today, he was handing over his work. He nodded to a huge pile of papers he had placed on the counter. 'Got room for them in your bag, have you, son?'

'Shit,' I replied.

'Told you, once I get started . . . Mocha?'

'Be nice,' I grimaced.

'You worried about this part, are you?' he said, standing up.

'I am. I just feel like this stuff has been covered a million times now.'

'Know what you mean,' he said. 'Have you seen that new book called *Casuals*? Looks good, as well. But it's another one on the subject.'

Mark went to order my drink. I picked up the pile, started flicking through. There was plenty of material. The early articles described how the world of 1976 had been so transfixed by punk that it left the most significant British youth cult for the past 25 years to start its journey in silence; how Casual culture was firmly entwined with football; how in stadiums up and down the country, the rules and the edicts of dress and behaviour (based on Mod notions of secrecy and elitism) were handed down.

There were other articles. One said it was impossible to trace the birth of the cult, for it was not one person or one group or one incident that sparked what Tony Rivers of the Cardiff Soul Crew calls 'the biggest youth phenomenon to hit this country in 25 years' – rather it was a variety of influences.

One theory said that in London the roots lay in the generation of young Caribbeans who, in the early '70s, had developed a style they named 'the Sticksman'. The Sticksman took to the concrete dressed smart-casual, meaning a Gabicci top, Farah slacks, Bally shoes, and jewellery on the neck and wrist. This look was popular in many areas, most notably London's Peckham, which in turn bled into nearby Bermondsey, and onto Millwall's terraces.

In Liverpool, other directions. I noted that Mark had sourced Kevin Sampson's July 1983 *Face* article in which he described the 1977 Liverpool youth in mohair jumpers, plastic shoes, camel duffel coats. What pushed them apart from the crowd was the wedge haircut they sported.

From this starting point came a new look: Lois jeans, then Inege, Fiorucci. Next, the labels Fila, Lacoste, Tacchini and Ellesse took centre stage before Burberry and Aquascutum seized the day.

Mark had found stories of how Liverpool fans had 'acquired' this expensive gear by following their team into Europe, and all the sport and clothes shops they could find.

There was Peter Hooton's important 1992 article detailing how the training shoe had been brought screaming back into fashion by the Casual, how this cult was now responsible for a massive billion-pound industry in trainers. I ran an eye down the page and various names sprang straight up at me. There were the Adidas legends – the Samba, the Stan Smith, the Forest Hills, the Trim Trab, the Gazelle. There was the Borg Elite from Diadora and from Puma the States and the Argentina.

There was also material on little-known cults such as the Perry Boys in Manchester. This gang sported a hairstyle known as 'the Failsworth Flick' and wore Fred Perry tops. The Stone Roses were Perry Boys. From little Mods do great bands grow.

Mark had done an excellent job but it couldn't alleviate my main thought on the matter – there were now a thousand books out there telling the exact same story. What made it worse was that one of them, *The Soul Stylists*, was mine.

Mark put my mocha in front of me. 'I know what you're saying about this being old ground,' he said, settling down again, 'but have a look at some of this stuff. Where is it, now?' He took the pile, leafed through it, finally found what he was looking for. 'Ah, gotcha, you little bastard. These guys are really interesting. One's this guy from London – Will, a shop owner, he's got some interesting things to say. And the others are from Wales and Scotland and, let's be fair, you don't get to hear their side very much.'

The first page he handed me was an email from Jonathan and Matthew Owen. I knew them both. They were brothers who had both run with Cardiff's Soul Crew. The previous year, I had spent time with them and others writing a piece on the Soul Crew for *FourFourTwo* magazine. After the piece ran, I had called Matthew, told him the fashion and football idea. I asked if it would be possible to go up again, and see him and his brother Jonathan to talk about clothes. They had said no problem, and invited me up for the play-offs in May 2003. Cardiff were playing QPR in the Second Division play-off final. I could arrive Saturday, talk to the boys that night, go to the game the next day. Sounded just fine.

It didn't work like that. I reached Cardiff at seven, was unable to speak by midnight. I stayed at Jonathan and Kate's house. Both were actors, Kate about to star in a prestigious BBC drama, Jonathan to begin filming *Dose*, a safe-sex film written by Dean Cavanagh and Irvine Welsh (which was BAFTA nominated).

On the Sunday morning after breakfast, Matthew and his friend arrived at the house. We sat at a table and started the interview but it soon became clear that the boys were so nervous about the game, the last thing they wanted to do was sit and talk about the past. How could they? The future was upon them.

That afternoon, Cardiff beat QPR 1–0, went up to the First Division. The town went ballistic. I got wayward by six, talking gobbledegook by ten.

The next grey morning, I told Jonathan about the email we had posted on the Internet, asking for fans' experiences with clothes and football, how in the main all we had received was loads of stick from sulky Northerners.

'I'll write you an email,' Jonathan said. 'I'll get Matthew to, as well.' They were Cardiff, they weren't jiving me. Like Mark, they came from a culture of principles. You say you're going to do it, you do it. This is what arrived at Mark's about a week after my trip.

Mark,
My name is Jonathan Owen. I told Paolo I would write an email about the Cardiff Casual scene and he told me to send it to you, so here we go.

It's a strange old thing that sometimes those in the Northwest can be really hypocritical about the whole Casual thing. I mean, they complain that it's this great big subculture that has been ignored for so long and then complain when writers of real quality like Paolo and Irvine wanna do stuff on them.

There is no doubt that it originated from large numbers of working-class youths dressing in a particular style to go to football in that region, whether it was the Bowie-clone scallies of Scotland Road in Liverpool, or the Perry Boy Mancs who had a hairstyle known as the Failsworth Flick specific to that part of Manchester. There is no doubt it was quickly adopted across the rest of the UK and many people developed regional characteristics that became specific to each club.

I mean Pompey fans always looked nautical to me! I know this sounds daft but whenever I saw the 657 they had navy jumpers with hooped white stripes. They looked fantastic. They were the first boys I saw in Armani and almost immediately, 'I wanted in!' So I spent the following weekend in Knightsbridge trying to find stuff. Which brings me to Londoners. They had a huge advantage in the availability of clothing particularly when labels became the be-all by '78 and '79. By '82, there was no one to touch Denton and the Arsenal boys, mainly because of their geographic location *and* economic situation. Thatcher went for the Liverpool docks in the '80s. She also went for the pits.

It was boutiques for us in Wales. Woodies was open by '82. Fortunately, that generation, which would have gone to the pits to work, saw boom time in Cardiff, which is where we all work nowadays, along with supporting the team.

We were 'the Welsh dressers' by the early '80s, a play on the world-famous furniture that has become trendy again with Nigella and the Islington set. The look Cardiff had by '88 was a uniform of Adidas Gazelles, C17 jeans and a Ralph Lauren top. Any kind of Armani jacket completed the job. Hair was usually shaved around the back and sides with a severe Steven Seagal, I kid you not! Slick on top or a Bros quiff, often highlighted. What makes me smile is when they say there is no comparisons to Mod. It doesn't take a professor in social history to see the parallel. Young working-class males adopting an obsession with specific clothing.

Snobbery was essential, along with African-American urban music – RnB, soul and house – as your soundtrack. Violence? Optional, although you wouldn't really want to get sand in your suit or a Stanley slash across the arse of your Armani jeans.

The best person to talk to about the Northwest is the writer Kevin Sampson. He was right there. I've seen photos of him, read the books. He's smack on and a gentleman.

When they call you a Mod, I'd take it as the highest compliment. To use it as a term to signify the difference is laughable. The line

```
between the two is exceptionally thin.
   Cheers
   Jon, Soul Crew
   PS You Millwall then, Mark?
```

I put the paper down. 'Hope you memorised that line there, Mark,' I said, 'the one that refers to Irvine and I as writers of "real quality" quote unquote.'

'Don't have much call for good books up in Cardiff, then?' he retorted.

'I like it,' I said, ignoring him. 'I like the fact we've got Cardiff in there, not just Liverpool and London. In fact, when I did that *FourFourTwo* article, Tony Rivers was saying that he was drawn to the Soul Crew simply because of what they were wearing and how glamorous they looked. I remember that feeling myself from school, when the boys came in with Ben Shermans and Sta-Prests on – I just thought they looked amazing.'

'It's good how he's expanded it as well,' Mark pointed out. 'Drawn the parallel with the Mod thing.'

'Yeah, he probably nicked that off my book, *The Soul Stylists*.'

'In your dreams, son.'

'OK, what else you got?'

'His brother, Matthew.'

'Let's have a look.'

```
Dear Mark,
One point I would like to make is that in the
late ' 80s, the Casual scene was very different
to now. It was all about being smart, looking
good, neat and tidy. It was not a scene that
was  necessarily  obsessed  with  labels,  but
rapidly  became  so  for  hundreds  of  self-
professed  'dressers'  (as  we  tended  to  call
ourselves at Cardiff) by the early 1990s. The
major  corporations  began  muscling  in  on  the
look  and  were  soon  stocking  a  plethora  of
labels   to   sell   to   fashion-conscious,
financially  blessed  young  male  posers  of  the
```

The Fashion of Football

South Wales Valleys, just like in the Northwest and London, etc.

When I first began trying to dress as a Casual or dresser, it seemed like you were trying to infiltrate an exclusive and elite bunch within, yet beyond, your own working-class tribe. The buzz of dressing to be part of that tribe was as good as the buzz of a football riot. Indeed, by the time I was sixteen in the late '80s, I would not dare walk within a five-mile radius of a football ground unless I looked distinctively Casual and casually distinct.

For me, starting from the bottom up, Casual clothing consisted of nice jeans i.e. Levi's, C17 (a must among the more discerning soccer lout), Armani (overrated and evidently overpriced in the jean department), the rarely worn yet avidly adored Simpson jeans.

Barker's was a clothing boutique situated in an arcade on St Mary's Street. (Not many away fans have walked down there. Plenty have run, though!) I never liked the shop much, it really was the prime example of tatty commercialism but it soon clothed half the fucking Bob Bank due to its catchy 'Sign of our Time' theme clothing.

To me, it undermined the whole idea of dressing smartly, which was to look like one of the boys by dressing according to your own peculiarities. Soon, the vagaries of football fashion became the mass-produced and mass-marketed overpriced spawn of the ad man and his merry shareholders.

Trainers – this area was probably the most important part, and the most valued opportunity to look the part by standing apart. This is well documented and my brother is right in saying

Adidas Gazelles were a must back then. We must not forget Samba and Forest Hills. New Balance were much fancied by a few of my mates who could dress a little and fight a little too. Nike were shite as far as I was concerned – too American, hence too commercial. Pumas were the business, as were Reebok with that British flag that reminded you that you were part of a scene that was a white working-class British phenomenon and there's fuck all wrong with that. But Adidas were the mother superior of footwear, still are.

Shirts or T-shirts were resplendent in the sunshine. Pity, we saw fuck all sun at football but when the sun shone so did the polo T-shirts by Ralph Lauren, Hugo Boss and Helly Hanson. The football Casual scene was very cliquey and finicky. In fact, I would not wear a particular brand if someone I hated was wearing it. In the late '80s, the area of Merthyr I was from was embroiled in a feud with these boys from an area called the Brecon Road. Because a few of them wore Helly Hanson, that was it, to this day I have never bought it.

Shirts. To me, Ben Sherman stands alone here, followed by Ralph Lauren. With shirts, the label does not matter, though, it is the style, which must be button-down collars, long sleeve and asymmetrical patterns, no dots or any hint of roundness!

Needless to say, Burberry was to shirts what Stone Island is to jackets, although wearing their gear is tantamount nowadays to wearing a sign saying hello, everyone, I too am a famous football hooligan.

Jumpers invariably consisted of varying colours of Polo by Ralph Lauren. That jumper was so fucking omnipresent that it became a

The Fashion of Football

question of what colour can I buy that no fucker else has? I never bothered with buying many, preferring to purchase the old school (by then) diamond Pringle V-neck. I am a big lover to this day of V-neck with button-down shirt underneath. Now that's class! Must not forget Soviet, a much-loved must for so many.

Until the mid-1990s, I couldn't care less for hats, but I did become a fan of the baseball hat, which looks nice with a long-sleeved shirt draped over cords.

Last but not least – jackets, which, like the trainer, formed the epicentre of the Casual look. All rival hooligans will check your coat and your shoe leather, and so looking the part was a chance to have one over on them. Indeed, to many, dressing better than a rival firm was as important as outfighting them. In the late '80s, I was very young, a teenager, and so fighting was not much of an option.

The smartest jackets were for winter time – Berghaus, Gore-tex (I loved that mountaineering jacket), Stone Island, plus Timberland made a few nice ones, too.

Summertime, it was Polo by Ralph Lauren, some of which could be worn in winter, Burberry and an expensive Armani number if you had the cash. Thinking about it, back on the old Bob Bank in the late '80s, the Polo by Ralph Lauren was our very own forerunner to the Stone Island syndrome, hence my belief that the Casual scene was very much hijacked and held hostage by the corporations by the time I was attempting to shed the quintessentially British disease of deference by showing the snooty-nosed middle classes I could look smart.

The notion that we all worked hard for our

clothing is very true for the most expensively dressed. My brother and a select few had good jobs and could afford to indulge in very expensive clothing from Conduit Street, London. But for the majority, we had to scrimp and save, and to a few it was a case of smash and grab, and we all encouraged it if it meant nice clothing at cheaper prices, if we're honest. There was no let up, either, I know so-called friends who would sell you cheaper jumpers with a home-made designer label. Some of these extol the virtues of clothing as the spawn of comradeship and bonding . . . bollocks, don't believe the hype, as they say.

Nevertheless, necessity is the mother of invention or being skint is the generous source of ingenuity, so to speak. I would budget and then choose more carefully, the irony being I would find myself looking as smart or even smarter than my brother on occasion due to my more ruthless shopping habits. I would trawl the market stalls, not for labels but for nice, smart straight-leg jeans in varying colours, which I loved wearing at a time when some were braving flares.

Please remember, some of my most prized items were often the cheapest, like jumbo cords that I picked up from an Asian market stall in Merthyr and a smart navy-blue jacket with the parallel white stripe at the edge of the zip, class. Neither ever had a label, but I didn't care, as to me, it was about feeling good about yourself and not a proclamation that you could afford expensive tastes. Dressing up was and is a pick-me-up, a mood-setter, so to speak. It was about individuality, street chic, not high-street consumerism.

For me, it will remain how you looked in a

The Fashion of Football

certain array of garments not 'look at me in this commercialised advertisement of insignias'. Fucking tragic when you think about it.

'I love that phrase,' I said. 'Adidas is the mother superior of all footwear. Great line. This stuff is good. It gives a really good list of the labels and you get a real taste of what clothes mean to him and his boys. I like the political angle as well. It's very real round their way. His brother Jonathan was telling me that when Thatcher kicks it, they're holding a big fuck-off street party. Matthew is like that as well, a real Lacoste leftie. He was telling me that in the '30s when the Communist Party was recruiting, they were told to wear smart suits otherwise the working-class guys wouldn't even look at them. And people tell me clothes are superficial, eh? It's like with Ronnie Lane [of the Small Faces]. If he had worn a shabby Oxfam blazer, dirty jeans, had long hair and never smiled, he would be up there with Nick Drake but . . .'

'OK, son. Calm down, take it easy, preaching to the converted here, mate, and I got to get back to work soon. Talking of which, this is from a guy I actually work with. He's Scottish, a Celtic man. I gave him some questions and this is what he's come back with. His name is Sam Monie, really good guy.'

'OK, let's have a look.'

Clothes on the terraces, for me, have always been about how sharp you look. At Celtic, the lads I went with were always moving with what was in at the time, taking the labels straight off the catwalk onto the terraces. Over the years, the names we all wore were stuff like Pony, Adidas, New Balance, Pepe, Levi's and tops by Ocean Pacific. Relay was big, very big. Once, we turned up wearing Christian Dior shirts and Valentino jeans and those nice tan Timberlands. I went from £25 Adidas trainers to £110 Timberlands without blinking. We were the dog's balls!!

Now what I see on the terraces is that same mix occurring yet again. Only the names have changed. You now have Aquascutum and Burberry, Prada and Gucci. The desire to look crisp on a Saturday afternoon is still there. We wanted to stand out, be admired, be separate from the ordinary fans in their team colours.

I was originally into the Mod scene. I loved the music as well, the two things – fashion and sounds – go hand in hand. It was a natural progression to move on to the Casual scene. I went to football more than anything else and that sharpness came with me from Mod to Casual.

Casual, that's what I was. To be seen wearing the best designer gear was what it was all about. 'Plastic Casual' we would shout at others in inferior gear. All the top boys had the best stuff and that's what we aspired to be – top boy. The ritual was to go down to the shops first thing in the morning to get the new top, shirt, trousers, trainers, whatever and then shoot back to the pub or town square and pose. All the talk was about what you had on. Where did you get it? Who made it? How much was it?

Then off to the game, where you would meet up with other Casuals and the comparisons would start again. At the game, you would look at what the enemy, the opposing fans, had on. We would shout through the wire fence separating us, 'With that shit kit on, you look like you shop at British Home Stores, ya plastic Casual, ya supporting a shit plastic football club!'

Now, I don't particularly go for one label, brand or style. Sometimes I like the smarter stuff, or I may go for the hip-hop, B-boy, skater look. It is still label-orientated,

The Fashion of Football

though. I can't be arsed to trawl for 'Dead
Stock' Adidas or whatever, as much as I like
them. Re-issues don't feel the same, so I go for
skate shoes, which is still a bit elitist. I
know when I go to JD Sports, they'll have the
latest Nike, Adidas and Puma, but they won't
have what I've got on, namely a lovely pair of
DVSs. That comes from me once being a Casual.
Labels I keep an eye out for are Stussy, X-
Large, Bathing Ape and Maharishi. Their kit is
in a class of its own.

I placed the email back on the table and said, 'See, this is why a lot
of people don't like the Mod thing. You see that bit where he's going
on about having a go at people for wearing inferior clothes, that's
why some people have problems with it. They see it as elitist, it runs
against their notions of equality.'

'Yeah, but it's not serious, is it?' Mark replied. 'It's just another
way of taking the piss or having a go at someone.'

'I know but a lot of them really don't understand the art of taking
the piss, which is why they get really offended. It happened to me
all the time in the music press. Anyway, his stuff about getting the
clothes in the morning and then styling them in the afternoon is
very Italian. That's what they do in Sorrento, dress up and then walk
around the main square showing off their clothes.'

'He makes that Mod connection, as well.'

'Another one who's read my book. Anything else?'

Mark pulled out another sheet of paper. 'This guy is called Will, ran
a shop on the Walworth Road called Whitehall Clothiers, knocking out
all the stuff. He makes some interesting points. Have a look.'

Hi Mark,
This story begins when the writer Dave Rimmer
did an article in *The Face* magazine and it was
followed by a call from the *Evening Standard* to
say they would also like to have a chat. I told
him that the real start for us here in the shop
was when Farah slacks became big, then Gabicci,

then Lacoste, which was always the best quality. Gabicci was named after a holiday resort in Italy, it's called Gabicca, I think [probably Gabicce Mare, Marche]. Anyway, it was a massive garment in and around Brixton.

With the Lacoste stock, the supplier would only let certain people have it in this area. What's never mentioned is that girls were also wearing this stuff. They were really into Farahs, Lacoste and Lois Jeans, which was a massive seller, so it was a great time, with lots of coordination then.

As a retailer, it was a dream time. If you can get the kids into buying a range, you have cracked it. Obviously, it had its place on the terraces, but also the pop world helped, with the Wham! boys wearing the Fila shorts etc. Good sellers, them, at £25 a pop. There was only one music show at the time, *Top of the Pops*, and a lot of suppliers were trying to get their products worn by singers and groups on that because if you did that, you had cracked it.

Originally, Farahs were worn on the golf course – Howard Clark was their big model at the time. Consequently, Pringle jumpers also followed from the course. Lacoste came from the tennis world, as did Fred Perry. Ivan Lendl became a figure for Adidas and, of course, Björn Borg, who was wearing Diadora. As for Nike, the first style I can remember was one called Martin Mulligan, named after an Australian tennis player.

At this time, I have to say that London was in advance of everywhere else, at least six months ahead in some cases. I used to have firms ringing me up from Liverpool, and Portsmouth especially. I didn't realise how influential it was in a street-fashion way.

It was a smart period, a lot like the Mod scene in some ways. We were lucky to be a small shop at this time. We weren't lumbered with loads of stock 'cos the styles changed pretty quick, and we could get it in and sold before most of the high street stores, who were really asleep, in all honesty. Also, with all the bombings in the West End, people tended to stay local, so we benefited from all of that.

Another thing I've noticed is that it was also a black *and* white thing, worn by all cultures. A lot of black kids today are into Avirex leather jackets and you don't see many white kids wearing that but this was right across the board really. We even had fellas of 55 wearing it and no one thought it odd, a bit of a taxi-driver look, if you know what I mean.

People forget how expensive some of the clothes were. A Borg Fila tracksuit was £125, a lot of money now, in all honesty. You could see it was breaking the mum's heart to part with that sort of money, but it had to be done. Björn Borg let us down a bit by packing it in. It's like with Beckham now, whatever he wears, it's got to have an effect.

At the moment, he's an individual with his own style, sometimes smart, sometimes urban. As a retailer, we need him to pick one label and we can then cane it! Mind you, we had to have security on the door, we were taking a lot of dough, and there was always the chance someone was gonna be on their toes out of the shop with some of the gear.

The scene started to wane for us around 1985-6. Those days, a style could be around for a couple of years but now, especially in

the kids' age ranges, it's over in six months.
They were great years.

'I like the fact he brings girls into it,' I pointed out. 'This girl was having a go at me the other day, asking where the girls were in all this business. He also brings in the taxi-driver look. He's talking about that Del Boy look, isn't he?'

'That's right, the Farah slacks, nice top and some tomfoolery.'

'Jewellery?'

'What else? There's also a mate of mine, Danny Walters, who was a main mover round my way. He's writing his memoirs at the moment. He told me that a lot of the Millwall mob wore lab coats on the terraces, as they didn't want to fuck up their expensive gear. He also sent me a Casuals alphabet.'

'Really?'

'It goes something like Aquascutum, Burberry, Cecil Gee, Dior, Ellesse, Fiorucci, Gucci, House of Fraser, Ice, Jaeger, Kappa, Lyle and Scott, Pringle and Yves Saint Laurent. Zee was the last one. A few missing but you get the idea. He used to get his stuff from Will in Whitehall Clothiers, and then run over to the record shop opposite and get the latest tunes. He also went to a shop called Moda. Moda was a real social club. People met on a Saturday to work out what to wear, where to go.'

'I've met that Moda guy. I tried to interview him but he would never get back to me.'

'Wonder why. Anyway, have a read of some of Danny's stuff.'

One shop we 'visited' was Rufus. Back in the '60s, they sold the Ivy League gear and then they gradually started to stock the Casual labels. We used to go 'fishing' down there on a regular basis. You got a rod, stuck it thru' the letter box, hooked something and reeled it in, mate! The best place for the trainers was Munich 72, down towards Southwark Park Road.

Around this time, I produced a 'newspaper' called the *Walworth Remix*, where I detailed who was wearing what, going out with who, where we

The Fashion of Football

were all drinking. It became quite a famous little thing for a while. People were actually getting into rucks in pubs in the hope that I would write about it and they would get in the paper! We only did three or four issues. Unfortunately, one night I got stopped by the Old Bill who were interested in what I was carrying. He had a look thru' the paper and people started to get worried 'cos now the Old Bill knew what they was up to! I am thinking of re-launching it actually, now everyone is older . . .

I handed back the paper to Mark. 'I love the fishing-rod story,' I said. 'That's how they should liven up those country programmes on TV. OK, take your rod, stand back, now whip it through the window . . . that's it, hook one of those shirts . . .'

'Class, isn't it? And that stuff about the lab coats? You know who the Casuals fought a lot with, round about '79, '80, don't you?' Mark said.

'Go on.'

'Mods. You know the revival lot from 1979? Them. Huge rucks sometimes. Some Casuals used to go to Carnaby Street looking for them.'

'You're joking.'

'Nah, check this.' He slid another email towards me.

'This is a guy called Paul Hallam. Big DJ on the Mod scene and a Millwall fan. He's just bought that pub Filthy McNasty's in Islington. Anyway, he goes up to Birmingham to DJ and then has to catch the train back to London. Check this.'

Innocence and stupidness meant that I never thought to think that boarding a train out of Birmingham at 5.30 on a Saturday afternoon when Aston Villa were hosts to West Ham would be foolhardy and downright dangerous. I was eighteen, dressed in a tight suit, wearing cycling shoes, carrying two boxes of records and looking downright camp. I couldn't have looked further removed from the packed carriages of ICF [West Ham gang] and wannabes that accompanied me.

As I got on the train after the ICF, I was forced to stand for most of the journey. In my carriage, a pretty girl who looked as confused but probably not as frightened as me and a businessman reading a newspaper were the only other passengers apart from those who were sporting wedge haircuts and talking of blood in the Holte End [Villa Park].

For the first ten minutes or so, nobody seemed to notice me. I put my hold-all and records up on the luggage rack and stood trying to fit in with the crowd. Tales of taking Portsmouth in a Cup game and of pub-football rivalry were far more interesting than an 18-year-old suited-up ponce. Then somebody about 15 feet away spotted me.

'Odd bod Mod! Odd bod Mod!' came the chant from a Gabicci-wearing Casual. I stupidly turned my head as if to acknowledge it was me that they were talking to. 'Mod wanker, what you doing on here?' my new acquaintance asked. I smiled, making me look even more camp and vulnerable.

'How do you know he's a Mod?' asked Casual number two, whose wedge was blonder and floppier than the first.

'Look at the shoes, they're Mod shoes and he ain't one of us,' commented Casual number one.

Suddenly some British Transport Police came into the carriage, averting attention from me. I was forgotten for a short while. Then my luck changed. The businessman got up and got off the train. Very bravely, I took his seat and slipped in opposite the pretty girl. My records

The Fashion of Football

were safe up top and I was comfortably tucked into the corner.

The conversation turned back to the recent ICF play about 'knockers' and 'Did you see Dave, Alan, whoever in the TV show?' The wedge to end all wedges came along the carriage and asked who'd seen his performance on the programme. More banter followed. They had forgotten all about me.

'Was there a fight today?' the pretty girl suddenly asked. Why was she talking to them???

'No, we don't fight. We just go for the football, the booze, and then go home and fight with the wife.'

'Are you married?' she asked.

'We're all married to West Ham, darling.' Cue to all to start singing 'I'm Forever Blowing Bubbles'.

More talk of local rivalry and then somebody realises that Millwall (my team) are playing away that day. The plan was laid. 'We can get to Euston, head up to King's Cross, have a beer and wait for the bastards to come in.'

I am a Millwall supporter and, bearing in mind I was wearing an ice-blue suit *sans* wedge, they would all have assumed that I was far too gay to like football. I don't know why it took them so long but we were heading towards the London suburbs before somebody spotted my records up top.

'Whose fucking records are those?' I looked out the window. 'I said whose fucking records are those?'

'Er, mine.'

'What you got in them then, Mod?'

I shrugged. There wasn't much point in explaining that I'd recently picked up a fantastic Calypso-Ska compilation on early

Second Half

Island or a British Beat version of Mel Tormé's 'Comin' Home Baby'. 'Records,' I replied weakly.

'What's in the Mod box?' one taunted.

Great. I was going to lose my records and my life. Great.

Then a bigger bloke appeared who had been sitting in the row of seats behind me. He was slightly older than most of the wedges and had shorter hair, and had on a rather smart-looking crew-neck jumper with a smart-looking shirt beneath. 'You a Mod?'

Wasn't much point in denying it. Short of wearing a parka or having The Who tattooed on my forehead, there wasn't a lot to suggest otherwise. Non-Mods didn't dress like this for at least another ten years.

I nodded weakly.

'I was a Mod once,' he said. 'Did you see The Jam at Brighton last year?'

I hadn't but nodded and hoped he didn't ask me any questions about it.

'Do you know . . .' and then reeled off a list of Mods who I was probably destined to meet in the very, very near future. Although our chat was brief and my part of the conversation was generally limited to nodding or shaking my head politely, it gave me the opportunity to deny the Casuals a chance to destroy me or my records. Euston was approaching and thoughts were more focused on ambushing Millwall and getting down the pub than on taunting the young Mod.

The train stopped and off they all piled. The ICF chanted a few more songs and off they disappeared into the night. I sat for about ten minutes until a guard asked me to get off the train. Where was he when I needed him? Off I trundled and back to the safety of Mod World.

What was bizarre was that today or indeed perhaps any time since the early to mid-' 90s, I could have travelled on the train unnoticed by the football crowd. I have in recent years been to Millwall and seen Noel Gallagher lookalikes, full on twenty-first century Mods with backcombs and not dressed too dissimilar to the young 18-year-old Mod some years earlier, without anybody batting an eyelid. But back in the early '80s, football had a distinct uniform and it wasn't the uniform of Mod, for sure.

'Close escape,' I said. 'Actually, I forgot to tell you this but on one of the websites, this guy reckons that the police started visiting a few Stone Island outlets because so many of the guys were wearing the gear. That explains why they didn't want to get involved with this book.'

'It does make sense,' Mark replied, 'but they could have said something, though, instead of giving us the old silent treatment.'

'Tell me about it. Look, reading Paul's stuff, do you think we should be looking at the music connection a bit more? There's a guy I know called Mick Robinson. Runs the Hotel Pelirocco in Brighton. He was in a Casual band called The Accent and I'm pretty sure they actually played at Chelsea football ground. It's a good tie-up.'

'Well, if you can get hold of him, have a word.'

'In his shell-like, in his ear?'

'Exactly.'

As it happened, Mick Robinson (or Ginger Mick, as he is known) and his partner Jane kept a flat in North London quite near to me. I arranged to meet him at a local pub, The Larrik. It was a Monday night in cold February.

Mick was a Soul Stylist, someone who had gone through the Mod, Suedehead and Casual line with football ever present. He was Chelsea through and through, as was Jane. At their hotel Brighton, climb the stairs to the first floor and on the left-hand side you will see a huge 40 x 40, head-and-shoulders picture of Alan Hudson with one of the best haircuts in the world.

In the early '80s, Mick had formed a band called The Accent along with two other Casuals. Stuart, who ran a Casual clothing shop called Stuart's in Shepherd's Bush, managed the band. In 1984, as the band started to make a name for itself, Chelsea were promoted from the Second Division. Their last home game was party time. 'We got wind that they were going to have a promotion party with music,' Mick recalls. 'We were down there one day and, by a fluke chance, we saw Ken Bates. He was a bit more accessible then, so was the ground. You could walk in any time. Anyway, we said to him, we're in a band, can we play before the game? And he just went, all right then, leave your number with the secretary and arrange it. Which we did.

'They gave us passes, put all the gear up before the game and that was it. We played Stamford Bridge. In fact, you could say the band started off in stadiums and worked its way down!'

The band set up on the touchline and played four songs at about two in the afternoon. What's interesting is that prior to playing they also sought out a main Chelsea fan called Icky, asked his permission to play. It was when Icky gave them his blessing, not Bates, that the gig was on.

'We thought we were going to get things thrown at us,' Mick reveals, 'but we got a pleasant round of applause. We played when the ground was filling up so there were probably five to ten thousand there. We played in front of the East Stand but surprisingly we weren't that nervous.' The gig was perhaps the highlight of their career. Bands who rally round cults always have a limited shelf-life.

'Initially, it worked using the clothes thing,' Mick said, 'because it got us a bit of press but, eventually, once they had written about it, there was nothing else to say. Plus, musically, I don't think we were that competent. We couldn't take it any further. It just petered out.'

We started talking about other bands that had connections with football. Both of us thought that The Faces were the first to really draw football into rock culture. Their lead singer, Rod Stewart, had nearly gone into the game via trials with Brentford. At their concerts, Rod would often kick balls into the crowd and every year he would be photographed at the England v. Scotland game. In interviews, whilst other musicians talked up their concept albums or love for glam rock, Rod spoke about football with passion and sense.

'I remember going to the Reading Festival to see The Faces in '73,'

The Fashion of Football

I told Mick, 'and John Peel was DJing and at about five in the afternoon he started giving out the results, which was kind of weird. Apart from Rod, very few musicians spoke about football. It was too un-hip.'

'Different days now,' Mick replied.

'I know,' I said. 'I'm getting quite bored of everyone going on about it. Although, that guy Tony Rivers who runs with the Soul Crew said something interesting. He said he liked all these people getting involved if it meant that his club, Cardiff, was going to benefit financially. Which is a good point.'

'Yeah, I suppose it wasn't until Oasis that it picked up again,' Mick said.

'Well, you had that awful New Order record which everyone thought was great. But, yeah, Oasis, their fashion at first was definitely terrace gear,' I said. 'They were a bit like The Faces as well except that instead of one band member harping on about football, it was three of them – Noel, Liam and Guigsy. In fact, one of their best songs, 'Acquiesce', was written for Manchester City but then Noel kept it back for the band.'

A funny story came to mind. 'When I was writing my biography of the band, Noel invited me along to meet Francis Lee at the Man City training ground,' I told Mick. 'The club wanted to talk to him about business or some kind of tie-up. Anyway, we get there and Franny Lee is sitting at a table so we go over. Franny says, "Hello, Noel."

'Noel goes, "How ya doing? This is Paolo."

'Franny looks at me and says, "What's your name?"

'"Paolo," I replied.

'"Ah, Paolo. You Noel's chef then?" He was absolutely serious. Foreign name, must be a chef. Hilarious. Anyway, after Oasis, everyone got into football. It was like part of the routine in interviews, say you're Britpop, you take drugs and you're into football. Some bands were genuine, though. The Super Furrys did that single about Robin Friday, "The Man Don't Give A Fuck".'

'Did you ever hear that band Glamorous Hooligan? They were definitely football heads, wearing all the gear,' Mick said.

'I know the guy, Dean Cavanagh. He's a script writer now. Didn't think about them. I think they were signed to Warners or an off-shoot or something. Great name for a band. Actually, Mick, we've forgotten the main men,' I said. 'Chas 'n' Dave – "Ossie's on his way to Wembley, Tottenham going to do it again".'

Mick laughed. 'You'd do better to listen to The Accent.'

* * *

The next day, I was back in Bar Italia, reporting to Mark on the interview with Mick. 'It went well,' I told him. 'It's a great connection – a mix of music, clothes and football, the eternal trinity – plus we spoke about other bands who were part of the football thing. In fact, Mick and I ended up discussing the merits of none other than Chas 'n' Dave. Due for a comeback soon, that lot, I'm telling you.'

'You know I was once a Casual, don'tcha?' Mark said.

'Didn't know that.'

'Yeah, I was bang into it when I was much younger.'

'Where did you get your stuff?' I asked.

'Well, say you went away on a school trip and . . .'

'Hang on a sec, hang on a sec, I've got an idea.'

'Go on, son, what you got?'

'Well, you know how you're always saying that what you do is proper work, getting up at five in the morning, having to deal with all kinds of people etc., etc. and that I have it real easy, getting up when I like, sitting at home writing when I feel like it?'

'Yeah.'

'Well, why don't you write something for the book? See how easy it is then.'

'OK, son, I will. I'll get on the old keyboard tonight.'

'Good. I'll expect your report on my desk first thing tomorrow.'

Mark Baxter on the World of Casuals

I was part of the label madness that was the world of the Casuals. Everyone in my immediate circle was. You *had* to be one. You were either a Casual or you were classed as a State [i.e. in a state, badly dressed]. At its height, we became obsessed with tracking down all the latest designs and labels that hit big-time in and around South London. As with all clothing cults over the years, be they Mod, Skin or

The Fashion of Football

Suedehead, there was always one or two kids who set the pace. They'd wear something first and, within a week, we all had it on. Word would go round that a shop on Tanners Hill in Lewisham had cheap Lois jeans, 'but keep it to yourself, we don't want everyone sussing it', and you would bomb down there and, when you arrived, there were big queues of the like-minded outside, and you thought you had the inside information! Nothing stayed a secret for too long, there were simply too many punters chasing the same cloth. The big purchase for me at the time was buying a burgundy Lacoste polo shirt at Whitehall Clothiers on the Walworth Road. I remember it costing me £35, which was a lot of money to me back in 1980, but I *had* to have it. To not buy it would have left me on the sidelines among the kids wearing the cheap 'Le Shark' copies and you wouldn't want that.

We used to try and outdo each other in getting the latest 'in' gear first. Buying trainers in Europe whilst away on school trips, and then wearing them down at Millwall and really enjoying everyone asking you where you got them, and you'd reply, 'Switzerland, mate. Can't get 'em over here.' As with all these trends, people move on and I eventually began to favour a more Mod look but, at the time, I loved it.

But you know what? In some ways, I wish it hadn't happened. In my opinion, it's to blame for leaving us with a generation who wear nothing but 'sportswear' and, what's more, they wear it badly. If you look out of any top-deck bus window going from the West End to Peckham, as I do on a daily basis, you look out on a sea of polyester and nylon going by. Tracksuit bottoms, tracksuit tops, hooded tops, crop trousers, polo shirts, T-shirts, all covered with logos of every size. Then there are the 'glorias' in every conceivable colour, all topped off with a baseball cap.

I think I must have slept through a law being passed where it was decreed that if you are between 12 and 25, you can't go out without a bloody baseball cap on! There's the 'chavs' in Burberry, Aquascutum, Nike, Adidas, etc., there's your skater boys being all ironic in their Ed's Garage retro caps or something super-trendy like Bathing Ape, and then there's the more sorted fashion conscious, trotting about in Von Dutch or a snide Louis Vuitton one.

What's worse is that the art of being an individual has disappeared. OK, occasionally you see someone on the street, at football or in a club, and they stand out so much that the image of them stays with you for a long time. One such sighting was a fella I spied in among the Millwall away supporters at Selhurst Park on Boxing Day of last year. He cut through the crowd of baseball caps and track suits, coming towards me wearing a three-quarter-length white mac, Prada shoes and sporting a good haircut. He looked great and it made my heart glad to know that there are people out there who can still stop you in your tracks by looking different.

Sportswear is obviously king now. Nike and the like have won the war for the young pound. The influences have all got mixed up. Football culture with hip hop, hip hop with skater wear. To me, saturation point has been achieved. It's totally global, from Europe to the States.

To an old Mod like me, they all look . . . sloppy, baggy, loose, crumpled, dishevelled . . . . I know I sound like my old man, giving it the

The Fashion of Football

'I despair of the youth of today' speech but I reckon I'm cock on, mate. Last Sunday, I was having a quiet pint at a riverside boozer down in Rotherhithe and two fellas, not particularly young, walked in. They were covered head to toe in Burberry and Aquascutum. Caps, shorts, polo shirts, even socks. It could have been snide, it could have been kosher, I don't know and frankly don't care. The funny thing is, the two visions in check obviously thought they looked good, tasty even. I personally thought they looked ridiculous. No style, no class, the clothes were wearing them, not the other way round. They were settling for the lowest common denominator, thinking, 'everyone has got the same stuff as me on, that'll do nicely'.

Well, it doesn't, and us old Casuals have a lot to answer for.

'What do you reckon? Read it?' Mark asked. Bar Italia, again.

'I did, yeah, and I see your point. But explain something. Chavs? Glorias? – which I presume is something to do with Gloria Jones?'

'You don't know what chavs are? Where the hell have you been for the past year? You put chav into Google and you'll get about 50,000 websites about them. Chavs are like the real underclass and glorias, Gloria Gaynor, trainer. Simple, eh?'

'Your piece made me think about something. Once, in an interview with the DJ Terry Farley, he said that he misses walking down the street and seeing six kids dressed in a way he had never seen before.'

'That's what I mean. Everyone's dressed the same, no one's got any individuality.'

'Blair's Britain, mate, the bland leading the bland. So how did you find writing? Easy, eh?'

'I'll be straight with you. I did find it difficult but, you know what, I really enjoyed it, if that makes any sense.'

'It makes absolutely perfect sense. It's what I've been going through these past 21 years.'

Second Half

■ ■ ■

The Wolverhampton Wanderer

In the summer of 1997, Mark Baxter was standing outside his clothes shop in Camberwell watching the world go by when a car pulled up and out jumped a man Mark recognised as the singer and songwriter Kevin Rowland. 'Here, mate,' Rowland said. 'Look after my car, will you?' Then he dashed off. Five minutes later, Rowland returned, thanked Mark, got back in the car and drove away.

'That is the only time I have met the great man,' Mark told me. 'Love the music, of course. Cracking stuff. The first Dexys album is a blinder. So you think he'll be good for the book, eh?'

It was nine in the morning and we were on a train bound for Brighton, Rowland's current home town. That day, we were interviewing him about clothes, about football, about growing up with obsessions. We were doing so because I knew three things about Rowland. First, he had been a staunch Wolves supporter in the '60s, following them all over the country. Second, he was obsessed with clothes and style. And third, he had an outstanding memory. If anyone could recall what the fans were wearing on the terraces during the '60s and early '70s, this was the man.

'His memory is amazing,' I told Mark. 'When I was doing my *Soul Stylists* book, he told me the month and year the *Daily Mirror* first used the word Skinhead. My girlfriend went to the British Library, looked up the dates: right on the button. I think it is maybe something common to musicians. I've certainly noticed great memory skills in a few others. That and very high sex drives, of course.'

'Best leave that subject to the *News of the World*, eh, son?' Mark said.

Today, the big man was more than happy. He had the day off work, the sun was out and he was on his way to one of his favourite towns. 'Tremendous,' Mark said, stretching out a bit. 'Get up at a good time for once, not bleeding five in the morning, go down to

Brighton, hang out with a top man and then home for the football. Millwall are on tonight. Lovely.'

Mark's enjoyment and enthusiasm at doing this interview reminded me how easy it is to take such things for granted. Doing this job for years, you lose sight of your luck – which is usually when it deserts you.

The pair of us jumped a cab at Brighton Station, arrived at the flat Rowland has lived in for many years. He answered the door dressed simply in jeans and a jumper. The first thing he did was to make us tea. The second thing he did was to start explaining how he had first been entranced by Wolves in 1959 when, as a child of six, he witnessed the club's victory procession through town following their capture of the old First Division title. 'Wolves were the Manchester United of the day,' he stated. Then he turned to Mark. 'What team are you? Tottenham as well?'

'Nah, I'm Millwall, season-ticket holder, been going since 1969.'

'Season-ticket holder,' Kevin said admiringly. 'I remember going to the old Den quite a few times. I remember one game, Derek Dougan scored and a Millwall fan ran on the pitch and punched him.'

'Yeah,' Mark replied. 'They do get a little lively down there.'

Kevin took a sip of tea, assessed Mark again. 'I know you from somewhere,' he said. 'Didn't you use to have a clothes shop in Camberwell?'

It was the first and only time that I have seen the garrulous Mark rendered absolutely speechless.

'Was it down a little alleyway, the shop?' Kevin continued.

'That's right,' Mark said, 'and you pulled up in a car and asked me to look after it. I'm amazed you can remember. Staggering.'

As the man once sang, some things he won't forget. What followed next was an hour and a half chat which, for Mark and I, encapsulated all the themes contained in this book. Kevin Rowland's testimony that day recalled not only the clothes, the shops, the popular styles of the day but also vividly brought to life terrace culture, recalling the songs, the passion but above all the *feel* of being a football fan. So this is what he's like.

Paolo Hewitt: When did you first start getting serious about football?

Kevin Rowland: It wasn't really until we moved to London when I was just, I think, ten or eleven. In between primary and secondary school, we moved to London. And I had planned to support a London team. I planned to support Tottenham, Chelsea, Arsenal or something like that, although I didn't really like football that much. We moved to Harrow and I went to school. I was from Wolverhampton and my accent was really broad, and so I came in for stick straight away. There were Tottenham fans, Chelsea fans, Arsenal fans there. And I was really unlucky because Labour were campaigning to get in, I think, about October '64. There had been Tories in until then.

PH: This was after the Profumo Affair?

KR: Exactly. Anyway, there was this election in '64 and they had drama at this school. It was a big, modern place, a Catholic school, and they got us all up talking about who you were voting for. I knew my mum and dad were voting Labour, so I just said Labour to them. The drama teacher was quite taken with my accent and she goes, now, say what your name is and where are you from, and I went [adopts heavy Midlands accent] my name is Kevin Rowland and I come from Wolverhampton. And that became a fucking catchphrase. All the kids were going, my name is Kevin Rowland and I come from Wolverhampton. I became a cockney within about a fortnight. I became a cockney really quick, but I thought, I'm not going to support your fucking football teams, you know, I'm going to support the Wolves. I kept that little secret defiance inside.

Wolves had just sacked Stan Cullis, like about a month after I had got there. He had managed them since the war. And it wasn't like it is now, where managers are getting sacked all the time. It was very unusual to sack a manager and the papers were in an uproar. 'They've sacked Stan Cullis.' And he'd had all that success with them. And now Wolves were bottom and it wasn't going to get any better. It was terrible. When he got the sack, it was about September or October. I was, like, second or third smallest in the school at that time. Shot up later.

Third or fourth year comes up to me. Oi, you're from Wolverhampton, ain't ya?

I went, yeah.

They sacked Stan Cullis, didn't they?

I went, yeah, and then, bang! He whacked me. They kept doing me, you know. So all this stuff was somehow formative of me. At the same time, there were all these Mods in Harrow and I was really interested in watching all them and what they were wearing and how their hair was.

Then I had my brother Pete, who said to me, Wolverhampton is far tougher than London. You drop half a dozen of these fucking Mods in the middle of Queen's Square, they would be battered. And I'm like [adopts keen kid's voice], yeah, yeah, that's right, that's right. So I believed all this stuff, I really believed it. And I kept this secret thing going on. We went to see Wolves play at Tottenham and we lost 7–4. That was the 1964–65 season. Great game, great game. And there wasn't that many Wolves fans. They didn't travel as much in those days. There was probably about a coachload and that's all there was.

PH: Do you remember what you guys were wearing?

KR: It wasn't until, I mean, to be honest, again, I was still very small, ever so small. We will talk about clothes but I've just got to tell you the experience of it. But I do remember the vibe of it. I think, with the Tottenham fans, there was a big difference between London and the Midlands then. And Wolves fans were kind of probably considered uncouth by a lot of the Tottenham fans. They were rough around the edges, whereas the London ones would be more smooth. I remember big sideburns and all that kind of stuff.

PH: The Wolves fans?

KR: Wolves, like big bushy ones and women as well, all bleached-blonde hair and all that kind of stuff. I remember it was quite good-natured, there wasn't any trouble. There was this song, 'Two, four, six, eight, ten. Fucking hell, we lost again.' That's what Wolves were singing over there.

I saw another game around that season. A mate of mine was a Fulham fan and I went to see Fulham v. West Bromwich Albion and I did notice again this big difference between them and London, they were really quite smooth compared to these sort of quite uncouth and wild Midlanders. Then Wolves got relegated to the old Second Division and I started going quite a bit. There was like Charlton, Millwall. I do remember Wolves were likely to wear things like combat jackets and stuff like that, really. I remember some of the London fans wearing things like deerstalker hats about that time. I think we played Fulham in a Cup game or something. I was about 12 or 13 by that point and getting beaten up, and it was the first time I started to realise, oh, blimey, this is quite serious. I think it was about two of us and about ten of them jumped us.

What happened is that when we went down to the Second Division, a new pride came in. It was so weird. A new pride came out. You would go to away games and the away support had really increased because it gave us something to fight for. It is a weird thing, isn't it?

Mark Baxter: It is very similar at Millwall. If we got in the Premiership, it would be one season, go down, but when we're fighting to survive . . .

KR: Exactly the same thing. I mean, there was hardly more than a coachload at Tottenham in 1964–65. But in the 1965–66 season, all of a sudden there are loads of Wolves fans. I remember a Palace game, and the Wolves fans coming round and handing out bits of paper where they had typed a lyric to a song. At the top, they had put in brackets 'To the tune of "Land of Hope and Glory"'. It was like [sings to the tune] 'Wol-ver-hamp-ton Wan-de-rers, we will follow you. When you play away from home, we will see you though.' I remember, after that game or one of the other games, walking around wearing the colours and feeling really proud. We started to win those games, as well. The first season we finished third or fourth. And then the next season we came right up, you know. I remember walking around Baker Street, probably with my brother, and I saw another Wolves fan, he had a scarf on, and he saw me and he went, 'Wolves fans of the world unite. We alone know what it's like.' Remember that song? That was a hit at the time, 'Lovers of the World Unite'.

At about 12 years of age, I left that Catholic school and I went to this building school in Willesden. And I remember going to see Wolves play Arsenal. I went on my own to that one. There were a couple of Arsenal fans from the school and, as I was getting the Tube, they jumped on the train. And I went into the North Bank and found out there was a load of Wolves fans on the other side, so I walked over to them. I wanted to be with the Wolves fans because, in my mind, they were like these noble people from Wolverhampton. I remember joining them and, in the middle of the North Bank, there were maybe eight, nine Wolves fans. And they were probably older than the Arsenal fans, more like maybe 24, 25. Big fucking sideburns. They were still wearing early '60s London clothes. They had quiffs and stuff like that. They were really, I don't want to be derogatory, but they looked pretty wild. Almost looked gypsy-like. There was a lot of that around Wolverhampton. They looked kind of gypsy-like, really unkempt, you know, compared to all these cockneys that were around them. And there were all these cockneys around them and everywhere, like, I think this is around 1966–67. They were wearing, like, gabardine raincoats, really nice. Beautiful navy, you know, fly-front. And maybe a crew neck underneath, you know, and maybe a button-down shirt. You could just see the top of it. I am not sure what the shirts were, you know, they were wearing nice 501s and they all had their hands behind their back and all that, you know.

One of them was going, come on, there's no Old Bill around. Let's fucking have 'em. But they wouldn't touch us for some reason. And then one of these cockneys went to me, you from Wolverhampton, mate? And I went, yeah, I was a long time ago. I am from Wolverhampton. And he went, oh, I used to live in Sutton Coldfield. Do you know it? I went, yeah, yeah, I know it. And that was it really. There was no trouble there. But I saw a massive difference, like, between them and the Wolves fans. I used to dream and count the days until the games, you know.

PH: Didn't you go to the World Cup final?

KR: I did, yeah.

PH: Yeah? Tell us about that. You bunked in or something?

KR: Certainly did. Entrance F. I don't know what you call them, you know those sort of gates that are zig-zag metal that you can put your hand through? You know those ones?

MB: Concertina, sort of thing?

KR: Concertina thing. For some reason, it was slightly wider at Entrance F. And if anybody pulled it, you'd just about get your head through. If you can get your head through, you're in. And that's how I got in. I was coming back from a holiday with my mum and dad. We'd been to Selsey Bill or somewhere like that, and we were driving back and I said to Dad, can you drop me off at Wembley, the stadium? You know, it was all on the radio, and he said, yeah, I will drop you off. And me mum was in the front, have you got tickets? You've got no tickets, and I went, no, I think I can get in, you know. And she said, you can't get in, you'll be arrested. And me dad went, oh, they'll only throw him out if they catch him. And he dropped me down the bottom of Wembley Way. And I run up. But the game had already started, you know.

PH: When did you get in, the first or the second half?

KR: Second half. I think the second half had started. And I saw Muhammad Ali. He was over fighting Henry Cooper. The game had already started and he couldn't get in. He didn't know where to go actually. I think he was in the wrong bit. So I went to that, yeah, I went to that. That was amazing. I don't remember much clothes culture because it was mostly old blokes.

PH: That's the impression you get from those times about football. It was an old blokes' thing, really.

KR: There was a lot of old blokes. You'd see a lot of old blokes on the way to the game. Loads of old blokes and [pauses, then corrects himself] – no, no, no, it was everybody actually, wasn't it? It was everybody. Do you remember rosettes? I had a Wolves rosette. And I had a rattle, painted gold and black. Painted it myself.

MB: I got a blue and white one from years and years. Still got it. Makes a right noise.

PH: What were you dressed in, in '66?

KR: I was 13. I was into clothes but on a limited budget, very much so. A pair of Levi's, brogues, by then. Were they around? Yes, they were. Brogues and [points to Paolo] jackets like yours . . .

PH: Right, cord jackets.

KR: I think so. [Turns to Mark] That Wolves game we spoke about, at Millwall, '66, '67, where somebody ran on and hit Derek Dougan, they all came round for us afterwards and I was very interested in what they were wearing. They still had Moddy haircuts. If not centre-parting, quite high, [nods to Paolo] probably your length if not a little bit longer. Sideburns coming forward, kind of number. And they were wearing stuff like granddad vests. They were all going to do us but then it turned into a bit of a party. They started having a bit of a party because

The Fashion of Football

they knew they had taken our end completely and shoved us down the front. And they were singing that song, 'All Your Love' by The Troggs. Remember that? 'Give it to me, give it to me, all your love, all your love.' That was a big hit at the time. Got to number one, or had been to number one. And they sang, 'Give it to me, give it to me, LSD, LSD'. That was quite a surprise.

MB: Never heard that before.

PH: They were all on acid. That's probably why they didn't beat you up.

KR: It's like in the '80s when they all started taking Es on the terraces.

PH: These were Mods who became hippies?

KR: I don't think these were hippies. I think they were thugs because, remember, they came round to take our end.

PH: One old Mod I met once said he turned hippy because he took LSD, which in turn made him grow a 'tache and then listen to Jimi Hendrix.

KR: Some of them did and some of them didn't. I don't remember meeting many Mods who had turned into hippies. Mostly they turned into pre-Skinheads but maybe that was just the circles I was mixing in. A lot of them carried on wearing those kind of clothes. I remember V-neck jumpers. I remember like being in Harrow when I was about 15 and there were guys older than me, 21 or 22, with nice short hair, very well cut, nice cardigan, very, very smart still. My own experience outside of football was that, from '67 or '68, I started to get really obsessed with clothes. I started at another school in '68, another Catholic school in Burnt Oak called St James's. And this guy called Tim Brennan was not only the smartest kid in the school but one of the smartest in the area.

MB: There's always one like that.

KR: He didn't really follow football but one day he said to me that there was a shop where all the really smart geezers go. It's in London in Brewer Street. And he took me to the Squire Shop. I couldn't believe it. First of all, it was a tiny little shop. And I remember the other thing I couldn't believe was seeing shoes like that, exactly like that [points to Mark's burgundy brogues bought in, ironically enough, John Simon]. They looked weird but at the same time they looked fantastic. They were really clumsy looking compared to what was

Second Half

going on in the '60s, which, don't forget, was that dainty dandy kind of thing. [Tiny, wafer-thin soles, etc.]

And they had the shirts in there and then over the next sort of year the whole thing built and built and built, and, by summer of '69, there was that first article. [The one that used the word Skinhead for the first time in the *Daily Mirror*, September 1969] By late '69, that thing had exploded, you know, but really its peak was summer '69 for me. I remember thinking, I'm really part of something here.

PH: Were you still going to football then?

KR: Yeah, I was. I left school February '69 and I got a job in Dunn & Company, the clothes shop, so I had to work Saturdays. But I took the holidays in August of that year and I went up to Wolves, and I started to see what was going on up there. I went to a West Ham match, probably early '69, and I saw what they were wearing. They were wearing sheepskins and trilby hats, button-down shirts, cardigans. They were looking really good. They were all about 15 or 16 years old and I remember thinking, how the fuck do they afford a sheepskin, which was like fifty quid, a fortune in the those days.

PH: I know. Crombies were £40.

KR: Yeah, a good one, a proper one. So I went up to Wolves. The first game I went to was Coventry away and, to be honest, Wolves were a significant level of time behind London, in terms of fashion. The Wolves fans were wearing denim Levi jackets and jeans, or Wranglers. They were wearing their tops with Wranglers, whereas, in London, Wranglers were just nowhere. We went and got the train up there and I was wearing a Harrington jacket. I had short hair, with Sta-Prest trousers, a button-down shirt. The Wolves fans were all wearing denim jackets, blue denim jeans, but they were Skinheads. They had short hair. It was just amazing. All the fans congregating outside Coventry Station waiting, loads and loads and loads of young kids.

PH: When you say these kids were young – 14, 15?

KR: About 14, 15, 16, 17 and some older. Anyway, we were outside Coventry Station and the police are actually starting to panic because there were so many. They didn't seem to have football under control at that point. Football violence was really starting

The Fashion of Football

to get big then. It really was getting massive. This is '69. This is my experience of it. About '69, it's big. I mean like I say, there were 5,000. I am only guessing but there were a few thousand Wolves fans there outside Coventry Station. The police just couldn't control them. And they were all singing, 'Harry Roberts, Harry Roberts is our friend . . .'

MB: [Sings] 'He kills coppers . . .'

KR: 'He kills coppers', that's the one. 'Harry Roberts is our friend, is our friend.' Is he still around, Harry Roberts?

MB: He's still inside, yeah. Trying for parole. When there's a bit of trouble at Millwall and the police come up, they always sing that song.

KR: So, we were all singing, 'Harry Roberts is our friend'. And then everyone was just running through Coventry after that because it was exciting when you're 15. It was very exciting. How are you going to resist that? You can run through the shops, do whatever you want. Police couldn't control us. Then we went to the game, I think we were in the West Stand.

I remember what the Coventry fans were wearing as well. They were wearing granddad vests and I thought at the time they looked ridiculous. I tell you why. Hippies were wearing granddad vests. In London, that's what hippies wore. You wouldn't be seen dead in one. Yet, these Coventry Skinheads were wearing them, although they didn't seem to be wearing the denim thing. They had some kind of jeans, I think. Jungle greens were popular in London. I used to wear them. Jungle greens. West Ham fans wore those. They were almost like, they were a little bit like combat trousers.

PH: And what were they singing?

KR: There was a big change then. I remember in '67, staying with my cousins in Coventry, and going to matches and hearing songs like, 'Go home you bums, go home you bums, go home you bums, go home you bums' or 'I hear the sound [claps hands], I hear the sound [claps hands], of distant bums, over there, over there'. It was still polite-ish.

I can remember George Curtis, who was a big Coventry player who had broken his leg or something, and then he came back. It was his first game back. It was '67 when I was there and I remember, 'A welcome back for George. A welcome back for

George. A welcome back for George'. It sounded quite polite.

And then coming back to Midlands football in 1969, a significant change had taken place. A massive change had taken place between '67 and '69. Massive. Everybody, it seemed, was so much more up for it, everybody wanted to be part of the violence. It was part of the match experience by then.

PH: Maybe it was to do with transport improvements because, after '66, motorways were opened so football fans could travel a lot more easily, and maybe that's why it turned uglier. Away fans having more of a presence.

KR: That's probably true.

PH: And after the World Cup, was there a huge explosion of interest in football? A bit like this England rugby thing at the moment.

KR: Massive. Massive. Like I say, that 1964–65 season, Wolves bringing a coachload. Then a year later, when we're in the Second Division, and all of a sudden there's hundreds.

PH: I did a book called *The Soul Stylists* and this guy was saying he was a Leicester fan and the first time he saw the first Skinhead was when Chelsea fans came to Filbert Street. Because fans could travel, the fashions would spread.

KR: Definitely, definitely, absolutely 210 per cent. That's how these Wolves fans sort of dressed like that. But they were a long way behind.

PH: And could you get the right gear in those towns?

KR: In Wolverhampton, there was a shop called Eddie's. I've got cousins there and they told me there was a shop called Eddie's that did sell it.

PH: So, I suppose in each place there must have been one shop in every town.

KR: I mean, it started to come in but they wouldn't have it right. They'd have, like, brogues but not like that [points to Mark's shoes]. They'd have the brogues that people were wearing in London in about '67 or '68. You could get Levi's anywhere. Levi's were nationwide, they weren't a problem. Get them in any Millets. You could get denim jackets anywhere. What happened is Ben Shermans and Brutus came out pretty quick and started to come in. And they were all wearing those Jaytex shirts. So, yeah, where were we?

The Fashion of Football

PH: 1969.

KR: I went to a Derby game, Wolves and Derby. I was off work. I tell you what was popular as well – a lot of people would wear suit jackets and jeans.

MB: I've spoken to a couple of Chelsea and QPR fans, and they've said that was big on the terraces.

KR: Especially in London. Chelsea wore that a lot, very, very smart. A suit jacket and jeans. Interestingly, the Sloanes started wearing that in the sort of late '70s or '80s. Not quite as smart, though. It was a bit more of a country-look thing, do you know what I mean? And I suppose about five or six years ago, it came into fashion again. It's mainstream fashion now, isn't it?

I remember those Duffer of St George guys started wearing it. The blokes who worked in there. About six years ago, they were all like suit jacket and jeans. But I would also have my friends in Harrow, who were Chelsea fans, Tottenham fans, Arsenal fans. I would sometimes go to those games, you know. Chelsea is a significant one.

PH: Definitely.

KR: I remember going to see Wolves at Chelsea about May '69 and going to the other end, to The Shed or whatever it was called. And I first heard about this gang called the Rising Sun Crew because there was a pub nearby called The Rising Sun. And when I first heard about them, I couldn't understand it because somebody told me that they never bought programmes, they never wore colours. It was the first time I had ever heard of that. It became a big thing later on but at this time it was unique. They stayed in the pub until the game started and they came in afterwards. But they wouldn't go in The Shed. They went the other end. And that's the first time I had really seen that. And they never sang songs. They looked really cool and they wouldn't be seen dead in The Shed or anything.

PH: What sort of things were they wearing?

KR: I knew you'd ask me that. For some reason, I can't remember. I think standard clothes, you know. Probably a bit more subtle. Slightly longer hair, they were a little older than your average Shed boys as well.

That was the first time that I had ever heard of a bunch of fans starting the game the other end, you know. Yeah, they often come around because, in those days, incredibly, you could just walk around, all the way around. Chelsea certainly.

MB: Millwall was the same.

KR: Yeah, you could just walk all the way around. In the summer of '70, a friend of mine, Pany, who is a Greek guy and a Chelsea fan, told me about a Chelsea fan who was just way ahead of everybody else with clothes. He had started undoing the buttons on the collar of his button-down shirt, which gave it the look of a West End fashion shirt, which is what the 'hairies' were wearing, which previously you definitely wouldn't want your shirt to look like. But he started undoing it and then growing his hair long. And he was still wearing brogues and everything, but his hair was long. It had grown right out. And that was the start of that, really. People started growing their hair long. Shirts were the first thing to go. People started buying West End fashion shirts and then they started buying penny-round collar shirts and the trousers started to go. By '72, it was all out. It was great big wide trousers. It was Toppers, suede shoes, you know. I had a great big pink tweed trench coat that was massive. Great big lapels out here, but flared right out, great big pockets.

MB: Where did you get it?

KR: It might have been from Take Six. Take Six was a big shop and it was easy to steal from as well. It was high fashion.

MB: It wasn't really run-of-the-mill stuff, was it?

KR: It was high fashion, you know, multi-coloured patterned shirts with wide collars. It was the start of that '70s look, which was quite similar to a '40s look. Do you remember? The wide lapels and the wide trousers, do you know what I mean? With quite high-waisted pants. That was the first time that sort of nostalgia started to come in as well, wasn't it?

MB: I always equate Take Six with the West End because around where I live, Camberwell, it was all little boutiques, all just independent shops, really. Stocked the latest gear or what they thought was the latest gear. But Take Six was the sort of shop you saw in the West End.

KR: I tell you another – Village Gate. There were a few Village Gates around London. There was one on Old Compton Street, I think, because the Squire Shop had pretty much changed. The

The Fashion of Football

commendable thing about the Squire Shop, or the interesting thing about it, was as soon as that Skinheady thing started to happen, they changed. They started to change. They were still selling it but they started to do wide-lapel jackets. And that's what people were wearing as well. Wide lapels in corduroy and velvet. [Pauses.] Does anybody want a cup of tea? I'm going to make myself one.

Half-time

KR: There was something else I remember. By 1970, the Skinhead thing was massive. In '69, the Skinhead thing had been in the papers, so that made it bigger and bigger. In 1970, I left that job in the shop and I was, like, free Saturdays, so I would go up to Wolves on a regular basis through '70 to '71, maybe. By the summer of 1970, it was massive. There were just thousands of them and it seemed the same at every match you went to. Every match, there were Skinheads. It just seemed like the whole stand would be full of them.

PH: And if a guy with long hair had ever walked into that, he would have been ripped apart?

KR: No, he wouldn't have been because he would be considered not part of it. He would have been something different. And I know that because, to jump right forward for a minute to 1971–2, I had sort of long hair, and a great big coat and great big, wide trousers and big shoes. If I wasn't wearing Toppers then, it was big boots with what looked like a wooden heel. Feather-cut hair, all massive blow-dried. I remember going to an Albion–Wolves game and travelling up from London to meet me cousins at West Brom. They were at the pub. I get off at the station, walk under this railway bridge and suddenly there's a load of Albion fans coming. And how it would work in the those days is that you would know who was who because of their faces. If you didn't know their faces, you would know they were opposing fans. So, I see a load of Albion fans coming and think, oh, fuck, I've had it. But they went straight past me, and then I realised. It was because we in London were about a year in front of them fashionwise. They just thought, oh, he's a long-hair. He's not part of it. They were still Skinheads and might pick you off if they felt like it but, generally, if you weren't a part of it . . . I mean, there was a uniform that you wore that everyone recognised.

Second Half

PH: Signals?

KR: Yeah, there was signals. And if you weren't part of that thing, you were outside of it, you might get it [a beating] if you were unlucky, but you wouldn't generally. So that's how it was. It seemed like pretty much the whole country, although, like I say, in the summer of 1970, in London, there was a few people starting to change. They were starting to grow their hair.

PH: Would that be a reaction to the Skinhead thing being in the papers and going mainstream?

KR: Definitely, definitely. Everybody grew their hair a little bit, whereas there were a few who were right at the very front who started growing their hair longer. They didn't stop when it got to [nods to Paolo] your length, they just went with it. I remember going to London games with my cousins, places like West Ham and Chelsea, and by then London clubs had got longer hair, whereas the Wolves fans still had short hair and they still hung around in Crombies. They stood out like sore thumbs. The Londoners had just moved on so much. I remember one Wolves fan saying, they can smell us, and I felt like saying, it's not they can smell you, mate, it's because you look completely fucking different.

PH: Do you recall any Skinhead footballers?

KR: There weren't. Footballers were considered generally pretty naff in dress sense. I mean, you'd be very hard pushed to find a pop star with short hair in those days. That's how it was, '68 and '69. I remember going home on the bus with Tim Brennan and he's going, why are there no short-haired groups on *Top of the Pops*? And I thought, yeah, why not? And the only one that had been in the last year or so was Steve Ellis [lead singer with Love Affair]. He was the only one with short hair. That was what, '67 or '68. You didn't see short-haired footballers. You didn't see short-haired pop stars. There was a stigma about it.

PH: Funnily enough, I was thinking there, when you were talking about the long-hair thing, about Charlie George. He had that.

KR: Maybe he was the exception. But the important thing to remember is that they had grown it out from the Skinhead. It wasn't just because players had long hair. The fans would have had long hair, anyway.

Is there anything else? I made some notes earlier. See, I

stopped going by the summer of '72. I used to go up to Wolverhampton a lot before that.

PH: You were living in Harrow?

KR: Yeah, I was in the print for a while. I went with my dad on the building. He had his own building firm by this point. And I worked at C&A for a while. All different jobs, really. So, yeah, summer of '72, that was it. UEFA Cup final [Wolves v. Spurs]. I went to both legs. And, by then, it was definitely out-and-out feather cuts and wide trousers. It was all Take Six. That was massive in London, anyway. I remember one of my cousins in Wolverhampton goes, fucking shit at Wolves, all we get are the fashions that come third-hand. They go to Manchester first and then come back down to us. And it was all through the football.

That's another thing. Me and my friend from Harrow decided to hitch up to Blackpool for the weekend, I think it was '71. We met these fans, I think at Keele Services. They were Liverpool fans. They were going down to see a game. I think it was Arsenal or something, and they were telling me about how they used to get fans up there, Arsenal or Tottenham. They would get them and take their clothes off. Beat them up and take the clothes off them, take their shoes.

PH: That's amazing because, in the '80s, there was a big hoo-ha about young American kids holding up people for their trainers.

KR: It's funny, that thing about the Yanks. There was a report recently that you're far more likely to get beaten up in this country than you are anywhere in the US. Apart from gun crime, this is a much more violent place. There was so much violence back then. It was all the time. You couldn't walk down the road without trouble.

PH: You're right about that. In Woking, they just used to pull up in the car, and four guys would jump out and you had to run. If you got away, you got away. If you didn't, you got beaten. For nothing.

KR: For nothing.

PH: For living.

KR: For living. It was mad, wasn't it?

PH: It was crazy.

KR: It's quite a relief to sort of be out of that.

MB: That's what I'm saying earlier about that culture. Before, I was always running around, causing a bit of grief, just little petty things. And then my dad banned me from going to Millwall for three months as a kind of punishment. And it made me think, what the fuck am I doing? There's got to be more to it than this. That is how I started drifting that way.

KR: That's the same with me, exactly the same with me. At the time, footballers were getting £300 a week. And I don't know how much I was getting. You know, ten quid, twelve quid and that was good money. I remember thinking, they are getting all that money and they don't really care as much as we do. I went to the UEFA Cup final, first leg up at Molineux. We go to the second leg at Spurs. I don't know which end we were in but the police had divided it with a barricade thing – half Wolves, half Tottenham. And I remember absolutely hating these Tottenham fans so much. I remember just getting up on top of the barricades and screaming over to them, and really, really wanting to fucking kill them. And the anger. [Pauses.] It frightened me how angry I was and how passionate I was about it. And, that summer, I went off it. That was the summer of '72, I went off.

I went to Butlins in Clacton. I did a season there working, washing up and all that sort of stuff. I started to puff a bit more and not too long after that I had my first trip. I was in Scotland, in Aviemore, and I had a trip up there. I think it was after that I really stopped going. I think I might have gone to one game after that, maybe '72. I went to Arsenal and I saw that one of them had sprayed his Dr. Martens a bright colour, like fluorescenty. It was well weird. My life was changing and that was it. I stopped going, and I started to change and do my own thing, which ended up being music. I moved to Liverpool and then Birmingham after that. I think I had the attitude that football was stupid. And I hardly ever went until '88. My brother was going and he got me a ticket. Wolves, by that time, were in the old Fourth Division. I go now but I'm too old to understand street fashion, so I can't really give you anything on that.

PH: I think you've given us more than enough. Thank you so much.

MB: Yeah, cheers, Kevin, that was a real treat.

■ ■ ■

The Formal Label Slave's Dressing-room, 2004

Hair is by Vidal at one of Sassoon's salons.

Shirt is from Etro, the Italian fashion house founded as Etro SpA in 1968 by Gimmo Etro. It's a candy-striped button-down with the extra-long collars and it carries the classic Italian thick buttons.

Trousers are black tailored from Vivienne Westwood. Westwood was born in the Peak District in 1941, later moving to Harrow, north-west London. When her marriage to Derek Westwood broke up, she fell in love with a friend of her brother's at Harrow Technical College by the name of Malcolm McLaren. Together, they open a series of clothing shops, the most notorious being Sex, on the Kings Road. The Sex Pistols would be launched from this shop.

After parting company with McLaren, Westwood starts her own clothing range. It's ridiculed in the press but very influential on the streets. Same as it ever was. She is named British fashion designer of the year two years running, in 1990 and 1991. She collects her OBE from the Queen wearing no knickers and gives the photographers a flash to prove it! Her son, Joseph Corre, co-owns the highly successful underwear boutique Agent Provocateur.

Shoes are by Prada. The company was founded by Mario Prada in 1913 in Milan, making luxury leather goods. His granddaughter, Miuccia, joins the family business in 1978. Miuccia can't help herself. In 1989, she revolutionises the company by introducing her ready-to-wear collection. Nine years later, she launches her menswear, which proves a huge commercial success and is acclaimed critically.

The Casual Label Slave's Dressing-room, 2004

Hair is cut by a student at one of Vidal Sassoon's hair academies, thus guaranteeing a cutting-edge design. The company was founded by the East Ender Vidal Sassoon. He was a tough man. As a child, he spent time in a children's home, as a teenager, he fought the fascists on Cable Street and, as a 17 year old, he spent a year in the Israeli Army fighting Palestinians in the desert.

It was his parents who pushed him into hairdressing. Sassoon came to prominence in London in the early '60s. In 1963, putting together his love of architecture with his craft as a hairdresser, he created his famous angular-bob hairstyle, beloved by the model Twiggy and the designer Mary Quant. This cut established Vidal as the most influential hairstylist of the decade. The company has gone from strength to strength over the past 40 years.

T-shirt is from a range at Comme des Garçons, a Japanese company founded by Kawakubo Rei in 1973. Rei presented her first major show in Paris in 1981. Since then, the rise of Comme des Garçons has not been accompanied by a fall. They have just 'co-branded' with the UK's own Fred Perry company to produce the classic Fred polo-shirt with extra coloured piping.

Trousers are by Maharishi. Designed by Hardy Blechman in 1995 – his SnoPant range proving to be the most popular – the fabrics used are three-ply, weatherproof cashmere and waterproof wool.

On the feet are brown leather Birkenstock sandals. The name Birkenstock has been associated with footwear right back to 1774. Their sandal was born in 1964, designed by Karl Birkenstock, and introduced to America by Margot Fraser in 1966. It was an immediate success. Queues outside the Birkenstock shop in London's Covent Garden testify to the shoe's continued popularity.

United Colours of Beckham

Already, it is dusk.

The sun, falling into the ground from a sky of magic silver-blue, suddenly dips and unexpectedly casts black sticks of mystery around my feet. The dark angular shadows forcibly remind me of a presence that has hovered over us since we began this book. That shadow's name is David Beckham.

David Robert Joseph Beckham was born in August 1996, during a game between Manchester United and Wimbledon. Beckham, an unknown quantity up until that point, received the ball just by the halfway line, looked up and, with one heaven-sent strike, sent the ball sailing over goalkeeper David Seaman's (oops, sorry, force of habit) Neil Sullivan's head and into the goal.

The selling of David Beckham began that day and it was a process he was all too willing to help along. From a young age, David Beckham has always wanted to be famous. He saw fame as positive, something not to fear but to embrace, to eagerly seek its blessings. The cult of celebrity that permeates every level of British society today started with Beckham. For this Essex-born boy, it was as desirable as winning games. When fame did come to him, so did the media. In subsequent profiles, two obsessions were revealed: football and clothes.

'Crazy about fashion, always, always,' Beckham insisted in a *GQ* interview. 'It was a bit bad, actually, in the early years.' It's an intriguing quote, one the interviewer sadly chose to ignore. (This was understandable in that the interviewer was a celeb himself, if being Elton John's boyfriend qualifies you for such a position.)

Beckham added that he had grown up admiring the style of the legendary Rat Pack, the gang that comprised Frank Sinatra, Dean Martin, Peter Lawford and Sammy Davis Jnr. Their look revolved around Ivy League suits, button-down shirts and brogues. They looked like bank managers but partied like playboys. Perhaps it was then that Beckham learnt how clothes could be used as camouflage.

If he did, he learnt his lesson well. Since his elevation to national hero, Beckham has used clothes to send out signals. It is one of the few avenues of expression open to him. Disciplined by agents and advisers to keep his true thoughts a secret so as to never alienate mainstream society, Beckham has instead used clothing to communicate his mind.

The first example came when he was photographed, with his wife Victoria, wearing a sarong, a radical move by a man operating in such a macho culture. Soon after this picture came news of the gay community's delight with this provocative statement. David's response was to leak his pride at his high standing within the gay community – although his wife was quick to add that he was 'an animal in bed', lest anyone get the wrong idea.

'I'm not scared of my feminine side,' he said at the time. 'I think quite a lot of things I do come from that side of my character.' Beckham was true to his word, as well. The birth of his children has seen him naturally assume a modern-day father's role. It is he who stays at home to tend to his offspring if illness strikes, not his wife.

In doing so, he forcibly challenged the sanctity of Liverpool manager Bill Shankly's oft-used quote about football being much more important than life or death. As far as Beckham was concerned, that was bullshit. His children came above all else.

Such statements strengthened his standing within many circles. So did a few of his haircuts, especially the very feminine, braided look he wore with an Alice band, another signal which reached out to the gay community. It was only when the opposition started pulling at his locks that Beckham was forced to shave his head.

Haircuts have always been important to the man. When Beckham hit that goal against Wimbledon, the press locked tightly onto him, surrounded him with an army of cameras which have yet to leave his side. Pictures from around this time reveal a fashion sense closely related to late '70s terrace culture. His hair is not a wedge (but is approaching one) and he seemed to favour duffel coats, echoing Kevin Sampson's description of the very first Liverpool Casuals, who, in turn, had been inspired by the cover of David Bowie's album *Low*, on which he sports such a coat.

Later on, Beckham made a distinct shift, started using jewellery and accessories, such as a bandanna. He was moving with the times, tapping straight into the urban culture that defines much of Britain's youth today. So strong were Beckham's signals (at one game, he reserved a seat for his fave artist, Usher) that a Channel 4 documentary, *Black Like Beckham*, spent half an hour exploring this side of his character.

When we spoke to Terence Parris, a black Briton himself, he told us, 'I think that undoubtedly his influences are black but I think it's quite a shame that people have to say that because black is so integrated into urban culture you should just call it urban mainstream. Long before that *Black Like Beckham* . . . it has been known in our circles for some time now how influential he has been. He's got a huge record collection but his agency, who I know very well, have tried to keep him as mainstream and as Middle England as possible.'

There might be doubts about his overall skill – a strange thing to say about a man who has played Champions League football for both Manchester United and Real Madrid – but, politically and culturally, his wardrobe seems to suggest he is right on. Just as Perryman's haircut had induced a sense of recognition amongst his fans, so Beckham's clothes and style have at one point made a certain section of society gasp, 'He's one of us.'

Everyone loves David Beckham in equal measure. That's some feat, and it made us want to talk to those who had contributed to or spent time analysing the Beckham phenomenon. First stop, Dylan Jones, editor of *GQ* magazine.

* * *

I had known Dylan for ages. I think our first meeting was in Austria way, way back when we were both covering a band called Black Britain. One night at dinner, I dismissively told him that the idea of launching a men's magazine in Britain would never work. Which is probably why he has never called me in to write anything for him. Revenge is still a dish best served cold . . .

Dylan was working for *i-D* magazine at the time, about to assiduously work his way up the career ladder, stopping off at *The*

Face and *Arena*. His work was good, solid. He soon came to be admired by the publishers. It was he they called in to steady the good ship *GQ* after James Brown's experimental time in charge. Dylan pushed sales up and found time to write books, present TV shows and produce columns for national newspapers.

In his time as editor, *GQ* has heaped loads of awards on Beckham, voting him man of the year, best dressed man, haircut of the year, shoe wearer of the year, etc. Their heavy patronage of the man revealed how far football had come. *GQ* rarely hits the stands today without some football-related story lurking within its pages.

We met Dylan at his office in Hanover Square. He wore a nice three-button-necked collared, flowery shirt (David Saddler?) and his answers were considered, incisive.

'I think Beckham is fantastic,' he started off saying. Like Mark and I, Dylan saw his wearing of a sarong and his outlandish haircuts as a radical challenge to football culture.

'I think his feminisation is funny and clever and fascinating,' Dylan said. 'He is quintessentially working class, he's heterosexual, a brilliant sportsman, he's famous, self-deprecating, he's the most famous man in Britain, so it makes it very easy for him to walk around in sarongs or do funny things with his hair. Football hooliganism is back in a big way and so anybody who subverts that is a good thing. I think it's fabulous but then if you had someone more effeminate who had attempted the things he has, they would be a laughing stock.'

Mark felt the same way. What intrigued him was how Beckham had crossed over to every section of society, been accepted by the whole crowd, not just parts of it. Dylan remembered a three-week trip around Ireland he had taken after the 2002 World Cup. 'All the kids, *all of them*, I mean *everyone*, they had the Beckham haircut,' he reported.

I wondered out loud when it was that footballers had first found designer culture. Dylan pointed to the late '70s, early '80s, the rise of the Casual and the obsession with designer labels. He went on to say that in many ways Beckham was a product of his time, arriving on the stage after a huge period of change in which a consumer society was established and a giant media created.

'In the '60s and '70s, these things, such as football and fashion, were not of interest to anyone in Fleet Street and there wasn't the style press,' he said. 'It all changed in the '80s. You had *i-D*, *The Face*, Next, Paul Smith, youth-culture TV programmes – suddenly you have a lot of airspace, lots of pages to fill and people consumed this stuff with absolute glee. And the subject you're writing about has actually had a huge impact on what is happening in fashion now because that old Mod thing about the minutiae has become incredibly important. Details are very important now and that is coming back in a major way because people don't want to walk around with logos emblazoned on their chests.'

How important is the footballer to the likes of Prada these days? I wondered.

'Well, the endorsement or the patronage of someone like Beckham is incredibly important,' Dylan replied. 'Gucci is a good example of that. But then Beckham is very smart. He has an innate taste and he doesn't just follow designers, he's very eclectic. In the mid-'90s, the generic footballer look was black silk tie with a big, fat knot, black silk shirt, black silk suit. It could have been from a high-street chain or it could have been from the top end of Bond Street but it looked naff because it was that gauche, nouveau riche "I've got a lot of money and I am going to buy into the designer lifestyle". But Beckham hasn't done that. He's made a few mistakes but he spends a lot of money on fashion and he is a clothes horse. He's been a huge boost for menswear.'

Anyone else on Beckham's level?

'We shoot a lot of footballers,' Jones reveals, 'but very few of them have an innate sense of style. Ljungberg is good. Rio Ferdinand is all right. Jamie Redknapp we used to do a lot a few years ago. But then look at TV pundits. None of them are well dressed. John Barnes – talk about crimes against fashion. The sartorial elegance of football punditry is no better than it was 20 years ago. I think Beckham is an anomaly and fascinating because of that. He is more influential in his style than any pop star right now.'

It was a line we were hearing a lot – the footballer taking over the pop star's role as fashion's mover and shaker. We heard it a week later when we went to see William Hunt, a man who has designed suits for Beckham in the past.

Hunt grew up in Manchester, studied architecture but quickly moved into civil engineering. 'Which is a great discipline in life,' he states, 'because it teaches you how to get from A to B. If there's something in your way, you're going to go around it, above it, under it, through it, or you're going to fucking shift it. And so it gives you great determination. You never talk about a problem, just the solution.'

He was first transfixed by fashion through the films of Gene Kelly. Hunt started frequenting dance clubs where he would be 'the first on the dance floor and the last one off'.

He also dressed like Kelly. He then moved to London and started dressing in suits with pink shirts and a big brooch. Cinema again acted as inspiration when, after watching the film *West Side Story*, he started designing clothes. 'In that film, I saw this guy in a black suit with a lilac lining and a lilac shirt, and I'm still styling on that design today,' he reveals.

He began his career by making his own suits, creating an image which he wore into a clothes shop called Demob on London's Beak Street. The shop owner saw him and exclaimed, 'That's a great outfit, where did you get it?' William refused to tell him. 'Because you didn't tell anyone where you got anything,' he explained. 'You keep it for yourself. You go and find it yourself. But the guy explained that if I made him a dozen of these suits he'd pay me a certain amount of money. I was thinking, that's a fantastic amount, it's more than I earn in three months. I went away, came back three weeks later. The guy paid me and said, right, same again next month.'

William did well, made enough to open up his own shop on Neal Street, Covent Garden. Such was its success, he was able to follow Richard James to Savile Row. The operation has prospered.

When we met him, he was about to open a new shop on the street with clothes inspired by the current vogue for golf. (It has meanwhile opened its doors to the public.) At which point, I turned on the tape recorder and here's what was said:

Paolo Hewitt: OK, so this book we're doing is . . . what is this book we're doing?
Mark Baxter: Well, it's all over the place now, isn't it?
PH: [Laughing] Well, the idea was to look at the link between football and fashion, and not just the players but the fans as well. One of the reasons we wanted to talk to you was because of your involvement

The Fashion of Football

with Beckham. It seems to us that he really epitomises how football has supplanted pop music now in terms of influence.

William Hunt: Definitely. I mean now they are the new rock stars, aren't they? Footballers are the new rock stars.

PH: How did someone like Beckham come to you? How did all that come about? I wouldn't have thought he would have heard of you.

WH: Well, firstly, I don't want to go up because once you go up then you can only come down. We've always tried to swim along with the current of things. I remember first meeting David because we were doing Victoria's stuff through the Spice Girls.

PH: So there comes the pop connection.

WH: Yeah, exactly. We started making stuff for the Spice Girls and the pinnacle of that really was getting a credit on their movie, which I thought was hilarious, I thought it was fantastic. We had the very, very last credit on their movie. OK, everyone slagged it off but it was only fun, you know, it wasn't trying to change anything. And so Victoria met David and then the next thing is we were doing a lot of tailoring and stuff for the girls, and then I get a call from Victoria, can you come and do me new boyfriend?

PH: Are you a football . . .

WH: I'm a Man United fan, since I can remember. I went to 37 games last year, home and away, and Europe. A bit disappointed this year, I've only been to about four games this year.

PH: Too busy?

WH: Yeah, yeah, but I'll catch up. I'll get on that run in the new year. So, basically, with Beckham, I saw this kid with the makings of being a good-looking boy but he was a bit gangly and a bit spotty and a bit greasy-haired and stuff but he kind of metamorphosed, didn't he?

PH: What was he wearing at the time?

WH: Boss. They all wear Boss, don't they? Every single one of them wears Boss.

PH: It's like part of their contract, isn't it? Play for us for three years, earn this amount and you must spend some of it on designer labels.

WH: The thing is about footballers, they are institutionalised guys. They are all in an institution. They are not going to express themselves. Their influences are quite minimal, you know. Or they certainly were ten years ago.

Second Half

PH: Can you expand on that a bit because it touches on something Mark and I have been trying to work out, which is that most, if not all, footballers are working class, which is the one class that initiates all the fashion changes, has done so since time immemorial and, yet, looking at most of them, it's as if that whole culture has gone right over their heads. So, when you say institutionalised, what do you mean?

WH: I think they are institutionalised because if you are a football manager, you don't want your boy out there doing it for himself. You want them so that you can say, you do this, you do this. You want them grouped and tightly knitted, you know. There's a few guys who are a bit more influential or a bit more independent. I think one of the big breakthroughs for it all was David meeting Victoria, really. Because she just span it out. Opened his eyes up to stuff. And, basically, she was a catalyst for him becoming the person that he became.

PH: But he says in interviews that he was always into clothes.

WH: But here we've got a young kid, 18 years old, 19 years old seeing the world. Here we've got another kid who's like a year or two older but seeing a massively different world of fashion and style and pop. Yeah, he was into his clothes but if somebody comes along and shows you something different . . . and that's what happened there.

PH: When he came to you, did he leave the decisions to you or did he . . .

WH: No, he just said, I want this. I want that. I said, have you thought about this? Oh, great. Yeah, OK, fine. And we just showed him this and showed him that.

MB: Was he open to ideas?

WH: Absolutely. There's no rocket science to it. He's a good-looking guy, got a good body, you can put anything on him and he looks great in it. And if you can make it easy for him, he'll do it. He doesn't come in and say, I need this. Pink stripes and red this and blah blah blah.

PH: Who else do you do apart from Beckham?

WH: God himself, Alex Ferguson.

PH: As a Man United fan, that must be a kick for you, Alex Ferguson?

WH: Well, it's great. I mean, first, you know, Alex is a friend of mine

The Fashion of Football

but I'm a fan, the same as Martin Fry is a friend of mine but I am also a fan. One day, you'll have your fan's hat on, the next day you'll have your friend's hat on. We do Harry Kewell. We do Mario Melchiot, who's a lovely fella, you know.

PH: Do you find footballers are coming to you with ideas or is it you giving it to them?

WH: No, we have our ideas and, you know, you can't come to us and say, I want this with a blue collar on it and a red thing because what we do is very specific, and these are the styles that we do and these are the fabrics that we offer.

PH: And if you like it, you like it.

WH: Yeah, and if you don't, then we're not the right place for you.

PH: You don't force your ideas on people.

WH: It's quite subtle, our stuff now. I don't think we have to force anybody. If it came to it, I would make a stand and say, no, you need this, because that's my job, that's my area of expertise.

PH: When did you first start going to United?

WH: On and off from about seven years old. You go because your big brother takes you and then he fucks you off because he doesn't want to hang out with you any more. And then football got a bit uncool, didn't it, for a while? People stopped going. I know I stopped going about sort of mid- to late '80s. And then I felt, well, I need something in my life again. I'm getting mad about it now. But then again, so is everyone else. It's the exposure. Get your product on TV and then everyone wants to go and see it.

PH: What sort of things were the fans wearing when you first started going?

WH: They're still wearing it, United. I mean they've got the least stylish fans in the world. United fans are the ugliest fans I have ever seen in my life. They are. I mean you look around and you just think, oh my God, you know, it's scary. I've never met any good-looking United fans. If you were to quote a stylish bunch, then you couldn't go looking in Old Trafford.

PH: When you were doing Beckham could you help yourself and not talk football to him?

WH: No, we talk about football, yeah, of course you do, yeah.

PH: Do you ever talk to him about his performances, tell him he was crap?

WH: Oh, yeah, absolutely. And he'll say, that's a shit suit, fuck off. Even when you get Alex Ferguson, you talk about football. I mean, are you not a manager when you go and watch a game? I am. I run and kick every ball. I'm exhausted after a game.

PH: Who's a good dresser that you know, playerwise?

WH: Do you know who is a really, really stylish guy and doesn't know it, and nobody gives him any credit for it? Gary Neville. Gary Neville is a really good-looking bloke. And just doesn't know it. He's good looking in a De Niro way. He's got the sort of hard face, and the bit of a bent nose and stuff.

PH: And who else was well dressed at United? I'm talking past as well as present.

WH: Denis Law has always been a very stylish guy. I was talking to him the other day – I think he's 63 years old now – and he's still pretty dapper. He's still got the shock of that red-blond hair, very stylish, very slight. Charlie George was not handsome but he was just different. He had a bit of a swagger. Osgood had swagger. But they weren't crushingly good looking. They weren't pop stars, were they, do you know what I mean? These guys, there was no Jim Morrisons there. I'm gonna have to get back in because I've got some clients coming in. You got enough?

MB: More than, thanks.

David Beckham penetrated the fashion world with the same force that he uses to launch his 40-yard passes. Following his elevation to a subject of national obsession, Beckham started endorsing a wide range of clothing, from Adidas sportswear to MA-1 jackets, from Police sunglasses to his own range of boys' clothing for Marks & Spencer. Such is his power for advertisers that during half-time in the recent Euro 2004 game between France and England, he appeared in three separate TV adverts. He was also of interest in other fields. The writer Julie Burchill was so impressed with him she wrote a treatise on the man, whilst the Brit artist Sam Taylor-Wood was allowed to film him sleeping. The resulting tape can be seen at London's National Portrait Gallery. Mark saw it one Sunday, and rang and told me that night, 'You won't believe this but it's hypnotic. You've got to see it. I mean, you know what I'm like. I've read about it and gone, yeah right. More Brit Art crap. But I'm

The Fashion of Football

telling you, once you start watching it you can't take your eyes off it. I stood there for about half an hour. Mad.' Beckham was quick to make use of his power. It was he who single-handedly persuaded the FA to let Giorgio Armani design the England squad's suits for the 2002 World Cup and the recent Euro 2004 tournament. Those Burton's suits were no longer good enough.

He could, of course, have approached the designer Neil Cunningham to create something. Neil runs a prestigious shop in Sackville Street where he sells his lavish creations to an extremely rich clientele. His shop is around the corner from the likes of William Hunt and Richard James, and although he welcomes new blood, new talent, he has felt a notable drop in standards on 'the Row'. Too many shops employing too many straight men, he believes. Only girls or gays should work in such establishments. At least they care about clothes.

Neil had often seen Mark around the area so was happy to talk when the big man approached him for an interview. One March morning, he made us coffee and we sat talking in his deep red and rich shop. Neil recognised Beckham's influence, thought it very strong. He told us about a friend of his, a Newcastle tough man, an ex-boxer who now works as a bailiff. One day, he turned up wearing exactly the same hair-band that Beckham had been sporting in games.

'I couldn't believe it,' Neil said of his friend. 'It was one of those squiggly ones and I was completely knocked out. What's interesting about Beckham is the flamboyancy. Wearing the diamonds the other day when he went to see the Queen but then also kicking in that rappy, straighter, tougher side.'

Coincidentally, Neil had another connection to football. He had recently been commissioned to supply clothes for the popular TV series *Footballers' Wives*. The brief, he revealed, was to create clothes of a trash-glam style, a demand he believed had begun with the outlandish nature of the Beckhams' wedding.

'It's like going back ten years, in a way,' he says of his clothes for the show. 'It is so preeny and peacocky, and years ago it would have been seen as so vulgar and so grotesque. But they have completely made it OK. When you have a couple of thrones at your wedding . . . I mean, we saw such a change in the whole style of weddings, post-Posh and Becks. Up until then, that wedding would have been seen as nothing less than grotesque. Instead, it just changed how you go about doing it. If you want it to be crap and vulgar and totally over-glorifying yourself, you can do it now. And the amount of sort of dandyism that is coming out in the chaps is quite, quite fascinating.'

Then everything changed. Beckham's shadow actually started fading. It didn't seem possible. When we began this book, the man was omnipresent. Everywhere you looked, Beckham was there, bearing down from huge ad hoardings, staring out moodily from the front covers of magazines, trying to hide in front-page news, working his charm in countless TV documentaries, selling himself on the covers of books and videos and DVDs which all purported to tell his story. As England captain, his hard work on the field and ability to produce the goods when it counted had earned him huge respect from the crowd. He was seen as the leader of a new, promising generation of footballer who would bring the country the triumphs and the pride it craved. Although he had fallen out with his one-time mentor, Alex Ferguson, Beckham, against all the odds, had quickly made a big impact at Real Madrid. He scored goals, made goals. Players such as Roberto Carlos purred about his skill and work ethic. Even the notoriously hard-to-please Spanish press put their thumbs up: 'We thought we were getting a prima donna, instead we got a champion horse,' one praised.

But then 2004 arrived and with it a massive sea change. Beckham's form dipped badly. Real Madrid endured the worst season ever in their 104-year history. They didn't win a thing. Worse, their bitterest rivals, Barcelona, overtook and finished above them in the League, automatically qualifying for next season's Champions League. Unlike Real Madrid.

During this torrid time on the field came another storm, this time from outside. Beckham was publicly accused of infidelity, a massive blow to his image as devoted family man and one to make his sponsors very wary. Still reeling from these front-page revelations, Beckham travelled to Portugal to captain England in the Euro 2004 tournament. At the time, most experts believed England had as good a chance of victory as any other country. They were wrong. An ineffective midfield, allied with an inability to retain ball possession, prevented them reaching further than the quarter-finals. Beckham himself never seemed to get going. Often, he seemed tired, somewhat lost even, as the battle raged around him.

Worse, Beckham's poor performances were highlighted further by the explosive, brilliant play of the 18-year-old Wayne Rooney. By the tournament's end, Beckham must have felt like the boxer Tim Witherspoon whose last memory of his flamboyant manager, Don King, was when he stepped over his prostrate body to congratulate his opponent.

As Beckham faced the press after the tournament's conclusion, he did so knowing that it was Wayne Rooney the advertisers now desired, not him. It was Rooney all the kids wanted to be when they rushed out on their playgrounds, their waste grounds and muddy fields to play football, not Beckham. It was Rooney's name you would see on the back of children's shirts now, not his. A week later, at the Royal Academy of Arts, someone scrawled 'You Loosers' on a massive photo of Beckham's face.

As I close this chapter, for David Beckham . . . already it is dusk. Now he must bring back the days of sunshine.

POSTSCRIPT

The Final Whistle and Flute

On 15 April, in the year of our Lord 2004, Mark Baxter married Louise Nicholson at Peckham registry office. 'Perfect match,' he told me. 'She's even madder on football than I am.'

Afterwards, we went to his house, drank Chivas Regal Scotch. It was the tipple that Rod Stewart consumed in his time with The Faces. That was my excuse, anyway.

It had been an amazing month for the bride and groom. First, the wedding bells and then Millwall, against all the odds, reached the final of the FA Cup. Mark wasn't that surprised. Back in January, at the start of the competition, he had actually dreamt about Michael Caine handing over the FA Cup to Millwall manager Dennis Wise. 'But the funny thing was,' he told me, 'the Cup had no lid on it.'

As the tournament progressed, so did Millwall, aided by a draw that not once pitted them against Premiership opponents. By April, the impossible now seemed possible. Millwall were to play Sunderland in the semi-finals, having avoided both Arsenal and United. Mark went to the New Den at six in the morning to buy his tickets. Examining them on the way home, he was startled to see that the FA Cup depicted on his ticket was without a lid – just as it had been in his dream. He phoned me straight away. 'It's the sign,' he kept repeating. 'The sign.'

When they then beat Sunderland to reach the final, I swear there were tears in my eyes that day. I sat in London thinking what a fantastic day he and Lou were having, how much the pair of them deserved it and how this is what football did best, made lives triumphant, victorious, filled them with joy and happiness. It is the elixir everyone hopes to taste and this season it was given to Millwall fans. The fact that this riled a few uptight and snobby football scribes – 'no one wants Millwall in the final' – made their achievement even sweeter.

Mark knew, of course, that his team stood little chance against Manchester United in the final and he wasn't wrong. I don't think Millwall had one shot on goal during the whole game. Mark and Lou didn't care. They had travelled to Cardiff with friends and family – Mark took his mum – and watched their team in an FA Cup final. It was a day they never thought would happen and they enjoyed every second of it.

When Mark got home, he rang and told me, 'We out-sang the United fans, out-shouted them, probably out-drank them and came home.' I was happy for him and devastated that I hadn't put money on his team the day he told me about his dream. Since working with Mark, Millwall had become like a second team to me, along with Woking, where I grew up, and Naples, where my mother was born. Not far into the season, I started looking out for Millwall results, began video-taping the Nationwide round-up late on Monday nights so I could watch them in action.

After all, it had been some journey Mark and I had been on, a real adventure into two worlds – football and fashion – which, along with music, have been absolutely central to both our lives, both our identities. We had learnt a lot, discovered plenty. Examining the footballer from a clothes angle had yielded much, especially about his symbolism.

For us, George Best and Bobby Moore provided the perfect representation of the '60s. Best was that decade's youth, its glamour, its explosion of talent; Moore symbolised the English nature, the formality, the conservatism allied with talent. Today, it is David Beckham and Wayne Rooney who reflect the soul of the nation.

Beckham could be seen as the Tony Blair of football, a man who has pushed things forward but still remains unable to deliver on the big promises. His refusal to accept any blame for the Euro 2004 experience brought to mind Blair's behaviour over Iraq.

Wayne Rooney, on the other hand, is a throwback in time, the first major player in years to have come off the terraces and onto the

The Final Whistle and Flute

pitch. His swift ascension into football history at such a young age comes on the back of a growing feeling that the class he hails from may well be returning to vogue. The novels of John King, Michael Collins' book *The Likes of Us*, Nick Love's film *The Football Factory* are all signs that maybe the chavs are set to become the next black.

Although Rooney looks just as likely to be barring you from entering a club as he does his opponents from victory, the clothing industry is currently circling round him with keen intent. Mark sees such activity as evidence of a new generation assuming power within the industry. The likes of Carlo Brandelli at Kilgour, French & Stanbury recognise that footballers supply the best route to mass-marketing and profitability. Tradition is important but so is profitability. Dunhill, a brand more associated with Soho House than Chelsea Football Club, have reached out to the Blues and struck a deal. The magazine which had given me such heart palpitations on its arrival had been set up specifically to match footballers with brands, to further the footballer's current pre-eminence in the scheme of things. The worlds of football and fashion entwine ever stronger.

The end was nigh. On Friday, 9 July 2004, Mark and I met to go over the finished copy, look for mistakes, things we'd missed out, the final job on the book before it was sent to Edinburgh for publication. (Incidentally, any wrong 'uns are down to him.)

After the work was done, we went for a drink at Bar Italia, toasted each other. I was off to Italy to sleep, Mark was back to work, dreaming of promotion for Millwall. Outside on the pavement, I was still insisting on 'one for the road' but Mark declined. Work was hectic these days and all the big man was looking forward to was a long lie-in the next day.

'Hammered, I am,' he said. 'Absolutely hammered.'

'You should try writing,' I told him.

'So should you,' he shot back. We laughed, bade each other sweet adios.

As I walked away, I heard him say over my shoulder, 'Have a good rest, son. You deserve it. But remember, you got the Tubby Hayes biography when you get back.'

There was a large chuckle but by the time I turned around, the big man was gone.

■■■
Library

Barrett, Norman S. *Purnell's Encyclopedia of Association Football*, Purnell, 1975

Best, George *Blessed: The Biography*, Polar Publishing, 2002

Buchan, Charles *Charles Buchan's Soccer Gift Book*, IPC, various years

Cohn, Nik *Today There Are No Gentlemen: The Changes in Englishmen's Clothes Since the War*, Weidenfield and Nicholson, 1971

Gold, Johnny *Tramps Gold*, Robson Books, 2001

Harris, Steven *Dear Alan, Dear Harry*, Harris Books, 1999 (available from PO Box 26363 London N8 9ZJ at £6.99)

Hewitt, Paolo *Fifty – The Fred Perry Story*, De Facto on behalf of Fred Perry, 2002

Hewitt, Paolo and McGuigan, Paul *Robin Friday: The Greatest Footballer You Never Saw*, Mainstream Publishing, 1998

Hewitt, Paolo and Rawlings, Terry *My Favourite Shirt: The Ben Sherman Story*, Ben Sherman, 2004

Hewitt, Paolo *The Soul Stylists: Six Decades of Modernism – From Mod to Casuals*, Mainstream Publishing, 2000

Hopcraft, Arthur *The Football Man: People and Passions in Soccer*, Simon & Schuster, 1988

Hudson, Alan and Macleay, Ian *The Working Man's Ballet*, Robson Books, 1998

Lawrence, Amy *Proud To Say That Name: The Arsenal Dream Team*, Mainstream Publishing, 2001

Mace, Paul *Bring Back The Birch: The Alan Birchenall Story*, Polar Publishing, 2000

McIlvanney, Hugh *McIlvanney on Football*, Mainstream Publishing, 1997

Mendes, Valerie, and De La Haye, Amy *20th Century Fashion*, Thames & Hudson, 1999

O'Neill, Terry *Celebrity: The Photographs of Terry O'Neill*, Little, Brown, 2003

Rawlings, Terry *Harmony In My Head: Steve Diggle's Rock & Roll Odyssey*, Fire Fly Publications, 2003

Thornton, Phil *Casuals*, Milo, 2003

Venables, Terry *Venables*, Michael Joseph, 1994

Watts, Judith (ed.) *The Penguin Book of 20th Century Fashion Writing*, Penguin, 1999

The Fashion of Football